T0214400

Lecture Notes in Computer Science 11121

Commenced Publication in 1973
Founding and Former Series Editors:
Gerhard Goos, Juris Hartmanis, and Jan van Leeuwen

More information about this series at http://www.springer.com/series/7412

Islem Rekik · Gozde Unal
Ehsan Adeli · Sang Hyun Park (Eds.)

PRedictive Intelligence in MEdicine

First International Workshop, PRIME 2018
Held in Conjunction with MICCAI 2018
Granada, Spain, September 16, 2018
Proceedings

 Springer

Editors
Islem Rekik
University of Dundee
Dundee
UK

Ehsan Adeli
Stanford University
Stanford, CA
USA

Gozde Unal
Istanbul Technical University
Istanbul
Turkey

Sang Hyun Park
Daegu Gyeongbuk Institute of Science
 and Technology
Daegu
Korea (Republic of)

ISSN 0302-9743   ISSN 1611-3349   (electronic)
Lecture Notes in Computer Science
ISBN 978-3-030-00319-7   ISBN 978-3-030-00320-3   (eBook)
https://doi.org/10.1007/978-3-030-00320-3

Library of Congress Control Number: 2018953820

LNCS Sublibrary: SL6 – Image Processing, Computer Vision, Pattern Recognition, and Graphics

This Springer imprint is published by the registered company Springer Nature Switzerland AG
The registered company address is: Gewerbestrasse 11, 6330 Cham, Switzerland

Preface

Big and complex data is fuelling diverse research directions in the research fields of medical image analysis and computer vision. These can be divided into two main categories: (1) analytical methods and (2) predictive methods. While analytical methods aim to efficiently analyze, represent and interpret data (static or longitudinal), predictive methods leverage the data currently available to predict observations at later time-points (i.e., forecasting the future) or predicting observations at earlier time-points (i.e., predicting the past for missing data completion). For instance, a method that only focuses on classifying patients with mild cognitive impairment (MCI) and patients with Alzheimer's disease (AD) is an analytical method, while a method which predicts if a subject diagnosed with MCI will remain stable or convert to AD over time is a predictive method. Similar examples can be established for various neurodegenerative or neuropsychiatric disorders, degenerative arthritis, or in cancer studies, in which the disease or disorder develops over time.

Why Predictive Intelligence?

It would constitute a stunning progress in the MICCAI research community if, in a few years, we contribute to engineering a 'predictive intelligence' able to map both low-dimensional and high-dimensional medical data onto the future with high precision. This workshop is the first endeavor to drive the field of 'high-precision predictive medicine', where late medical observations are predicted with high precision, while providing explanation via machine and deep learning, and statistically, mathematically, or physically-based models of healthy, disordered development and aging. Despite the terrific progress that analytical methods have made in the last 20 years in medical image segmentation, registration, or other related applications, efficient predictive intelligent models and methods are somewhat lagging behind. As such predictive intelligence develops and improves (and this is likely to do so exponentially in the coming years), this will have far-reaching consequences for the development of new treatment procedures and novel technologies. These predictive models will begin to shed light on one of the most complex healthcare and medical challenges we have ever encountered, and, in doing so, change our basic understanding of who we are.

What Kind of Research Problems Do We Aim to Solve?

The main aim of PRIME-MICCAI is to propel the advent of predictive models in a broad sense, with application to medical data. Particularly, the workshop accepted 8- to 10-page papers describing new cutting-edge predictive models and methods that solve challenging problems in the medical field. We hope that the PRIME workshop becomes a nest for high-precision predictive medicine — one that is set to transform multiple fields of healthcare technologies in unprecedented ways. Topics of interests for the workshop included but were not limited to predictive methods dedicated to the following topics:

- Modeling and predicting disease development or evolution from a limited number of observations
- Computer-aided prognostic methods (e.g., for brain diseases, prostate cancer, cervical cancer, dementia, acute disease, neurodevelopmental disorders)
- Forecasting disease and cancer progression over time
- Predicting low-dimensional data (e.g., behavioral scores, clinical outcome, age, gender)
- Predicting the evolution or development of high-dimensional data (e.g., shapes, graphs, images, patches, abstract features, learned features)
- Predicting high-resolution data from low-resolution data
- Prediction methods using 2D, 2D+t, 3D, 3D+t, ND and ND+t data
- Predicting data of one image modality from a different modality (e.g., data synthesis)
- Predicting lesion evolution
- Predicting missing data (e.g., data imputation or data completion problems)
- Predicting clinical outcome from medical data (genomic, imaging data, etc)

In-brief

This workshop mediated ideas from both machine learning and mathematical, statistical, and physical modeling research directions in the hope of providing a deeper understanding of the foundations of predictive intelligence developed for medicine, as well as showed where we currently stand and what we aspire to achieve through this field. PRIME-MICCAI 2018 featured a single-track workshop with keynote speakers with deep expertise in high-precision predictive medicine using machine learning and other modeling approaches which are believed to stand at opposing directions. Our workshop also included technical paper presentations, poster sessions, and demonstrations. Eventually, this helps steer a wide spectrum of MICCAI publications from being 'only analytical' to being 'jointly analytical and predictive'.

We received a total of 23 submissions. All papers underwent a rigorous double-blinded review process by at least 2 members (mostly 3 members) of the Program Committee composed of 30 well-known research experts in the field. The selection of the papers was based on technical merit, significance of results, and relevance and clarity of presentation. Based on the reviewing scores and critiques, the 20 best papers were accepted for presentation at the workshop and chosen to be included in the present proceedings. The authors of the selected papers were invited to submit an extended version to the PRIME special issue in the *IEEE Journal of Biomedical and Health Informatics* (J-BHI).

July 2018

Islem Rekik
Gozde Unal
Ehsan Adeli
Sang Hyun Park

Organization

Program Committee

Ahmed Fetit	Imperial College London, UK
Avinash Varadarajan	Google AI Healthcare, USA
Changqing Zhang	Tianjin University, China
Daniel Rueckert	Imperial College London, UK
Dong Nie	University of North Carolina, USA
Dinggang Shen	University of North Carolina, USA
Ender Konukoglu	ETH Zurich, Switzerland
Gang Li	University of North Carolina, USA
Gerard Sanroma	Pompeu Fabra University, Spain
Guorong Wu	University of North Carolina, USA
Hamid Soltanian-Zadeh	University of Tehran, Iran, and Henry Ford Hospital, USA
Ilwoo Lyu	Vanderbilt University, USA
Ipek Oguz	University of Pennsylvania, USA
Jaeil Kim	Kyungpook National University, South Korea
Jon Krause	Google AI Healthcare, USA
Kilian M. Pohl	SRI International, USA
Le Lu	NVidia Corp, USA
Li Wang	University of North Carolina, USA
Marc Niethammer	University of North Carolina, USA
Mehdi Moradi	IBM Research, USA
Mert Sabuncu	Cornell University, USA
Morteza Mardani	Stanford University, USA
Polina Golland	Massachusetts Institute of Technology, USA
Qian Wang	Shanghai Jiao Tong University, China
Qingyu Zhao	Stanford University, USA
Serena Yeung	Stanford University, USA
Stefanie Demirci	Technische Universität München, Germany
Tal Arbel	McGill University, Canada
Ulas Bagci	University of Central Florida, USA
Yinghuan Shi	Nanjing University, China
YingYing Zhu	Cornell University, USA
Yu Zhang	Stanford University, USA
Yue Gao	Tsinghua University, China
Ziga Spiclin	University of Ljubljana, Slovenia

Contents

Computer Aided Identification of Motion Disturbances Related to Parkinson's Disease

Gudmundur Einarsson[1](✉), Line K. H. Clemmensen[1], Ditte Rudå[2],
Anders Fink-Jensen[3], Jannik B. Nielsen[1], Anne Katrine Pagsberg[2],
Kristian Winge[4], and Rasmus R. Paulsen[1]

[1] Technical University of Denmark, Copenhagen, Denmark
guei@dtu.dk
[2] Child and Adolescent Mental Health Center Mental Health Services,
Capital Region Denmark, Faculty of Health Science,
University of Copenhagen, Copenhagen, Denmark
[3] Psychiatric Centre Copenhagen (Rigshospitalet), Laboratory of Neuropsychiatry,
University Hospital Copenhagen, Copenhagen, Denmark
[4] Department of Neurology, Zealand University Hospital, Roskilde, Denmark

Abstract. We present a framework for assessing which types of simple movement tasks are most discriminative between healthy controls and Parkinson's patients. We collected movement data in a game-like environment, where we used the Microsoft Kinect sensor for tracking the user's joints. We recruited 63 individuals for the study, of whom 30 had been diagnosed with Parkinson's disease. A physician evaluated all participants on movement-related rating scales, e.g., elbow rigidity. The participants also completed the game task, moving their arms through a specific pattern. We present an innovative approach for data acquisition in a game-like environment, and we propose a novel method, sparse ordinal regression, for predicting the severity of motion disorders from the data.

Keywords: Game-aided diagnosis · Kinect · Parkinson's disease
Sparse · Ordinal · Classification

1 Introduction

Parkinson's disease (PD) is a long-term neurodegenerative disease, where the significant symptoms are tremor, rigidity, slowness of movements and difficulty walking. Currently, there are 7 million individuals affected on a global scale where the disease has a severe socioeconomic effect and reduces the quality of life. The condition has a significant financial impact on health care systems and society [16].

PD is now known to be caused by an interplay of environment and several genetic factors [11], but there is no known cure, only treatment to reduce symptoms. Treatment consists mainly of medication, surgery and physical therapy.

© Springer Nature Switzerland AG 2018
I. Rekik et al. (Eds.): PRIME 2018, LNCS 11121, pp. 1–8, 2018.
https://doi.org/10.1007/978-3-030-00320-3_1

Recent studies have also shown relief of symptoms via improved rehabilitation [1]. There is no diagnostically conclusive test available yet. The current diagnosis is clinical-questionaires and movement tests, and may be missed or misdiagnosed since the symptoms are common to other diseases/disorders. At the time of PD diagnosis, the disease has often progressed to an advanced stage with motor symptoms and neurophysiological damage.

It is of great importance to develop tools that can aid an unbiased diagnosis for PD in earlier stages of the disease. Some symptoms commonly appear before the motor-symptoms, such as depression, feeling tired and weak, reduced ability to smell, problems with blood pressure, heart rate, sleep disturbances and digestion [8].

Increasing the detection rate for early cases is very ambitious, especially if we do not resort to novel diagnosis tools. It would be easier, more accurate, and less prone to bias, to make a computerized diagnostic test a part of the regular screening processes. Using data from such a tool would allow us to model individual abnormalities more accurately, and make personalized and accurate predictions of disease status and progression, by comparing to earlier screenings. Another way to achieve this would be to have access to a proxy variable, that the patient can choose to send for analysis, such as data from a personal health monitor, movement data from a GPS tracker, mobile phone data, or data from a video game.

Our ambition is to predict the clinical ratings made by the physician of the underlying movement disorders from the motion tracking data, and to identify what part of the movement sequences are best suited for this task. This problem has several difficulties, of which the major ones are: (1) There are few observations compared to the number of variables. (2) The labels we want to predict are ordinal. (3) The classes are imbalanced.

In recent years the Kinect sensor has been widely used for retraining and physical therapy. Galna et al. presented such an application for PD patients [10]. A review of the usage of the Kinect sensor for medical purposes is presented in [13], of which most of the work is development and testing of physical therapy systems for various diseases and medical conditions. Of the studies covered in [13], three describe assessment of conditions, related to facioscapulohumeral muscular dystrophy (FSHD), stroke and balance in the elderly. The capabilities of the Kinect are limited, as reported in [9]; thus we do not expect to be able to detect or predict the presence of low amplitude tremors or movement disorders related to smaller movements.

We want to predict the score from the clinically collected movement data and identify the movement sequences related to PD. Due to the high number of variables, we propose to use a novel method, sparse ordinal regression. This method builds upon sparse discriminant analysis (SDA) [6] by adapting the data replication method to the sparse setting [4] to handle ordinal labels. We further extend the novel optimization approaches presented in [3] for sparse ordinal regression. The data replication method works on the principle of transforming an ordinal classification problem into multiple binary classification problems. These binary classification problems are solved together to find a common hyperplane that separates each pair of classes corresponding to adjacent ordinal labels. The difference between the hyperplanes corresponding to different classification boundaries are biases.

In the past years, multiple methods have appeared which can handle feature selection and classification problems of the type $p \gg n$, most notably Sparse Discriminant Analysis (SDA) by [6] and Sparse Partial Least Squares for Classification by [5]. Other algorithms commonly used to solve such problems, where the focus is not necessarily classification, are elastic net by [18] and sparse principal component analysis by [7]. Using an l_1-norm regularizer in the model formulation ensures that variable selection is performed in the model optimization process which gives leverage for the user to interpret the non-zero parameters in the model. Incorporation of an l_1-norm regularizer is influenced by the Lasso [15], which uses the l_1-norm to relax the vector cardinality function in the best feature subset problem for linear regression.

Ordinal labels appear in a multitude of applications, e.g., surveys, medical rating scales and concerning online user reviews. We believe that the methodology can be applied to a variety of other problems in the future.

The main contributions of this paper consist of a novel game-like framework, the Motor-game, for assessing arm-movement in individuals with movement-related disorders in the arms. We further propose a novel method for performing classification from this data, sparse ordinal regression, allowing us to summarize a whole run into a single score.

2   Methods

We have developed a game-like environment, which we call the *Motor-game*, where we use the Microsoft Kinect sensor [17] and the associated software framework to do motion tracking of the players (See Fig. 1) [2].

The motor-game is designed to capture a range of motions from the hands and arms. There are three levels in the Motor-game, where here we focus on

Fig. 1. *Left*: Screenshot from the motorgame. The player sees his pose reflected as a stick figure and needs to make the stick figure's hands hover over the buttons as fast as possible. *Right*: View from behind a player playing the motor-game.

data from the first level. The first level has 22 *tasks*. In the first 11 tasks, a button appears on the right side of the screen, and the player needs to react, *catch* the button and keep the hand stable there for one second. The following 11 tasks are similar but for the left hand. For each player, the buttons appear in the same location, meaning that their hands have comparable positions between playthroughs. The distances between appearances of the buttons vary, forcing the player to perform large and smaller motions. Using the tracking software from the Kinect, we obtain 30 measurements per second of ten joints, hands, wrists, elbows, shoulders, center of shoulders and head, in the upper body. One of the main reason to make this data collection process in a game-like environment is to keep the players motivated to perform as well as they can, and to make the process more enjoyable, similar to games that have been made for physiotherapy in PD patients [10]. In [6], Clemmensen et al. presented the sparse optimal scoring problem (SOS), which is the formulation we employ to solve sparse ordinal regression. SDA is like a supervised version of Sparse Principal Component Analysis (PCA). We seek to find discriminant vectors to project the data to a lower dimensional representation, where we balance the objectives of minimizing variation within classes, maximizing variation between classes and feature selection. For PCA, where we do not have labels, we seek directions to maximize variation. New samples are then traditionally classified according to the nearest centroid after projection. We reformulate the SOS criterion presented in [6] for ordinal labels:

$$\underset{\theta \in \mathbf{R}^2, \beta_{\mathrm{Ord}} \in \mathbf{R}^{p+K-1}}{\arg\min} \|Y_{\mathrm{Ord}}\theta - X_{\mathrm{Ord}}\beta_{\mathrm{Ord}}\|_2^2 + \lambda_2 \beta_{\mathrm{Ord}}^T \hat{\Omega} \beta_{\mathrm{Ord}} + \lambda_1 \sum_{i=1}^{p} |\beta_i|$$

$$\text{s.t. } \frac{1}{n}\theta^T Y_{\mathrm{Ord}}^T Y_{\mathrm{Ord}}\theta = 1. \tag{1}$$

When we solve the problem in Eq. 1 we seek a sparse discriminant vector β_{Ord}, which we can then use to project the data from feature space to a one-dimensional representation. In the ordinal case, we cast our problem as a binary classification problem, which only yields a single discriminant vector β_{Ord}, simplifying the interpretation of the solution. β_{Ord} is a vector of length $p + K - 1$, (where p is the number of variables and K the number of classes). The first p parameters correspond to the original variables that we can interpret. The extra $K - 1$ parameters are the additional biases introduced by the data replication method, allowing us to classify the projected points, based on where they end up concerning the biases.

[6] show that for a given β_{Ord} one can find θ in polynomial time. For a given θ the problem formulation is an elastic net problem, and the problem can be solved with the LARS-EN algorithm by [18]. We, however, approach the optimization from the point of proximal gradient (PG) methods and alternating direction method of multipliers (ADMM), using the soft thresholding operator to deal with the sparse regularizer in the same manner as [3].

A natural assumption for an ordinal classifier of K classes, is to have $K - 1$ non-intersecting classification boundaries, where boundary i separates classes 1 to i from classes $i+1$ to K. In our case, that means finding a hyperplane and a set of biases to shift the hyperplane between classes. We extend the data replication method of [4] to the sparse setting, by adapting the optimization, such that it does not regularize these new bias parameters.

We construct a new data matrix X_{Ord} and labels Y_{Ord} according to the data replication method. We then define a new $(p+K-1) \times (p+K-1)$ regularization matrix $\hat{\Omega}$.

$$\hat{\Omega} := \begin{bmatrix} \Omega & 0 \\ 0 & 0 \end{bmatrix}, \qquad \beta_{\text{Ord}}^{T} := \begin{bmatrix} \beta_1 & \beta_2 & \dots & \beta_p & b_1 & b_2 & \dots & b_{K-1} \end{bmatrix}, \tag{2}$$

where Ω is a $p \times p$ positive semi-definite regularization matrix for the parameters corresponding to the p original variables. The final adjustments relates to the l_1-norm in Eq. 1. In the soft-thresholding step of the ADMM and PG algorithms used to find β_{Ord}, we only apply soft-thresholding to the first p elements.

The resulting β_{Ord} vector is show in Eq. 2. The first part is composed of a traditional discriminant vector, corresponding to the first p elements, and then $K-1$ biases, denoted b_i, for $i \in \{1, 2, ..., K-1\}$. The proofs of convergence to stationary points, of the algorithms in [3], extend naturally to our approach.

3   Data and Experiments

We conducted a study, where we collected data from 63 individuals, of whom 33 were healthy controls and 30 PD patients. Detailed description of the cohort can be found in [2]. Each participant played the Motor-game two times; the first one is a trial run to get familiar with the game. Motion tracking data was collected during the playthroughs. A physician then evaluated the participants on various rating scales, of which we are concerned with the results from the *Simpson-Angus-Scale* (SAS) [14], in particular, item 4, which involves elbow rigidity. Furthermore, the PD patients were evaluated on the *Movement Disorder Society Unified Parkinson's Disease Rating Scale* (MDS-UPDRS) [12]. On MDS-UPDRS we are most focused on items 3.3b rigidity of right hand, 3.4a finger tapping in the right hand and 3.5a hand movement for the right hand. We picked out these items since they were *a priori* thought to have the most substantial correspondence with the data from the Motor-game. Items from the rating scales reflecting motor symptoms in hands and arms were included. Exclusion was made if there were too few participants affected. See Fig. 2 for prevalence and severity of the observed motion conditions in the data. We refer to the ratings as clinical scores. A more detailed description of the dataset and the Motor-game can be found in [2].

For analyzing the movements of the participants, we used the tracked position of their wrists, we denote x_{ij} as the position at timepoint j in task i. For the first 11 tasks, we used the avatar screen coordinate vertical position for the right wrist. The choice of this coordinate is because the avatar has been scaled according to an initial estimate of the player's arm length, making on-screen positions comparable between players. For the following 11 tasks, we used the

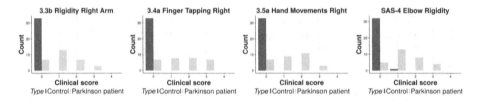

Fig. 2. Prevalence of labels in the dataset for the conditions we focus on. The first three plots from the left correspond to MDS-UPDRS items 3.3b *rigidity right arm*, 3.4a *finger tapping right hand* and 3.5a hand movement right. The final item corresponds to *elbow rigidity* on the SAS scale.

corresponding coordinates for the left wrist. For each of the 22 tasks, we used measurements for the first second of play. The first second of the game is enough for the person to respond and start moving. We can see the contrast between a fast and slow reacting participant in Fig. 3. This yields, in the end, a total of $p = 20 \times 22 = 440$ variables per participant. We denote m_{i_S} as the mean of the first three measurements for task i and m_{i_E} as the average for the last three measures for task i.

$$\tilde{x}_{ji} := \frac{x_{ji} - m_{i_S}}{|m_{i_S} - m_{i_E}|} \qquad (3)$$

We further scale the j-th measurement x_{ji} from task i as depicted in Eq. 3. Due to variation in the end and starting position, this scaling ensures that the data is more robust to reactions of the participants.

We normalize the data before applying sparse ordinal regression by subtracting the mean for each variable and scaling the standard deviation to one. We report the balanced accuracy for leave one cross-validation, where we allow the regularization parameters λ_1 and λ_2 from Eq. 1 to be in the set $\{0.1, 0.01, 0.001\}$. We perform this experiment for the four labels shown in Fig. 2. Note that the

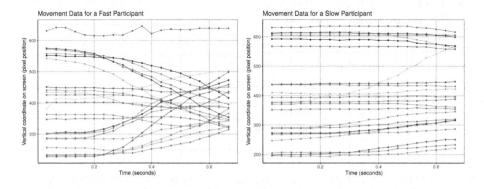

Fig. 3. Data used for the experiment, vertical position of two subjects' hands over the first second of the 22 tasks. On the left we have a participant that generally reacts fast, on the right we have a more slow reacting individual.

three variables for MDS-UPDRS were only measured for the Parkinson patients; thus the controls were assumed to have a score of zero.

4 Results

The leave one out cross-validation balanced-accuracy ranged from 38.8% for *hand movement right* to 48.1% for elbow rigidity. The corresponding confusion matrices are shown in Table 1. We can see that the predictions are somewhat accurate, although the LOO-CV most likely overestimates the real accuracy. Note that the best forecasts for class zero are in MDS-UPDRS 3.4a and SAS-4. We assume that the controls have a score of zero in the MDS-UPDRS variables since they were not measured, this may not be entirely correct, a few individuals in the control group had a score of one for SAS-4.

Table 1. Confusion matrices for predictions (with best performing regularization parameters) from the item left out in the leave one out cross-validation. Most of the predictions are concentrated around the correct label, but most of them have difficulties with the higher labels.

3.3b — True

Predicted	0	1	2	3
0	22	2	4	1
1	13	9	3	0
2	4	1	0	0
3	1	1	0	2

3.4a — True

Predicted	0	1	2	3
0	26	2	4	2
1	13	6	1	4
2	1	0	3	0
3	0	0	0	0

3.5a — True

Predicted	0	1	2	3
0	20	3	6	1
1	11	4	3	0
2	8	2	1	1
3	1	0	1	1

SAS-4 — True

Predicted	0	1	2	3
0	23	1	4	1
1	11	9	3	1
2	1	4	1	0
3	2	0	0	2

5 Conclusions

We have presented a novel approach for assessing the severity of upper body motor symptoms in PD. The novelty lies in the game-like environment, which has been proven to work both in the clinic, or in the patient's home and the sparse ordinal regression for prediction the severity of motion disturbances. Longitudinal studies are needed to establish further the potential of this approach. Monitoring the movement in correspondence with the presence of pre-movement related symptoms has potential to create novel tools for early detection of PD.

Acknowledgements. Gudmundur Einarson's PhD is funded jointly by the Lundbeck Foundation and the Technical University of Denmark. The study has received grants from The Capital Region of Denmark, Research Fund for Health Promotion and The Capital Region of Denmark, Mental Health Services Research Fund.

References

1. Ahlskog, J.E.: Does vigorous exercise have a neuroprotective effect in parkinson disease? Neurology **77**(3), 288–294 (2011)
2. Anonymous: Exploring alternative ways to assess Parkinson's patients (2018)
3. Atkins, S., Einarsson, G., Ames, B., Clemmensen, L.: Proximal methods for sparse optimal scoring and discriminant analysis. arXiv preprint arXiv:1705.07194 (2017)
4. Cardoso, J.S., Costa, J.F.: Learning to classify ordinal data: the data replication method. J. Mach. Learn. Res. **8**(Jul), 1393–1429 (2007)
5. Chung, D., Keles, S.: Sparse partial least squares classification for high dimensional data. Stat. Appl. Genetics Mol. Biol. **9**(1) (2010)
6. Clemmensen, L., Hastie, T., Witten, D., Ersbøll, B.: Sparse discriminant analysis. Technometrics **53**(4), 406–413 (2011)
7. d'Aspremont, A., Ghaoui, L.E., Jordan, M.I., Lanckriet, G.R.: A direct formulation for sparse PCA using semidefinite programming. In: Advances in Neural Information Processing Systems, pp. 41–48 (2005)
8. Duncan, G.W., et al.: Health-related quality of life in early Parkinson's disease: the impact of nonmotor symptoms. Mov. Disord. **29**(2), 195–202 (2014)
9. Galna, B., Barry, G., Jackson, D., Mhiripiri, D., Olivier, P., Rochester, L.: Accuracy of the microsoft kinect sensor for measuring movement in people with Parkinson's disease. Gait Posture **39**(4), 1062–1068 (2014)
10. Galna, B., et al.: Retraining function in people with Parkinson's disease using the microsoft kinect: game design and pilot testing. J. Neuroengineering Rehabil. **11**(1), 60 (2014)
11. Gan-Or, Z., Dion, P.A., Rouleau, G.A.: Genetic perspective on the role of the autophagy-lysosome pathway in Parkinson disease. Autophagy **11**(9), 1443–1457 (2015)
12. Goetz, C.G., et al.: Movement disorder society-sponsored revision of the unified Parkinson's disease rating scale (MDS-UPDRS): scale presentation and clinimetric testing results. Mov. Disord. **23**(15), 2129–2170 (2008)
13. Mousavi Hondori, H., Khademi, M.: A review on technical and clinical impact of microsoft kinect on physical therapy and rehabilitation. J. Med. Eng. (2014)
14. Simpson, G., Angus, J.: A rating scale for extrapyramidal side effects. Acta Psychiatr. Scand. **45**(S212), 11–19 (1970)
15. Tibshirani, R.: Regression shrinkage and selection via the lasso. J. Roy. Stat. Soc. Ser. B (Methodol.), 267–288 (1996)
16. Tinelli, M., Kanavos, P., Grimaccia, F.: The value of early diagnosis and treatment in Parkinson's disease. A literature review of the potential clinical and socioeconomic impact of targeting unmet needs in Parkinson's disease. London School of Economics (2016)
17. Zhang, Z.: Microsoft kinect sensor and its effect. IEEE Multimedia **19**(2), 4–10 (2012)
18. Zou, H., Hastie, T.: Regularization and variable selection via the elastic net. J. Roy. Stat. Soc. Ser. B (Stat. Methodol.) **67**(2), 301–320 (2005)

Prediction of Severity and Treatment Outcome for ASD from fMRI

Juntang Zhuang[1][(✉)], Nicha C. Dvornek[2,3], Xiaoxiao Li[1], Pamela Ventola[2], and James S. Duncan[1,3,4]

[1] Biomedical Engineering, Yale University, New Haven, CT, USA
j.zhuang@yale.edu
[2] Child Study Center, Yale University, New Haven, CT, USA
[3] Radiology and Biomedical Imaging, Yale School of Medicine, New Haven, CT, USA
[4] Electrical Engineering, Yale University, New Haven, CT, USA

Abstract. Autism spectrum disorder (ASD) is a complex neurodevelopmental syndrome. Early diagnosis and precise treatment are essential for ASD patients. Although researchers have built many analytical models, there has been limited progress in accurate predictive models for early diagnosis. In this project, we aim to build an accurate model to predict treatment outcome and ASD severity from early stage functional magnetic resonance imaging (fMRI) scans. The difficulty in building large databases of patients who have received specific treatments and the high dimensionality of medical image analysis problems are challenges in this work. We propose a generic and accurate two-level approach for high-dimensional regression problems in medical image analysis. First, we perform region-level feature selection using a predefined brain parcellation. Based on the assumption that voxels within one region in the brain have similar values, for each region we use the bootstrapped mean of voxels within it as a feature. In this way, the dimension of data is reduced from number of voxels to number of regions. Then we detect predictive regions by various feature selection methods. Second, we extract voxels within selected regions, and perform voxel-level feature selection. To use this model in both linear and non-linear cases with limited training examples, we apply two-level elastic net regression and random forest (RF) models respectively. To validate accuracy and robustness of this approach, we perform experiments on both task-fMRI and resting state fMRI datasets. Furthermore, we visualize the influence of each region, and show that the results match well with other findings.

Keywords: fMRI · ASD · Predictive model

1 Introduction

Autism spectrum disorder (ASD) is a neurodevelopmental syndrome characterized by impaired social interaction, difficulty in communication and repetitive behavior. ASD is most commonly diagnosed with a behavioral test [1], however,

© Springer Nature Switzerland AG 2018
I. Rekik et al. (Eds.): PRIME 2018, LNCS 11121, pp. 9–17, 2018.
https://doi.org/10.1007/978-3-030-00320-3_2

the behavioral test is insufficient to understand the mechanism of ASD. Functional magnetic resonance imaging (fMRI) has been widely used in research on brain diseases and has the potential to reveal brain malfunctions in ASD.

Behavior based treatment is a widely used therapy for ASD, and Pivotal Response Treatment (PRT) is empirically-supported [2]. PRT addresses core deficits in social motivation to improve social communication skills. Such therapies require large time commitments and lifestyle changes. However, an individual's response to PRT and other behavioral treatments vary, yet treatment is mainly assigned by trial and error. Therefore, prediction of treatment outcome during early stages is essential.

fMRI measures blood oxygenation level dependent (BOLD) signal and reflects brain activity. Recent studies have applied fMRI in classification of ASD and identifying biomarkers for ASD [3]. Although some regions are found to have higher linear correlations with certain types of ASD severity scores, the correlation coefficient is typically low (below 0.5). Moreover, most prior studies apply *analytical* models, and lack *predictive* accuracy.

The goal of our work is to build accurate *predictive* models for fMRI images. To deal with the high dimensionality of the medical image regression problem, we propose a two-level modeling approach: (1) region-level feature selection, and (2) voxel-level feature selection. In this paper, we demonstrate predictive models for PRT treatment outcomes and ASD severity, and validate robustness of this approach in both task fMRI and resting state fMRI datasets. Furthermore, we analyze feature importance and identify potential biomarkers for ASD.

2   Methods

2.1   Two-Level Modeling Approach

Dimensionality of medical images (i.e., the number of voxels) is far higher than the number of subjects in most medical studies. The high dimensionality causes inaccuracy in variable selection and affects modeling performance. However, medical images are typically locally smooth, and voxels are not independent of each other. This enables us to perform the following two-level feature selection as shown in Fig. 1. The proposed procedure first selects important features at the region level, then performs feature selection at the voxel level. Our generic approach can be used with both linear and non-linear models.

Region-Level Modeling and Variable Selection. Based on brain atlas research, we assume that voxels within the same region of a brain parcellation have similar values. Therefore, we use the bootstrapped (sample with replacement) mean for each region as a feature, reducing dimension of data from number of voxels to number of regions. Then we can perform feature selection on this new dataset, where each predictor variable represents a region.

Beyond dimension reduction, representing each region with the bootstrapped mean of its voxel values decreases correlation between predictor variables.

Another potential benefit is to increase sample size. We can generate many artificial training examples from one real training example by repeatedly bootstrapping each region. Since this generates correlated training samples, repeated bootstrapping can only be used in models that are robust to sample correlation.

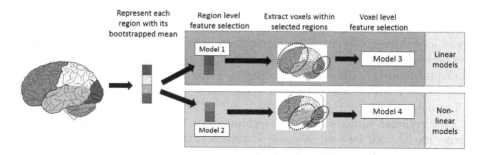

Fig. 1. Flowchart of the proposed approach. Each column represents a stage of the approach, region-level and voxel-level models. Top row shows linear models (e.g. elastic net regression), bottom row shows non-linear models (e.g. random forest).

Voxel-Level Modeling and Variable Selection. Region-level feature selection preserves predictive regions. However, representing all voxels within a region as one number is too coarse, and may affect model accuracy. Therefore, we extract all voxels within the selected regions, perform spatial down-sampling by a factor of 4, and apply feature selection on voxels.

Pipeline Repetition. Due to the randomness in bootstrapping for region level modeling, we repeat the whole process. For each of the four models (linear and non-linear models at region-level and voxel-level respectively), we average outcomes to generate stable predictions.

2.2 Linear and Non-linear Models

We can apply any model in the approach proposed in Sect. 2.1. To instantiate a generic approach for both linear and non-linear cases, we train elastic net regression and random forest (RF) independently, both trained at two levels.

Variable Selection with Elastic Net Regression. Elastic net is a linear model with both $l1$ and $l2$ penalty to perform variable selection and shrinkage regularization [4]. Given predictor variables X and targets y, the model is formalized as

$$\hat{\beta} = \mathrm{argmin}_{\beta}\left\{||y - X\beta||^2 + \lambda\left[\alpha||\beta||_1 + (1-\alpha)||\beta||^2\right]\right\} \tag{1}$$

where $0 \leq \alpha \leq 1$, α controls the proportion of regularization on $l1$ and $l2$ term of estimated coefficients, and λ controls the amplitude of regularization. $l2$ penalty is shrinkage regularization and improves robustness of the model. $l1$ penalty controls sparsity of the model. By choosing proper parameters, irrelevant variables will have coefficients equal to 0, enabling variable selection.

Variable Selection with Random Forest. Random forest is a powerful model for both regression and classification problems and can deal with interaction between variables and high dimensionality [5]. Although random forest can handle medium-high dimensional problems, it's insufficient to handle ultra-high dimensional medical image problems. Therefore, two-level variable selection is still essential.

Conventional variable selection technique for random forest builds a predictive model with forward stepwise feature selection [6]. For high dimensional problems, it is computationally intensive. Therefore, we use a similar thresholding method to perform fast variable selection as in [7] (Fig. 2). We generate noise ("shadow") variables from a Gaussian distribution independent of target variables. Shadow variables are added to the original data matrix, and a random forest is trained on the new data matrix. The random forest model calculates the importance of each variable. A predictive variable should have higher importance than noise variables. A threshold is calculated as:

$$Thres = \text{median}(VI_i^{shadow}) \quad s.t. \quad VI_i^{shadow} > 0, \quad i = 1, 2, ...n \qquad (2)$$

where n is the total number of shadow variables, and VI_i^{shadow} is the importance measure for the ith shadow variable. We use permutation accuracy importance measure [6] in this experiment. The threshold is calculated using positive shadow variable importance because permutation accuracy importance can be negative. We use the median to make a conservative threshold, because even noise variables can have high importance in high-dimensional problems, due to randomness of the model. After variable selection, we build a gradient boosted regression tree model based on selected variables.

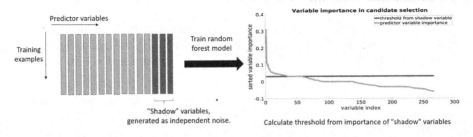

Fig. 2. Flowchart of variable selection with random forest and "shadow" method.

2.3 Visualization of Each Variable's Influence

To achieve both predictability and interpretability, we use the following methods to visualize influence of each region in the brain. For linear models, we plot the linear coefficients map.

For non-linear models, we visualize the influence based on the partial dependence plot. The partial dependence plot shows the dependence between target and predictor variables, marginalizing over all other features [8],

$$D_l(z_l) = \mathbb{E}_x(\hat{F}(x)|z_l) = \int \hat{F}(x)p(z_{\backslash l}|z_l)dz_{\backslash l} \tag{3}$$

where $D_l(z_l)$ is the partial dependence function for variable z_l, $\hat{F}(x)$ is the trained model, $z_{\backslash l}$ is the set of variables except z_l, $p(z_{\backslash l}|z_l)$ is the distribution of $z_{\backslash l}$ given z_l. Each $D_l(z_l)$ is calculated as a sequence varying with z_l in practice.

The influence of each variable is stored in a sequence. For visualization, we summarize the influence of a variable (Influence$_l$) by calculating the variance of $D_l(z_l)$ to measure the amplitude of its influence, and the sign of its correlation with z_l to show if it has a positive or negative influence on targets:

$$\text{Influence}_l = \text{Sign}\left(\text{corr}\left(D_l(z_l), z_l\right)\right)\text{Var}\left(D_l(z_l)\right). \tag{4}$$

3 Experiments and Results

3.1 Task-fMRI Experiment

Nineteen children with ASD participated in 16 weeks of PRT treatment, with pre-treatment and post-treatment social responsiveness scale (SRS) scores [9], and pre-treatment autism diagnostic observation schedule (ADOS) [10] scores measured. Each child underwent a pre-treatment baseline task fMRI scan (BOLD, TR = 2000 ms, TE = 25 ms, flip angle = 60°, slice thickness = 4.00 mm, voxel size $3.44 \times 3.44 \times 4$ mm^3) and a structural MRI scan (T1-weighted MPRAGE sequence, TR = 1900 ms, TE = 2.96 ms, flip angle = 9°, slice thickness = 1.00 mm, voxel size = $1 \times 1 \times 1$ mm^3) on a Siemens MAGNETOM Trio TIM 3T scanner.

During the fMRI scan, coherent (BIO) and scrambled (SCRAM) point-light biological motion movies were presented to participants in alternating blocks with 24 s duration [11]. The fMRI data were processed using FSL v5.0.8 in the following pipeline: (a) motion correction with MCFLIRT, (b) interleaved slice timing correction, (c) BET brain extraction, (d) grand mean intensity normalization for the whole four-dimensional data set, (e) spatial smoothing with 5 mm FWHM, (f) denoising with ICA-AROMA, (g) nuisance regression for white matter and CSF, (h) high-pass temporal filtering.

The timing of the corresponding blocks (BIO and SCRAM) was convolved with the default gamma function (phase = 0 s, sd = 3 s, mean lag = 6 s) with temporal derivatives. Participant-level t-statistics for contrast BIO > SCRAM were calculated for each voxel with first level analysis. This 3D t-statistic image is the input to the proposed approach. The input image is parcellated into 268 regions using the atlas from group-wise analysis [12].

We tested the approach on three target scores using leave-one-out cross validation: pre-treatment SRS score, pre-treatment standardized ADOS score [13], and treatment outcome defined as the difference between pre-treatment and post-treatment SRS score. For elastic net regression, we used nested cross-validation to select parameters ($\lambda \in \{0.001, 0.01, 0.1\}$, α ranging from 0.1 to 0.9 with a stepsize of 0.1). Other parameters were set according to computation capability. For random forest models, we set tree number as 2000. For region level modeling, each region was represented as the mean of 2000 bootstrapped samples from its voxels. For gradient boosted tree model after feature selection with random forest, the number of trees was set as 500. The whole process was repeated 100 times and averaged. All models were implemented in MATLAB, with default parameters except as noted above. Neurological functions of selected regions were decoded with Neurosynth [14]. For each experiment, results (linear correlation between predictions and measurements r, uncorrected p-value, root mean square error $RMSE$) of the best model are shown in Figs. 3 and 4.

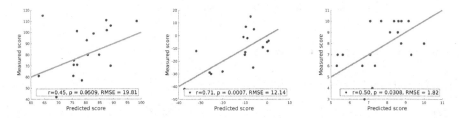

(a) Region-level elastic net model for pre-treatment SRS

(b) Voxel-level random forest model for change of SRS after treatment

(c) Voxel-level random forest model for standardized ADOS

Fig. 3. Results for various scores predicted from task fMRI, red lines are reference lines of perfect prediction $y = x$. (Color figure online)

3.2   Resting State fMRI Experiment

We performed similar experiments on the ABIDE dataset [15] using the UM and USM sites with five-fold cross validation. We selected male subjects diagnosed with ASD, resulting in 51 patients from UM and 13 patients from USM. We built models to predict the ADOS Gotham total score from voxel-mirrored homotopic connectivity images [16]. We set parameters the same as in Sect. 3.1. Results are shown in Fig. 5.

3.3   Result Analysis

Training and validation datasets were independent for all experiments. The proposed two-level approach accurately selected predictive features, while elastic net and RF directly applied to the whole-brain image failed to generate predictive results in all experiments (correlation between predictions and measurements <0.1). The proposed approach generated very high predictive accuracy on various datasets and different scores, achieving better accuracy than state-of-the-art.

For SRS scores, we found no predictive models in the literature. Kaiser et al. reported regions of correlation r = 0.502 [11] in *analytical* modeling, while our *predictive* model achieved r = 0.45 (Fig. 3(a)).

For standardized ADOS score, the best result in literature achieves r = 0.51 between predictions and measurements with 156 subjects based on cortical thickness [17]. Our model achieved r = 0.50 with 19 patients (Fig. 3(c)) based on fMRI.

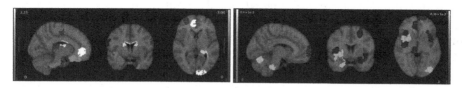

(a) Region-level elastic net model for pre-treatment SRS

(b) Voxel-level random forest model for change of SRS after treatment

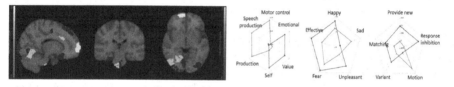

(c) Voxel-level random forest model for standardized ADOS

(d) From left to right: results of Neurosynth decoder for model in (a) (b) (c).

Fig. 4. Regions are colored in red for positive influence and blue for negative influence. (a–c): Influence of regions for various scores based on task fMRI. (d): Functions decoded by Neurosynth. (Color figure online)

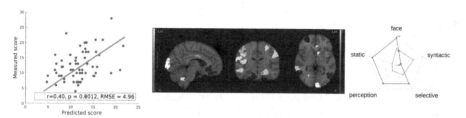

Fig. 5. Left: Results of region-level elastic net regression model for resting-state fMRI experiment. Middle: Linear coefficients of model. Right: Functions decoded by Neurosynth, red for positive regions, blue for negative regions. (Color figure online)

For raw ADOS score, Björnsdotter et al. found no significant correlation with brain responses in fMRI scan [18]. Predictive models based on structural MRI achieved correlation of r = 0.362 between predictions and measurements [19]. In our experiment with resting-state fMRI, we achieved correlation r = 0.40 (Fig. 5).

To predict treatment outcome from baseline fMRI scan, Dvornek et al. achieved correlation r = 0.83 between predictions and measurements [20]. We achieved r = 0.71 (Fig. 3(b)). However, the study by Dvornek et al. takes pre-selected regions as input and loses interpretability because it does not perform region selection. In contrast, our proposed approach takes a whole-brain image as input and can select predictive regions for interpretation and biomarker selection. Furthermore, the proposed approach is generic and any non-linear model (including Dvornek's method) can be applied.

Neurosynth decoder results (Figs. 4(d) and 5 right figure) show that selected regions match the literature [11]. The selected regions are slightly different across experiments due to different tasks, datasets and target measures. Many regions are shared across experiments, such as prefrontal cortex and visual cortex.

4   Conclusion

We propose a generic approach to build *predictive* models based on fMRI images. To deal with high-dimensionality, we perform two-level variable selection: region-level modeling, and voxel-level modeling. This generic approach includes elastic net and random forest models to fit both linear and non-linear cases. The proposed approach is tested on both task-fMRI and resting-state fMRI, and validated on different scores. The proposed predictive approach achieves higher correlation than state-of-the-art predictive modeling in many experiments. Overall, the proposed approach is generic, accurate, and achieves both predictability and interpretability.

Acknowledgement. This research was funded by the National Institutes of Health (NINDS-R01NS035193).

References

1. Baird, G., et al.: Diagnosis of autism. BMJ **327**(7413), 488–493 (2003)
2. Koegel, L.K., et al.: Pivotal response intervention i: overview of approach. TASH **24**(3), 174–185 (1999)
3. Anderson, J.S., et al.: Functional connectivity magnetic resonance imaging classification of autism. Brain **134**(12), 3742–3754 (2011)
4. Zou, H., et al.: Regularization and variable selection via the elastic net. J. Royal Stat. Soc. **67**(2), 301–320 (2005)
5. Liaw, A., et al.: Classification and regression by randomforest. R news **2**(3), 18–22 (2002)
6. Genuer, R., et al.: Variable selection using random forests. Pattern Recogn. Lett. **31**(14), 2225–2236 (2010)

7. Zhuang, J., et al.: Prediction of pivotal response treatment outcome with task fMRI using random forest and variable selection. In: ISBI (2018)
8. Friedman, J.H.: Greedy function approximation: a gradient boosting machine. Ann. Stat. (2001)
9. Bruni, T.P.: Test Review: Social Responsiveness Scale, 2nd edn. (srs-2) (2014)
10. Lord, C., et al.: The autism diagnostic observation schedule-generic: a standard measure of social and communication deficits associated with the spectrum of autism. J. Autism Dev. Disord. **30**(3), 205–223 (2000)
11. Kaiser, M.D., et al.: Neural signatures of autism. In: Proceedings of the National Academy of Sciences U.S.A (2010)
12. Shen, X., et al.: Groupwise whole-brain parcellation from resting-state fMRI data for network node identification. Neuroimage **82**, 403–415 (2013)
13. Gotham, K., et al.: Standardizing ADOS scores for a measure of severity in autism spectrum disorders. J. Autism Dev. Disord. **39**(5), 693–705 (2009)
14. Yarkoni, T., et al.: Large-scale automated synthesis of human functional neuroimaging data. Nat. Methods **8**(8), 665 (2011)
15. Di Martino, A., et al.: The autism brain imaging data exchange: towards a large-scale evaluation of the intrinsic brain architecture in autism. Mol. Psychiatry **19**(6), 659 (2014)
16. Zuo, X.-N., et al.: Growing together and growing apart: regional and sex differences in the lifespan developmental trajectories of functional homotopy. J. Neuroscience **30**(45), 15034–15043 (2010)
17. Moradi, E., et al.: Predicting symptom severity in autism spectrum disorder based on cortical thickness measures in agglomerative data. NeuroImage **144**, 128–141 (2017)
18. Björnsdotter, M., et al.: Evaluation of quantified social perception circuit activity as a neurobiological marker of autism spectrum disorder. JAMA Psychiatry **73**(6), 614–621 (2016)
19. Sato, J.R., et al.: Inter-regional cortical thickness correlations are associated with autistic symptoms: a machine-learning approach. J. Psychiat. Res. **47**(4), 453–459 (2013)
20. Dvornek, N.C., et al.: Prediction of autism treatment response from baseline fMRI using random forests and tree bagging. Multimodal Learn. Clin. Decis. Support (2016)

Enhancement of Perivascular Spaces Using a Very Deep 3D Dense Network

Euijin Jung[1], Xiaopeng Zong[2], Weili Lin[2], Dinggang Shen[2(✉)],
and Sang Hyun Park[1(✉)]

[1] Department of Robotics Engineering, Daegu Gyeongbuk Institute of Science
and Technology, Daegu, South Korea
shpark13135@dgist.ac.kr
[2] Department of Radiology, BRIC, University of North Carolina, Chapel Hill, USA
dinggang_shen@med.unc.edu

Abstract. Perivascular spaces (PVS) in the human brain are related to
various brain diseases or functions, but it is difficult to quantify them in
a magnetic resonance (MR) image due to their thin and blurry appearance. In this paper, we introduce a deep learning based method which
can enhance a MR image to better visualize the PVS. To accurately
predict the enhanced image, we propose a very deep 3D convolutional
neural network which contains densely connected networks with skip
connections. The densely connected networks can utilize rich contextual
information derived from low level to high level features and effectively
alleviate the gradient vanishing problem caused by the deep layers. The
proposed method is evaluated on seventeen 7T MR images by a two-
fold cross validation. The experiments show that our proposed network
is more effective to enhance the PVS than the previous deep learning
based methods using less layers.

Keywords: Perivascular spaces · Enhancement
Deep convolutional neural network · Densely connected network
Skip connections

1 Introduction

Perivascular spaces (PVS) are thin fluid-filled spaces in the human brain.
Recently, studies have shown that increasing the PVS number and thickening
the PVS are associated with brain diseases [1]. Also, it is revealed that the PVS
enlargement is related to cognitive abilities of healthy elderly men [2]. To demonstrate these hypotheses, it is necessary to quantify the relationship between the
thickness, length, distribution of PVS and the brain diseases or functions.

However, the PVS are not clearly visible in magnetic resonance (MR) images
acquired by traditional 1.5T, 3T or even by 7T MR scanners. Accordingly, Bouvy
et al. [3] and Zong *et al.* [4] proposed novel acquisition parameters of 7T MR
scanner that make the PVS more visible. However, it is difficult to find the

© Springer Nature Switzerland AG 2018
I. Rekik et al. (Eds.): PRIME 2018, LNCS 11121, pp. 18–25, 2018.
https://doi.org/10.1007/978-3-030-00320-3_3

parameters which can improve only the PVS while reducing the noisy in background. Thus, distinguishing small PVS is still difficult although several methods have been proposed to segment the PVS from MR images [5,6].

Accordingly, instead of carefully looking for a certain specific parameter of MR scanner, several studies have been proposed to enhance the PVS by using image processing methods after the MR images are acquired. For example, Uchiyama *et al.* [7] used the white top hat transform to highlight the tubular structures and proved that this enhancement is effective to detect the PVS. Hou *et al.* [8] proposed a method which improves the intensity of thin tubular structures using a nonlinear mapping function in Haar domain, and then removes noisy in background by using the block matching filtering. Although these methods help to extract the PVS by enhancing the intensity of PVS, they require heuristic parameter tuning such as controlling the filter size or defining the parameters of nonlinear mapping function according to the image.

In this paper, we propose an end to end PVS enhancement method which does not require the heuristic parameter tuning and the additional processing steps for distinguishing the PVS from noisy. Specifically, we suggest a very deep 3D neural network consisting of 39 convolution layers which are densely connected by skip connections. The proposed network using the dense skip connections effectively improves the prediction accuracy by utilizing rich contextual information derived from low level to high level features and alleviating the gradient vanishing problem. The prediction accuracy of our proposed network was evaluated on seventeen 7T MR images. Experimental results show that our deep network is more effective to enhance the PVS than the state-of-the-art deep learning based image enhancement methods.

1.1   Related Works

Deep learning based methods have achieved the best performance for the super resolution problem which converts a low resolution image into a high resolution image. For example, Dong *et al.* [9] proposed a method using three convolution layers and achieved better prediction results than the previous methods using sparse coding and regression. After that, several studies using deeper network [10,11] have been proposed to utilize higher level contextual features. Specifically, Kim *et al.* [10] proposed a recursive neural network to reflect a large contextual information without additional weight parameters and Tong *et al.* [11] proposed a network using densely connected blocks with skip connections to reflect the various levels of features for the prediction.

In this paper, we apply the deep neural networks, mainly have been applied to the super resolution of 2D images, to the enhancement of PVS in 3D MR images. The PVS are thin and oriented at different angles in three dimensions, and thus it is difficult to distinguish the PVS from noisy in a 2D image. In addition, since the difference between a MR image and its enhanced MR image is relatively larger (see Fig. 2) than that between the low resolution image and the high resolution image in super resolution, sophisticated contextual features need to be learned. Therefore, we design a very deep 3D network including six dense blocks and dense skip connections to reduce the feature redundancy and utilize the rich contextual information in three dimensions. Although several 3D networks [12–14] recently have been proposed for the super resolution of MR images, those models use shallow structures while our model includes six dense blocks and skip connections between them. The closest model to our proposed network is the network proposed by Tong *et al.* [11], but our model consists of 3D layers and there are some differences in the structure such as not using a deconvolution layer. To the best of our knowledge, this is the first work to use the deep learning based method for the PVS enhancement.

2   Method

We introduce a deep learning based method which generates an enhanced 7T MR image from a 7T MR image. Learning a deep network that maps the whole 3D MR image is infeasible due to memory limitations. Thus, if an image is given, we sample 3D patches at a regular interval, and then perform the prediction in each patch using a deep 3D convolutional neural network, and finally generate the whole enhanced image by merging the predictions on the 3D patches. Since the predictions near the boundary of patch may not be accurate, the predictions on the central region are collected to generate the whole enhanced image. The sampling interval is determined so that the prediction is obtained in every voxel.

In the training step, we sample the 3D patches from 7T MR images and those from their enhanced 7T MR images in a training set, and then learn the deep 3D convolutional neural network which learns the relationship between patches. The proposed network consists of an initial convolution layer for learning low level features, several dense blocks for learning middle level to high level features, a bottleneck layer for reducing the number of feature maps, and a prediction layer for generating the enhanced 3D patch. Figure 1 shows the proposed network and detailed descriptions follow in the subsections.

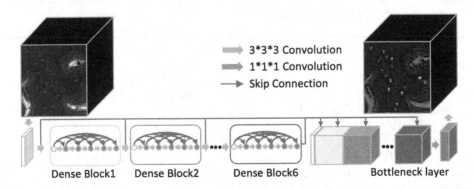

Fig. 1. The proposed deep 3D convolutional neural network for PVS enhancement.

2.1   Densely Connected Deep Neural Network

The proposed network learns the relationship between the patch X sampled from a 7T MR image and the patch Y from its enhanced 7T MR image. The relevance is parameterized by weights $\mathbf{w} = [w_1, ..., w_N]$ and residuals $\mathbf{b} = [b_1, ..., b_N]$ between layers where N is the number of convolution layers, and X is transformed into $P(X, \mathbf{w}, \mathbf{b})$ by those parameters. In training, the parameters $\mathbf{w}$ and $\mathbf{b}$ are updated by an optimizer so that the mean squared error between $P(X, \mathbf{w}, \mathbf{b})$ and Y is minimized.

The proposed network consists of 39 convolution layers ($N = 39$). First, the input patch X is passed through a convolution layer and then six dense blocks where each dense block consists of 6 convolution layers to produce low level to high level feature maps. Specifically, 8 kernels with a size $3 \times 3 \times 3$ is used for the convolution layers and a rectified linear unit (ReLU) layer is connected for nonlinear mapping behind each convolution layer.

In each dense block, as proposed by Huang et $al.$ [15], the feature maps generated in previous layers are concatenated and pass through a convolution layer to generate new feature maps. The new feature maps are also concatenated to the previous feature maps and then pass through the next convolution layer. Thus, the number of feature maps linearly increased by the number of kernel. Since we use six convolution layers with 8 kernels, the number of feature maps increased by 8 in six times and the dense block generates 48 feature maps. The concatenation of the feature maps not only reduces the number of parameters but also alleviates the vanishing gradient problem. Finally, the 8 feature maps generated from the last layer are used as the input of the next dense block.

After passing through all six dense blocks, the prediction can be performed by using the feature maps from the 6th dense block. However, in this way, the low level and middle level features extracted by the initial layer and the initial dense blocks are rarely reflected in the prediction. Thus, to use all levels of information for the prediction, we use skip connections between the following layer and the initial convolution layer and six dense blocks. Specifically, 8 feature maps obtained from the initial convolution layer and all 288 ($= 48 \times 6$) feature maps from six dense blocks are connected to the following layer in the network.

Connecting all these feature maps to the prediction layer for predicting a single channel output at once ($i.e.$, 296 to 1) is computationally inefficient and hard to keep the model compactness. Therefore, a $1 \times 1 \times 1$ convolution layer with 16 kernels is utilized as the bottleneck layer between the 6th dense block and the prediction layer to reduce the number of feature maps. Finally, the 16 feature maps generated from the bottleneck layer are passed through the prediction layer to predict the final output ($i.e.$, 296 to 16, and then 16 to 1). With through the bottleneck layer, prediction can be more accurate and efficient, since this layer use all feature map from low to high levels and reduce the number of feature map in computationally efficient way.

2.2 Implementation Details

Most PVS are located in the white matter and the non-brain region is large in a MR image. Thus, it is inefficient to sample the training patches in the whole image. We extracted the brain region by using the brain extraction tool [16] and then sampled 3D patches which contain a part of brain region for training. The patch size was determined as $60 \times 60 \times 60$ by considering the receptive field of our network. In testing, we similarly extracted the brain region using [16], and then estimated the enhanced image by performing the prediction on $60 \times 60 \times 60$ 3D patches containing the brain region and merging them.

Regarding the proposed network, the weights $\mathbf{w}$ were initialized by the method proposed in [17] and the biases $\mathbf{b}$ were initialized to 0. ReLU was used for the activation function and the batch size was set as 5. The Adam optimizer was used to minimize the mean squared error between $P(X, \mathbf{w}, \mathbf{b})$ and Y. The learning rate was initially set as 0.0001 and then decreased by 2×10^{-7} for each epoch. The experiment was ended up to 500 epochs. The method was implemented using Tensorflow and all training and testing were performed on a workstation with NVIDIA Titan XP GPU.

3 Experimental Results

3.1 Evaluation Setting

Seventeen 7T MR images were used for the experiment. For training and validation, we made those enhancement images by using the Hou et $al.$'s method [8]. The enhanced images were used for computing the mean square error in training, while used for evaluating the prediction accuracy in testing. We divided the images into two subsets and then performed a two-fold cross validation.

The prediction accuracy was measured by PSNR and SSIM between the predicted images and the enhanced images. The PSNR and SSIM were measured in the white matter as well as in the whole brain region since most PVS were in the white matter. The white matter was extracted by an brain tissue segmentation method [18].

To demonstrate the superiority of the proposed network (DCNN6+SC+B) using the six dense blocks, skip connections (SC), and bottleneck layer (B), we compared this with SRCNN [9] using three convolution layers with the kernel sizes 9, 5, and 5 and DCNN [13] using only one dense block for the prediction. To demonstrate the effect of skip connections between the dense blocks and the bottleneck layer, we provide the results obtained by the deep networks without the skip connections and the bottleneck layer (DCNN6 and DCNN6+SC). In addition, to demonstrate the effect of network depth related to the number of parameters and the size of receptive field, we provide the results obtained by using the proposed networks with two and four dense blocks (DCNN2+SC+B and DCNN4+SC+B, respectively) instead of six dense blocks.

For a fair comparison, we modified 2D SRCNN [9], which was proposed for the image super resolution problem, to the 3D network to address the PVS enhancement problem. Also, we modified the kernel size and the number of layers of DCNN [13], which was proposed for the super resolution of a brain MR image, to be comparable with our network.

Table 1. Mean PSNR (dB) and SSIM scores between the predictions and the enhanced images, and the training time for each method. The scores were measured in the white matter (WM) and in the brain region (Brain), respectively. SC represents the skip connections, B represents the bottleneck layer, and bold indicates the highest score.

	PSNR-WM	PSNR-Brain	SSIM-WM	SSIM-Brain	Time (hour)
SRCNN [9]	36.373	30.957	0.962	0.924	4.5
DCNN [13]	37.647	31.951	0.971	0.942	2.5
DCNN6	38.518	32.825	0.975	0.950	12
DCNN6+SC	38.636	32.918	0.975	**0.951**	14.5
DCNN2+SC+B	38.040	32.386	0.973	0.947	4
DCNN4+SC+B	38.420	32.718	0.975	0.949	8
DCNN6+SC+B	**38.739**	**33.015**	**0.976**	**0.951**	12.5

3.2   Result

Table 1 shows the mean PSNR and SSIM measured from the results obtained by the proposed method and the comparison methods, and the computational times for training. The result obtained by SRCNN was the worst since the small number of hidden layers could not produce the high level features useful for prediction. DCNN achieved better performances than SRCNN with less computations. The deeper network and the skip connections between convolution layers helped to use relatively high level features while reducing the number of parameters. Likewise, DCNN6 composed of approximately six times more layers achieved much better results since the deeper network could learn the higher level features on a large receptive field which could not be considered in DCNN.

The method using the dense skip connections (DCNN6+SC) further improved the performance by predicting the enhanced image with the low level to high level features together on a large receptive field. Using the bottleneck layer also helped to improve the performance slightly while reducing the computation (DCNN6+SC+B). According to the results obtained by DCNN2+SC+B, DCNN4+SC+B, and DCNN6+SC+B, we could confirm that the performance was improved as the depth of network deepened.

Figure 2 shows the qualitative results obtained by SRCNN, DCNN, and the proposed method. SRCNN or DCNN improved the PVS, but noises near the PVS were not suppressed effectively. On the other hand, the prediction results obtained by our proposed method were very similar to the enhanced images.

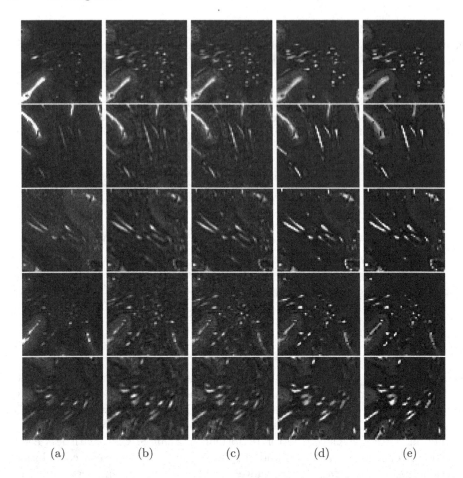

(a)   (b)   (c)   (d)   (e)

Fig. 2. Visual comparison between the proposed method and the comparison methods on several local regions. (a) Regions in original images, (b) the results obtained by SRCNN [9], (c) the results by DCNN [13], (d) the results by our proposed method (DCNN6+SC+B), and (e) regions in the enhanced images.

4   Conclusion

We have proposed a novel PVS enhancement method using a deep dense network with skip connections. We have demonstrated that the deep learning techniques usually used for the super resolution problem can be used for the PVS enhancement problem. The proposed method does not require empirical parameter tuning and additional processing such as denoising. The proposed deep network has outperformed the state-of-the-art deep learning networks and it has been proved that using various levels of features is helpful to improve the prediction accuracy. In the future, we will perform several experiments to prove how the proposed method can help in PVS segmentation and quantitative analysis.

Acknowledgement. This research was supported by the grant of artificial intelligence bio-robot medical convergence technology funded by the Ministry of Trade, Industry and Energy, Ministry of Science and ICT, and Ministry of Health and Welfare (20001533).

References

1. Zhu, Y.C., et al.: Severity of dilated Virchow-Robin spaces is associated with age, blood pressure, and MRI markers of small vessel disease: a population-based study. Stroke **41**(11), 2483–2490 (2010)
2. Maclullich, A.M., et al.: Enlarged perivascular spaces are associated with cognitive function in healthy elderly men. J. Neurol. Neurosurg. Psychiatry **75**(11), 1519–1523 (2004)
3. Bouvy, W.H., et al.: Visualization of perivascular spaces and perforating arteries with 7T magnetic resonance imaging. Invest. Radiol. **49**(5), 307–313 (2014)
4. Zong, X., et al.: Visualization of perivascular spaces in the human brain at 7T: sequence optimization and morphology characterization. NeuroImage **125**, 895–902 (2016)
5. Park, S.H., et al.: Segmentation of perivascular spaces in 7T MR images using auto-context model with orientation-normalized features. NeuroImage **134**, 223–235 (2016)
6. Zhang, J., et al.: Structured learning for 3D perivascular spaces segmentation using vascular features. IEEE Trans. Biomed. Eng. **64**(12), 2803–2812 (2017)
7. Uchiyama, Y., et al.: Computer-aided diagnosis scheme for classification of lacunar infarcts and enlarged Virchow-Robin spaces in brain MR images. In: Conference Proceedings of IEEE Engineering in Medicine and Biology Society (2008)
8. Hou, Y., et al.: Enhancement of perivascular spaces in 7T MR image using Haar transform of non-local cubes and block-matching filtering. Sci. Rep. **7**, 8569 (2017)
9. Dong, C., et al.: Image super-resolution using deep convolutional networks. IEEE Trans. Pattern Anal. Mach. Intell. **38**(2), 295–307 (2016)
10. Kim, J., et al.: Deeply-recursive convolutional network for image super-resolution. In: Computer Vision and Pattern Recognition (2016)
11. Tong, T., et al.: Image super-resolution using dense skip connections. In: International Conference on Computer Vision (2017)
12. Pham, C.H., et al.: Brain MRI super-resolution using deep 3D convolutional networks. In: International Symposium on Biomedical Imaging (2017)
13. Chen, Y., et al.: Brain MRI super resolution using 3D deep densely connected neural networks. In: International Symposium on Biomedical Imaging (2018)
14. Shi, J., et al.: MR image super-resolution via wide residual networks with fixed skip connection. IEEE J. Biomed. Health Inf., 2168–2194 (2018)
15. Huang, G., et al.: Densely connected convolutional networks. In: Computer Vision and Pattern Recognition (2017)
16. Smith, S.: Fast robust automated brain extraction. Hum. Brain Mapp. **17**(3), 143–155 (2002)
17. He, K., et al.: Delving deep into rectifiers: surpassing human-level performance on ImageNet classification. In: Computer Vision and Pattern Recognition (2015)
18. Zhang, Y., et al.: Segmentation of brain MR images through a hidden Markov random field model and the expectation-maximization algorithm. IEEE Trans. Med. Imaging **20**(1), 45–57 (2001)

Generation of Amyloid PET Images via Conditional Adversarial Training for Predicting Progression to Alzheimer's Disease

Yu Yan[1(✉)], Hoileong Lee[1], Edward Somer[2], and Vicente Grau[1]

[1] Institute of Biomedical Engineering, Oxford University, Oxford, UK
yu.yan@linacre.ox.ac.uk
[2] GE Healthcare, London, UK

Abstract. New positron emission tomography (PET) tracers could have a substantial impact on early diagnosis of Alzheimer's disease (AD) and mild cognitive impairment (MCI) progression, particularly if they are accompanied by optimised deep learning methods. To realize the full potential of deep learning for PET imaging, large datasets are required for training. However, dataset sizes are restricted due to limited availability. Meanwhile, most of the AD classification studies have been based on structural MRI rather than PET. In this paper, we propose a novel application of conditional Generative Adversarial Networks (cGANs) to the generation of ^{18}F-florbetapir PET images from corresponding MRI images. Furthermore, we show that generated PET images can be used for synthetic data augmentation, and improve the performance of 3D Convolutional Neural Networks (CNN) for predicting progression to AD. Our method is applied to a dataset of 79 PET images, obtained from Alzheimer's Disease Neuroimaging Initiative (ADNI) database. We generate high quality PET images from corresponding MRIs using cGANs, and we evaluate the quality of generated PET images by comparison to real images. We then use the trained cGANs to generate synthetic PET images from additional MRI dataset. Finally we build a 152-layer ResNet to compare the MCI classification performance using both traditional data augmentation method and our proposed synthetic data augmentation method. Mean Structural Similarity (SSIM) index was 0.95 ± 0.05 for generated PET and real PET. For MCI progression classification, the traditional data augmentation method showed 75% accuracy while the synthetic data augmentation improved this to 82%.

Keywords: Alzheimer's disease · Mild cognitive impairment
Data augmentation · Generative adversarial network · Deep learning
PET · MRI

1 Introduction

In recent years, amyloid positron emission tomography (PET) imaging has been applied in some medical imaging problems such as Alzheimer's disease classification and detection of amyloid plaques [1, 2]. The first PET tracer used to image β-amyloid

© Springer Nature Switzerland AG 2018
I. Rekik et al. (Eds.): PRIME 2018, LNCS 11121, pp. 26–33, 2018.
https://doi.org/10.1007/978-3-030-00320-3_4

plaques was ^{11}C-Pittsburgh-Compound-B (PiB) [3]. Due to the limited availability of ^{11}C-PiB with its short half-life, ^{18}F-labelled alternatives have been developed, which allow off-site production and regional distribution. ^{18}F-flutemetamol, ^{18}F-florbetapir and ^{18}F-florbetaben have recently been approved by the US Food and Drug Administration (FDA) for clinical use. Abnormal uptake in grey matter causes a disruption of the characteristic white matter pattern caused by non-specific white matter binding [4]. These scans are generally interpreted visually.

A separate group from healthy volunteers (HV) and patients with probable Alzheimer's disease (pAD), mild cognitive impairment (MCI) is an intermediate cognitive state between normal aging and dementia. Subjects with MCI, especially MCI involving memory problems, are more likely to develop AD and other dementias [5]. According to this progression, MCI subjects can subsequently be classified as progressive MCI (pMCI) or stable MCI (sMCI) [6].

Many deep learning methods have been proposed to classify different AD stages based on high dimensional features extracted from various neuroimaging biomarkers. Meanwhile, the focus for AD classification has gradually evolved from classification between healthy control and disease patients to classification between pMCI and sMCI. In a recent paper on MCI classification, Kim et al. developed a deep learning-based method for classifying tau-pet imaging patterns. MCI subjects were split into three subgroups with the Louvain method. This method discriminated subgroups 1 and 2 with accuracy 90.91%, and 80.49% for subgroups 2 and 3 [7].

A big challenge in the medical imaging field is how to cope with small datasets and limited amount of annotated samples [8]. One promising solution inspired by game theory for image synthesis is known as Generative Adversarial Networks (GANs) [9]. The method is based on the idea of training two networks, a generator and a discriminator simultaneously with competing losses. In the past few years, different variations of GANs have been applied to generate realistic natural images, and recently, the popularity of using GANs to generate medical images have also increased [10]. For example, Frid et al. [11] proposed a CNN based classification framework to classify different CT images, where GANs was used to generate high quality 2D liver lesion ROIs from a vector of 100 random numbers. The classification performance using only traditional data augmentation yielded 78.6% sensitivity and 88.4% specificity. By adding the synthetic data augmentation the results increased to 85.7% sensitivity and 92.4% specificity. Recently, Madani et al. [12] used a GAN to generate the 2D chest X-ray images from random noise, and the generated data were subsequently used to train a CNN to classify images for cardiovascular abnormalities.

In general, the availability of MRI is much higher than PET for a number of reasons. PET scanners are expensive to buy and operate, and thus less common. PET scans require subjects are exposed to ionising radiation during the test. More importantly, the number of test datasets is very limited when newly developed PET tracers are being tested. In this case, we aim at compensating this imbalance between available MRI and PET images by using a limited dataset.

To the best of our knowledge, direct generation of 3D amyloid PET imaging from structural MR has not yet been attempted. In this study, we focus on the application of conditional GANs to generate high quality volumetric florbetapir PET images from corresponding MRI images. In this way, we expect the natural variability in MRI scans and the image characteristics in PET to be combined. We also build a 152-layer ResNet classification model to distinguish pMCI and sMCI subjects, and quantify the difference in performance caused by the addition of this synthetic datasets in training. The summary of data generation model in this work is shown in Fig. 1.

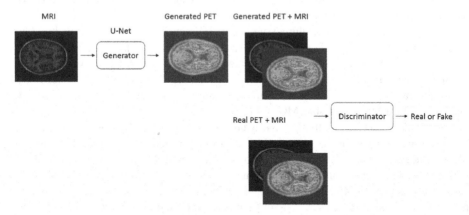

Fig. 1. Summary of data generation procedure using a conditional GANs

2   Materials and Methods

2.1   Data and Pre-processing

All image data were acquired from the Alzheimer's Disease Neuroimaging Initiative (ADNI) database (adni.loni.usc.edu). ADNI aims to improve clinical trials for the prevention and treatment of Alzheimer's disease. To date, over 1000 scientific publications have used ADNI data. ADNI has been running since 2004 and is currently funded until 2021.

In this study, 50 sMCI and 29 pMCI florbetapir images with corresponding T1 MRI were obtained from the ADNI database (set A). A second group of 29 T1 MRI images (21 of them with corresponding PET) from a different pMCI group were also downloaded (set B) and used independently. More details about the use of these datasets in training/validating/testing the cGANs and ResNet are provided in the relevant sections below. All the florbetapir images were pre-processed: MRI and PET scans from each subject were co-registered, and the PET scan was then reoriented into a standard $160 \times 160 \times 96$ voxel image grid, comprising 1.5 mm cubic voxels. This image grid was oriented such that the anterior-posterior axis of the subject is parallel to the AC-PC line. The MRI images have dimensions $256 \times 256 \times 196$ with a voxel size of $1 \text{ mm} \times 1 \text{ mm} \times 1.2 \text{ mm}$.

2.2 Amyloid PET Generation with Conditional Adversarial Training

GANs are generative networks that learn a mapping from random noise to output image. They are composed of two networks, a generator and a discriminator, trained in an adversarial way. The goal of the generator is to generate synthetic images, while the discriminator, evaluates them for authenticity. In conditional GANs, the generator learns a mapping between an input and an output image [13]. In this study, the generator is a U-Net based convolutional neural network with skip connections [14]. The discriminator is a convolutional Markovian discriminator (PatchGAN), which only penalizes structure at the scale of image patches. During the GANs training process, the generated PET was paired with the corresponding MRI and entered into the discriminator. The loss function of the conditional GANs is:

$$L_{cGAN}(G,D) = E_{x,y}[logD(x,y)] + E_x[\log(1 - D(x,G(x)))] \tag{1}$$

where x are MRI images and y are PET images. The first term is maximized when $D(x, y) = 1$, and the second is maximized when the $D(x, G(x)) = 0$, while it is minimised when $D(x, G(x)) = 1$, i.e. discriminator is not able to distinguish the generated images and real images. The generator G tries to minimize this objective against an adversarial discriminator D that tries to maximize it. In addition, conditional GANs also add an L1 loss term:

$$L_{L1}(G) = E_{x,y}(\|y - G(x)\|) \tag{2}$$

Therefore the complete form of loss function is:

$$L_{total}(G,D) = L_{cGAN}(G,D) + \varepsilon L_{L1}(G) \tag{3}$$

where ε is used to adjust the contribution of L1 loss, and it is set to 100 in the experiments reported here.

In order to measure the similarity between generated PET and real PET, We used SSIM due to its combination of errors in image contrast and overall structure [15, 16]. The structural similarity index (SSIM) was calculated as:

$$SSIM(x,y) = \frac{(2\mu_x\mu_y + C_1)(2\sigma_{xy} + C_2)}{(\mu_x^2 + \mu_y^2 + C_1)(\sigma_x^2 + \sigma_y^2 + C_2)} \tag{4}$$

where μ_x, μ_y, σ_x, σ_y, σ_{xy} are the local means, standard deviations, and cross-covariance for images x, y. C_1 and C_2 are regularization constants determined by pixel value range. The SSIM = 1 meaning that the two images are identical.

In this work, we used the 29 paired PET and MRI images from the pMCI group in set A to train the conditional GANs, and subsequently apply the mapping to the unseen 29 MRI images in set B to generate 29 synthetic PET images, thus doubling the size of the pMCI dataset. In set B, 21 subjects had available PET scans, which we used to test the cGANs by calculating SSIM values. For the implementation of the cGANs architecture we used the Keras framework. The experiment was conducted on computer cluster equipped with NVIDIA GeForce GTX 1080 Ti GPU.

2.3 MCI Progression Classification Architecture Using 3D ResNet

Deep Residual Network (ResNet) [17] is arguably one of the most important developments in the deep learning area in the last few years. ResNet makes it possible to train up to thousands of layers and still achieves competitive performance with fast convergence. The core concept of ResNet is introducing an identity shortcut connection that skips one or more layers.

ResNet have been used successfully for 3D image segmentation as in VoxResNet, where the authors use identity mappings as skip connections [18]. In our work, the ResNet architecture was modified based on the identity mappings version [19] that refines the residual block with a pre-activation variant.

The main difference between our network and the identity mappings version is the number of dimensions of convolutional kernels and pooling. Our ResNet architecture has 152 layers containing 50 3-layer blocks. The three layers are $1\times1\times1$, $3\times3\times3$, $1\times1\times1$ convolutions, where the $1\times1\times1$ layers are responsible for reducing and then increasing dimensions, leaving the $3\times3\times3$ layer a bottleneck with smaller input and output dimensions, as detailed in Table 1. Down-sampling is performed by conv3_1, conv4_1, conv5_1 with a stride of 2.

Table 1. 152-ResNet architecture for pMCI and sMCI classification

Layer name	152-layer
Conv1	$7 \times 7 \times 7$, 64, stride 2
Conv2_x	$3 \times 3 \times 3$ max pool, stride 2
	$\begin{bmatrix} 1 \times 1 \times 1 & 64 \\ 3 \times 3 \times 3 & 64 \\ 1 \times 1 \times 1 & 256 \end{bmatrix} \times 3$
Conv3_x	$\begin{bmatrix} 1 \times 1 \times 1 & 128 \\ 3 \times 3 \times 3 & 128 \\ 1 \times 1 \times 1 & 512 \end{bmatrix} \times 8$
Conv4_x	$\begin{bmatrix} 1 \times 1 \times 1 & 256 \\ 3 \times 3 \times 3 & 256 \\ 1 \times 1 \times 1 & 1024 \end{bmatrix} \times 36$
Conv5_x	$\begin{bmatrix} 1 \times 1 \times 1 & 512 \\ 3 \times 3 \times 3 & 512 \\ 1 \times 1 \times 1 & 2048 \end{bmatrix} \times 3$
	Average pool, 2-d fc, softmax

We trained our classification model using 50 sMCI and 29 pMCI real florbetapir images from set A. A 10-fold cross-validation was applied to the whole dataset. We tested three scenarios. In the first one only real images were used with no augmentation. The second one included traditional augmentation, which was done at each epoch. Specifically, the random rotation range is set to 20°, and images will be randomly flipped horizontally and vertically. These two experiments used 65 samples for training, 6 for validation, and 8 for testing. The third experiment used our cGANs augmented dataset, including the additional 29 PET images generated from the MRI scans in set B, resulting in 89 samples for training, 8 for validation, and 11 for testing. For training we used a batch size of 1 with a learning rate of 0.0001 for 100 epochs. We used Keras to implement our MCI classification framework. The experiment was performed on computer cluster with NVIDIA GeForce GTX 1080 Ti GPU.

3   Results and Discussion

3.1   Data Generation

In this study, we used volumetric MRI images to generate 3D PET images to enlarge pMCI group. Examples of real and generated PET images, with their corresponding SSIM values, are shown in Fig. 2. As can be seen from Fig. 2, the generated PET and real PET contain similar signal patterns. The mean SSIM obtained was 0.95 ± 0.05. Figure 3 shows generated PET images obtained from MRI scans for which the corresponding real PET was not available.

3.2   Classification Results

Classification results for pMCI against sMCI using 152-ResNet are shown in Table 2. We computed both the area under the receiver operating characteristic curve (AUC) and the accuracy (ACC). Three different cases are compared: classification with a network trained using only the real images, with no augmentation (top row); with a network trained using traditional augmentation (middle row) and using our synthetic images based augmentation method (bottom row).

Table 2. Classification ROC AUC and accuracy (mean $\pm$ std) with 152-ResNet

	AUC	ACC
sMCI vs pMCI (real images)	0.71 ± 0.08	0.63 ± 0.11
sMCI vs pMCI (traditional augmentation)	0.77 ± 0.11	0.75 ± 0.09
sMCI vs pMCI (real + generated images)	$\mathbf{0.81 \pm 0.07}$	$\mathbf{0.82 \pm 0.12}$

As can be seen from Table 2, the classification score for sMCI against pMCI using real PET images achieved accuracy 0.63, and with the aid of traditional data augmentation, the accuracy raised to 0.75. As we expected, the highest accuracy was obtained by using our proposed synthetic augmentation method, achieving an improvement of 7% over the traditional augmentation.

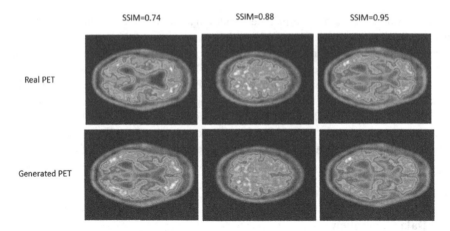

Fig. 2. Examples of real PET and generated PET images presented in different axial slices with SSIM score

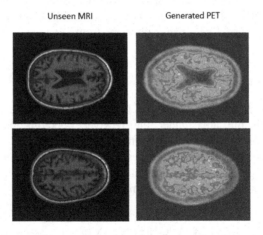

Fig. 3. Examples of unseen MRI and corresponding generated PET, corresponding real PET is not available

4   Conclusion

We developed a model for generating florbetapir PET from structural MR using deep generative networks, with generated data showing a high similarity to real corresponding PET. The generated data were then used for data augmentation for MCI classification on a limited dataset. We compared the synthetic augmentation method with a traditional augmentation method, and the synthetic augmentation outperformed the traditional augmentation. Future work will focus on using multi-modality imaging biomarkers for CNN classification.

Acknowledgements. We would like to acknowledge support from the China Scholarship Council (CSC) and The Engineering and Physical Sciences Research Council (EPSRC) and Medical Research Council (MRC) [grant number EP/L016052/1] and GE healthcare.

References

1. Cattell, L., et al.: Classification of amyloid status using machine learning with histograms of oriented 3D gradients. NeuroImage Clin. **12**, 990–1003 (2016)
2. Nordberg, A.: PET imaging of amyloid in Alzheimer's disease. Lancet Neurol. **3**(9), 519–527 (2004)
3. Klunk, W.E., et al.: Imaging brain amyloid in Alzheimer's disease with Pittsburgh compound-B. Ann. Neurol. **55**(3), 306–319 (2004)
4. Knesaurek, K., et al.: Comparison of SUVr calculations in amyloid PET brain imaging. J. Nuclear Med. **55**, 1873 (2014)
5. Villemagne, V.L., et al.: Amyloid β deposition, neurodegeneration, and cognitive decline in sporadic Alzheimer's disease: a prospective cohort study. Lancet Neurol. **12**(4), 357–367 (2013)
6. Thurfjell, L., et al.: Combination of biomarkers: PET 18F flutemetamol imaging and structural MRI in dementia and mild cognitive impairment. Neurodegenerative Diseases **10**(1–4), 246–249 (2012)
7. Kim, J., et al.: Mild Cognitive impairment classification using deep learning. Alzheimer's Dement. J. Alzheimer's Assoc. **13**(7), 1070–1071 (2017)
8. Greenspan, H., et al.: Guest editorial deep learning in medical imaging: overview and future promise of an exciting new technique. IEEE Trans. Med. Imaging **35**(5), 1153–1159 (2016)
9. Goodfellow, I., et al.: Generative adversarial nets. In: Advances in Neural Information Processing Systems (2014)
10. Odena, A., et al.: Conditional image synthesis with auxiliary classifier GANs. arXiv (2016)
11. Frid, M., et al.: GAN-based synthetic medical image augmentation for increased CNN performance in liver lesion classification. arXiv (2018)
12. Madani, A., et al.: Chest x-ray generation and data augmentation for cardiovascular abnormality classification. International Society for Optics and Photonics (2018)
13. Isola, P., et al.: Image-to-image translation with conditional adversarial networks. arXiv (2017)
14. Ronneberger, O., et al.: U-net: convolutional networks for biomedical image segmentation. In: International Conference on Medical Image Computing and Computer-Assisted Intervention (2015)
15. Wang, Z., et al.: Image quality assessment: from error visibility to structural similarity. IEEE Trans. Image Process. **13**(4), 600–612 (2004)
16. Choi, H., Dong, S.L.: Generation of structural MR images from amyloid PET: application to MR-less quantification. J. Nucl. Med. **59**(7), 1111–1117 (2017)
17. He, K., et al.: Deep residual learning for image recognition. In: Proceedings of the IEEE Conference on Computer Vision and Pattern Recognition (2016)
18. Chen, H., et al.: Voxresnet: deep voxelwise residual networks for volumetric brain segmentation. arXiv (2016)
19. He, K., et al.: Identity mappings in deep residual networks. In: European Conference on Computer Vision (2016)

Prediction of Hearing Loss Based on Auditory Perception: A Preliminary Study

Muhammad Ilyas, Alice Othmani, and Amine Nait-Ali[✉]

Université Paris-Est, LISSI, UPEC, 94400 Vitry sur Seine, France
naitali@u-pec.fr

Abstract. The major cause of deafness and hearing impairment around the globe is hearing loss. Hearing loss has become very common among young adults and kids due to the genetic disorder, temporary or permanent hearing impairments, aging, and exposure to noise. Meanwhile, the possibilities of treating hearing loss are very limited. It can be reduced by taking proper precautionary measures if diagnosed on time. In this paper, we study the possibility of preventing hearing loss based on the auditory system responses. The auditory perception is highly correlated with the human age. Consequently, predicting a big gap between the real age and the perceived one čan be an indicator of hearing loss. Our predictive model of human age is very robust with an RMSE value of 4.1 years and an EER value of 4%, indicating the applicability of our proposed method for predicting the hearing loss.

Keywords: Computer-aided · Healthcare technology
Predictive model · Hearing loss · Auditory perception

1 Introduction

Since many decades, research aims to study and analyze the reasons for the human hearing loss. Military and occupational physicians declared an index to decide for an individual to be at risk of hearing loss in the early age due to exposure to noise [11].

Hearing loss is the fifth leading reason for living with disability according to the World Health Organization [1]. It may lead to several diseases if not treated on time, such as cognitive decline [2], inclined incidence of dementia [3], social isolation [4], depression [5] and including falls [6]. Cognitive decline and hearing loss indicate a common cause on the brain and auditory pathway. Likewise, cognitive competence reduces cognitive resources for the auditory perception that increases the effect of hearing loss which is directly proportional to increasing age. In 2012 it was reported that at the age of 65 years and above, 164.5 million people suffered from hearing loss [7] and the number of individuals are increasing with a high ratio than the younger age [8]. Bringing this into account,

© Springer Nature Switzerland AG 2018
I. Rekik et al. (Eds.): PRIME 2018, LNCS 11121, pp. 34–41, 2018.
https://doi.org/10.1007/978-3-030-00320-3_5

experts concern about the precautionary measures for hearing loss [9,10]. In fact, hearing loss related to age has multi-factorial pathogenesis. Some pathogenetic elements are identified in microvascular disorders like hypertension, diabetes, and atherosclerosis. Hearing loss reduces the efficiency of cognitive skills related to age. To investigate the hearing loss, it requires a proper arrangement and cannot be possible for a subject to conduct by him/herself such as tympanometry, Audiogram, Auditory Brain Stem Response (ABR), Otoacoustic Emission (OE), and Auditory Steady State Response (ASSR). In tympanometry, a doctor inspects visually the ear with the help of otoscope, then a probe is placed in the ear. The probe generates an air pressure on the ear canal, changing pressures effects the eardrums and could be recorded for further processing. Audiogram also helps a physician to predict the hearing loss and the patient should physically appear for the test in the hospital. ABR measures the response along the auditory pathway by taking measurements from electrodes on the head. OE consist of measuring low-intensity sounds, generated by the cochlea. It can be measured with or without acoustic stimulation using a microphone. ASSR is often done in combination with the ABR test. This test also measures the brain response to sound. All the proposed test needs to be done in the hospital and is not possible to achieve without a physician. In this paper, we study the correlation between hearing loss and auditory perception. Thus, we present for the first time a new approach for predicting hearing loss based on auditory perception [11].

2   Related Work

A variety of research work explored the causes of hearing loss which are subdivided into two main categories:

Nonmodifiable risk factors comprise genetics, age, race, and gender. Among all these aspects, age plays a vital role. Hearing loss is directly proportional to increasing age. As the age increases, the value of hearing loss also increases. Nearly 23% of the population is suffering from partial or full hearing loss between the age of 65 and 75 years. The value of hearing loss increased to 40% for the age above 75 years and resulted in deafness and hearing impairment [12]. Recent studies show that hearing impairment and temporary threshold shift are increasing among children and teenagers. Around 12% of children from 6 to 12-years-old are suffering from hearing loss [13]. In parallel to that, the teenager and young adults are suffering from hearing impairment and tinnitus [14]. Studies have also shown that right and left ear respond separately to hearing loss. It is a proof of the genetic variance to respond to a sound [15]. The chances of hearing loss and impairment increase with individuals having blood group O. Research proves that boys have more chances of hearing loss as compared to females due to more involvement of activities [b]. There is a correlation between the higher level of noise and hearing loss, such that maximum noise exposure results in a severe hearing loss.

Modifiable Risk Components. Many modifiable components are related to hearing loss such as non-use of hearing protection, lack of exercise, smoking, unbalanced diet, diabetes.

Protection of ear can reduce the chances of hearing loss which is related to noise exposure. Most of the people, mainly teenagers do not take measures when required. Lack of knowledge, discomfort, safety measures and design pushes an individual to face hearing loss [16]. Smoking is also a cause of many health issues including hearing loss. Smokers are exposed to many toxic substances which efficiently effect hearing with loud noises. Nearly 3700 adults are reported to have hearing loss due to smoking. Nonsmoker sitting in the environment of smokers may also suffer from hearing loss [17]. Physical fitness and nutrition are also related to hearing loss. Having proper exercise teenagers and young adults can improve hearing capability and cardiovascular fitness [18]. Physical fitness and exercises can reduce temporary hearing loss which results because of noise exposure. Researchers suggest that with physical fitness, the inner ear gets more oxygen-rich blood, which reduces hearing loss and strengthens hearing [19]. Cognitive impairment related to hearing loss mesmerized researchers in the past decade. Evidence shows that hearing loss results in dementia. To assess and understand hearing is a tough job. Some clinical outlines can refer and indicate the assessment of hearing loss. There is very few web-based application for hearing loss detection [20,21] and all of them are complicated and time-consuming. As compared to the existing approaches, our approach is providing an alert system to predict and prevent hearing loss. It can help to reduce the cost, labor work, and time for early prediction of hearing loss.

3 Motivations

Auditory perception is the ability to interpret and identify the information that reaches the ears. Auditory perception plays a vital role in our daily life, being used almost in every task. It creates a link to interact with the outer environment, make us enjoy and responsive to probable threats.

The capabilities of the auditory system decrease with age. At 16 years old, the highest audible frequency is around 18000 Hz, while at 30 years old, it decreases to around 15000 Hz. Thus, there is a correlation between the auditory perception and the human age. Predicting the human age based on the auditory system responses provides a perceived age. When the perceived age is not close to the real age of the person, there is probably a hearing loss problem. It is, for this reason, we considered that there is a correlation between age and hearing loss. Thus, considering this as a factor, we proposed a computer-aided prediction of hearing loss based on the auditory perception.

The rest of the paper is organized as follows. In Sect. 4, we proposed auditory perception based prediction of hearing loss method. In the Sect. 5, the results and the evaluations of the proposed approach are discussed. Finally, in the last Sect. 6, we conclude this work and we deliver a set of perspectives and paths for our future works.

4   Proposed Approach

The proposed approach presents three main steps. First, the auditory system is stimulated using a dynamic frequency sound. Later on, the set of auditory system, responses are fed to the predictive model for age estimation. In case of a significant positive difference between the estimated age and the actual age, it will be considered that the test person may have a hearing loss. The flow diagram of our proposed approach as shown in Fig. 1. The protocol of the stimulation of the auditory system is presented in Sect. 4.1. The predictive model of Human age is presented in Sect. 4.2.

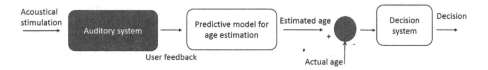

Fig. 1. Flow diagram of our proposed approach

4.1   Acoustical Simulation

The human auditory system is stimulated by generating a dynamic sound. The used protocol present a bilateral stimulation with the speaker. Our system required real-time interaction. Thus, the user should interact and respond to the system. For better accuracy, two tests are to be conducted:

- **First test:** the sound is generated from lower frequency to higher frequency (20 Hz to 20,000 Hz), and the user has to respond through keyboard action when he/she stops hearing. The correspondent audible frequency F1 is saved.
- **Second test:** the sound is generated from a higher frequency to lower frequency (20,000 to 20 Hz), and the user has to respond when he/she starts hearing. The correspondent audible frequency F2 is saved.

The human auditory system is stimulated by generating dynamic sound waves as shown in Fig. 2 according to the following model:

$$x(t) = A_0.sin(2\pi.\phi(t).t) \tag{1}$$

where $\phi(t) = \alpha.t + \phi_0$, A_0 stands for sound amplitude, t stands for time, ϕ_0 is the initialization frequency, and α stands for the increasing/decreasing frequency speed.

The two audible frequencies F1, F2 and the mean of both of them are saved and fed to the predictive model for age estimation.

Stimulation signal x(t)

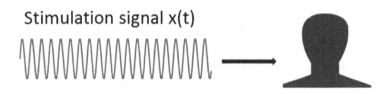

Fig. 2. Protocol of stimulation

4.2   Predictive Model of Human Age Based on Auditory Perception

The predictive model for age estimation is a regression model. Different regression models are compared to find the best one for age estimation using the auditory system responses. They are the Regression Forest (RF), the Support Vector Regression (SVR), the Adaboost regression and the Neural Network (NN) regression. For all the proposed regression models, we considered 10-fold cross-validation technique.

RF generates a forest of decision trees and uses average or majority voting to aggregate results over the set of trees. It is based on kernel functions by applying nonparametric algorithms for classification and regression. SVR minimize the error and increase the margin by finding the optimal hyperplanes. For AdaBoost, the experiments are done with backpropagation as "weak" learning algorithm. Adaboost techniques enhance the performances of machine learning algorithms for both classification (binary class, or multiclass) and regression. Neural Networks (NN) are used most of the time for classification and regression in both supervised and unsupervised learning.

5   Experiments

5.1   Dataset Collection

In this experiment, 156 healthy subjects participated to conduct the test as shown in Fig. 3. The dataset is balanced and which included subjects within a range of 6 to 64 years old. The ratio of males was more than females where 87 males and 69 females successfully conducted the test. The proposed protocol requires 2–3 min for a volunteer to conduct, successfully the test.

5.2   Correlation Between Auditory Perception and Hearing Loss

The performances of age estimation using machine learning techniques such as RF, SVR, Adaboost, and Neural network are shown in Table 1.

10-fold cross validation using RF shows the highest accuracy among the stated regression models. RF has a Root Mean Square Error value of 4.1 years and standard deviation of 2.98 years. That proves that our prediction model is very robust and shows a very a low error. Therefore, one can predict the hearing

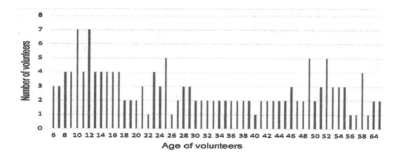

Fig. 3. Age distribution of the subjects

loss if the difference between the estimated age and the actual age $\triangle t$ is greater to n years (Eq. 2).

$$\triangle t = (\sigma_1 - \sigma_2) > n(years) \tag{2}$$

with $n = \triangle + \epsilon$ and $\epsilon =$ the minimum auditory distrust for subjects suffering with hearing loss presented by a number of years.

where σ_1 is actual age, σ_2 is estimated age, and $\triangle$ is the error rate of the system. The greater error rate indicates higher hearing loss.

Table 1. Age estimation regression models performances

Model	Root mean square error (years)	Standard deviation (years)
Random forest	4.1	2.98
SVR	5.9	4.01
Adaboost	12.3	10.9
Neural network	13.3	11.2

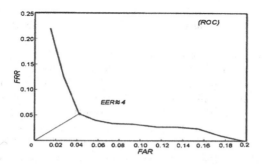

Fig. 4. ROC curve

Performance Evaluation. To evaluate our approach, we considered the False Acceptance Rate (FAR) and False Rejection Rate (FRR). We cannot evaluate a system by just the values of FAR and FRR such that a lower FRR and higher FAR performs better than a system having higher FRR and Lower FAR value. Hence, we need the Equal Error Rate (EER) to be used to evaluate the performance of a system. The lower is the EER, the higher is the performance of the system. In Fig. 4 shows Receiver Operating Characteristic (ROC). It can be noticed that the value of EER is 4% for 156 samples. Hence, this proves that our system is robust by providing a minimum error value.

6   Conclusion and Future Work

In our work, we studied the possibility of predicting hearing loss based on auditory perception. We demonstrate that auditory system responses are highly correlated with the age. Consequently, we built an accurate RF model that could estimate the age of a person with an RMSE value of 4.1 years and the EER value equal to 4%.

We are planning for future work to develop a computer-aided system to predict and prevent hearing loss. We are planned to test the system with subjects suffering from hearing loss to find the minimum auditory distrust. Our System can provide economic, health-care and well-being benefits.

References

1. World Health Organization. Deafness and hearing loss fact sheet. WHO, Geneva (2015). http://www.who.int/mediacentre/factsheets/fs300/en/. Accessed 1 Dec 2016
2. Lin, F.R., Yaffe, K., Xia, J., et al.: Health ABC study group. Hearing loss and cognitive decline in older adults. JAMA Intern Med. **173**(4), 293–299 (2013)
3. Hsu, W.T., Hsu, C.C., Wen, M.H., et al.: Increased risk of depression in patients with acquired sensory hearing loss: a 12-year follow-up study. Medicine (Baltimore), **95**(44), e5312 (2016)
4. Dawes, P., Emsley, R., Cruickshanks, K.J., et al.: Hearing loss and cognition: the role of hearing AIDS. Social isolation and depression. PLoS One **10**(3), e0119616 (2015)
5. Lin, F.R., Metter, E.J., O'Brien, R.J., Resnick, S.M., Zonderman, A.B., Ferrucci, L.: Hearing loss and incident dementia. Arch. Neurol. **68**(2), 214–220 (2011)
6. Lopez, D., McCaul, K.A., Hankey, G.J., et al.: Falls, injuries from falls, health related quality of life and mortality in older adults with vision and hearing impairment is there a gender difference? Maturitas **69**(4), 359–364 (2011)
7. World Health Organization. Hearing loss in persons 65 years and older. WHO global estimates on prevalence of hearing loss, mortality and burden of diseases and prevention of blindness and deafness. WHO, Geneva (2012). http://www.who.int/pbd/deafness/news/GE_65years.pdf. Accessed 2 June 2017
8. Olaosun, A., Ogundiran, O.: Hearing loss and the elderly - a primer. J. Natl. Sci. Res. **3**(13), 171–175 (2013)

9. Donahue, A., Dubno, J.R., Beck, L.: Accessible and affordable hearing health care for adults with mild to moderate hearing loss. Ear Hear. **31**(1), 2–6 (2010)
10. National Academies of Sciences, Engineering, and Medicine. Hearing health care for adults: priorities for improving access and affordability. The National Academies Press, Washington, DC (2016). http://www.nationalacademies.org/hmd/Reports/2016/Hearing-Health-Care-for-Adults.aspx. Accessed 2 June 2018
11. Fortunato, S., et al.: A review of new insights on the association between hearing loss and cognitive decline in ageing. Acta Otorhinolaryngologica Italica **36**(3), 155 (2016)
12. Centers for Disease Control and Prevention/NIOSH: Criteria for a Recommended Standard: Occupational Noise Exposure Revised Criteria. US Department of Health and Human Services, Cincinnati, Ohio (1998)
13. Niskar, A., Kieszak, S.M., Holmes, A.E., et al.: Estimated prevalence of noise-induced hearing threshold shifts among children 6 to 19 years of age: the Third National Health and Nutrition Examination Survey, 1988–1994. Pediatrics **108**(1), 40–50 (2001)
14. Chung, J.H., Des Roches, C.M., Meunier, J., et al.: Evaluation of noise-induced hearing loss in young people using a web-based survey technique. Pediatrics **115**(4), 861–867 (2005)
15. Klein, B.E.K., Cruickshanks, K.J., Nondahl, et al.: Cataract and hearing loss in a population-based study: the Beaver Dam studies. Am. J. Ophthalmol. **132**(1), 537–543 (2001)
16. Bogoch, I.I., House, R.A., Kudla, I.: Perceptions about hearing protection and noise-induced hearing loss of attendees of rock concerts. Can. J. Public Health. **96**(1), 69–72 (2005)
17. Cruickshanks, J., Klein, R., Klein, B.E.K., et al.: Cigarette smoking and hearing loss: the Epidemiology of Hearing Loss Study. JAMA **279**(279), 1715–1719 (1998)
18. Cristell, M., Hutchinson, K.M., Alessio, H.M.: Effects of exercise training on hearing ability. Scand Audiol. **27**, 219–224 (1998)
19. Kolkhorst, F.W., Smaldino, J.J., Wolf, S.C., et al.: Influence of fitness on susceptibility to noise-induced temporary threshold shift. Med. Sci. Sports Exerc. **30**, 289–293 (1998)
20. https://www.hear-it.org/Online-Hearing-Test. Accessed 3 June 2018
21. https://www.beltonehearingtest.com/. Accessed 3 June 2018

Predictive Patient Care: Survival Model to Prevent Medication Non-adherence

T. Janssoone[1(✉)], P. Rinder[1], P. Hornus[1], and D. Kanoun[2]

[1] Semeia, Paris, France
tjanssoone@semeia.io
[2] Clinique Pasteur, Toulouse, France

Abstract. Adherence in medicine is a measure of how well a patient follows their treatment. Not following the medication plan is actually a major issue as it was underlined in the World Health Organization's reports (http://www.who.int/chp/knowledge/publications/adherence_full_report.pdf). They indicated that, in developed countries, only about 50% of patients with chronic diseases correctly follow their treatments. This severely compromises the efficiency of long-term therapy and increases the cost of health services.

In this paper, we report our work on modeling patient drug consumption in breast cancer treatments. We test a statistic approach to predict medication non-adherence with a special focus on the features relevant for each approach. These characteristics are discussed in view of previous results issued from the literature as well as the hypothesis made to use this model.

Keywords: Adherence · Survival risk analysis · SNIIRAM

1 Introduction

During the last decades, patient-administered oral medications have become more and more prevalent [5,13]. This shift in anticancer treatments has increased the focus on adherence [14] defined as *"the extent to which patients take their medications as prescribed by their healthcare providers"*.

A common solution is to set patient support programs that include, for example, (1) providing information, patient counseling, (2) support and coaching sessions delivered by nurses (by phone or face-to-face), and (3) sending information to health professionals treating the patient. These programs have been shown to be effective, for example, pharmacist coaching has improved adherence by 12% [8] and an SMS based recall system showed a 10% improvement in adherence [15]. Yet, there are two main limitations to these interventions: (1) The use of human intervention is effective but very expensive limiting their reach, (2) The use of digital technologies (notifications and explanations) is too generic and sometimes too intrusive (daily reminders) which leads to patients losing interest. To optimize the relevance of these interventions, we propose using machine

© Springer Nature Switzerland AG 2018
I. Rekik et al. (Eds.): PRIME 2018, LNCS 11121, pp. 42–50, 2018.
https://doi.org/10.1007/978-3-030-00320-3_6

learning techniques on the consumption data of patients with breast cancer. We aim to give to each of them a risk index reflecting their adherence to the treatment. This allows us to predict the most appropriate moments to notify the ones really needing help. Thus, people will benefit from support adapted to their profiles and needs, and human interventions will be reserved for situations that are really critical.

To determine the categories of patients at risk and the appropriate moments to contact them, we develop predictive models built on anonymized data. These predictive models are trained on the reimbursement data of the French Health Insurance (SNIIRAM - the French National Health System).

In the rest of this paper, we first review previous approaches, then we introduce our models and discuss our results.

2   Related Work

Given the importance of the phenomenon of non-observance, many surveys have tried to identify their determining factors. This allows us to improve interventions and, therefore, compliance with the treatment. The review of many observation based scientific publications provides an interesting quantitative assessment of the research conducted on the subject [3,10]. This meta-analysis indicates that the increasing age of patients, and the treatment complexity level (multiple drugs, injections, ...) are essential factors of non-adherence. Similarly, low education and, more importantly, low income are correlated with lower adherence. Another study highlights the impact of patients' mental health shows that depressive episodes have a very negative impact on the patient's compliance to the prescriptions of health professionals [4].

Yet, other DiMatteo studies show that other factors also influence adherence. For example, in distinguishing between the objective severity of the patient's illness and their awareness of the severity of their pathology, they point out that the patient's beliefs influences the level of compliance, and not the actual severity of the condition. This enforces the importance of the role of patient education in strengthening their adherence to their treatment. Similarly, other analyses highlight the effects of modifiable factors in non-compliance. A meta-analysis thus shows the influence of the patient's entourage (support of their spouse, family, relatives and the wider social environment) in the proper monitoring of his treatments [2].

These studies provide a priori indications for detecting risk profiles of non-adherence. At the same time, they highlight the interest of identifying and accompanying these patients in taking their medication.

However, Franklin et al. underline the difficulty to use this information to predict adherence [6]. They evaluate different approaches, using logistic regression and boosted logistic regression, to define three categories of adherence predictors. Hence, they show that using census information or transaction data leads to poor prediction. However, they point out that using adherence observations during the first month significantly increases the accuracy of the results.

This nuance on the weight of each adherence prediction variable is confirmed in [9]. They use random survival forests highlights to find patient specific adherence thresholds to discriminate between hospitalization risks. Here again, the major variables are linked to patient history and previous transactions.

We propose in this paper to explore these solutions to predict the risk of a illegitimate stop during a treatment.

3   The SNIIRAM Database

3.1   Introduction

In order to optimize the use of human intervention and improve the use of digital technologies, we propose the use of machine-learning techniques on breast cancer patients' consumption data. The goal is to categorize patients into risk classes according to their characteristics. The long-term goal is to know the most appropriate moments to contact them for support. Thus, people will benefit from support adapted to their profile and their needs, and human interventions will be reserved for the situations for which they are really necessary. To determine these categories of patients at risk and these appropriate moments, we develop predictive models built on anonymized data.

These predictive models are trained and tested on the reimbursement data of the French Health System (SNIIRAM). SNIIRAM is one of the largest structured databases of health data in the world. The use of this massive data allows the application of complex models and the detection of weak signals. Useful data are, for example, hospitalizations, drug purchases or contextual patient information (age, government services, geographic information, ...). More details can be found in [16]. Previous work has already shown the value of massive data mining to aid diagnosis, either by taking all the information for a "static" approach [12], or, more recently, by also incorporating dynamic information [11]. Other studies have been conducted on the determinants of compliance, particularly for breast cancer.

Our study focuses on women's breast cancer on part of the SNIIRAM data. The cohort of the study consists of 50% of women (drawn randomly) who meet the following criteria:

- diagnosed with breast cancer
- having purchased at least one of the following molecules for the studied period: *Anastrozole, Capecitabine, Cyclophosphamide, Etoposide, Everolimus, Exemestane, Lapatinib, Letrozole, Megestrol, Melphalan, Tamoxifen, Toremifene* and *Vinorelbine*

Extraction concerns consumptions between 2013 and 2015 and is made up of three main categories:

- Pharmacy transactions (molecule, number of doses, date, ...)
- Hospitalizations (diagnosis, start date, end date, ...)

- Patient information (age, department, date of the diagnostic of eventual long-term illness (referred as *ALD*), pathologies, ...)

The aim of the study is to follow the entire care course, so the studied population must be representative. A discussion with the experts of the CNAMTS (French National Fund for the Health Insurance of Employees) allowed to fix a threshold: a period of 6 months without consumption of at least one of the target molecules is sufficient to consider that the person was not receiving a treatment.

A preprocessing has been done on the 'seniority of ALD' variable which represents the number of days since the diagnosis of the disease (stated in ALD 30). This variable has the characteristic of containing some extreme values, which bias the estimation for models assuming a linear effect. Thus, a common logarithm is used for the study to eliminate this bias. This still allows to keep the order of magnitude of the duration (in days, weeks, months or years).

3.2   Phases of Treatment

The raw data has been reworked to show the different phases of the treatment. A phase is a period of continuous intake of a molecule or hospitalizations for chemotherapy or radiotherapy. This allows the reconstruction of the patient's care path.

The criterion for identifying an end of a phase is the existence of a period of two months after the median time covered by the last purchase (or hospitalization) without a new purchase of the molecule (or hospitalization of the same type). For medication, days of hospitalization are excluded from this period. For example: the median time between two chemotherapies is three weeks. If there is a period of 2 months and 3 weeks without chemotherapy, this is considered a break in the phase.

The phase of treatment is regarded as censored by one of the legitimate stops (death, switch of treatment, some kind of serious cardiac issue or beginning of palliative care) if this event occurs less than two months after the date of the last theoretical dose. For example, if a patient bought a box of 30 pills on January 1st, the event has to occur before March 31 ($30 + 2 \times 30$). The date of the last theoretical dose is obtained by calculating the median interval between two purchases of the molecule or two hospitalizations of the same type: this median behavior is considered to be in conformity with the posology. Thus, the median time is 30 days between two box purchases of 30 doses of tamoxifen. The end of this period after the last box purchased corresponds to the date of the last theoretical take. The date of death is present in the initial data, the switches are identified by the beginning of a new phase of treatment and palliative care as a main diagnosis (which is spotted with a "Z515" tag in the database). Censorship of data caused by the end of the extraction period (end of December 2015) is also considered a legitimate stop. If the data extraction end date is less than two months from the last theoretical consumption, then, in the same way as for legitimate stops, the processing phase is considered censored.

For each phase, the following data is calculated:

- Start and end dates, number of intakes or hospitalizations, molecule or type of hospitalization
- End of treatment type (switch, death, stop, right censorship)
- Patient information (comorbidities, number of consultations in the first year of treatment, age, ...)
- Interventions on the breast (mastectomy) during the three months before the studied phase

In this paper, we propose evaluating different ways to model whether the end of a phase is legitimate or not. We focus on the consumption of *Tamoxifen* as it is the most used molecule. In addition, this molecule is prescribed for up to 10 years, so no patient is supposed to have stopped their treatment during the observation period (3 years) because due to the end of their prescription.

4   Our Model: Survival Analysis

To measure the rate of non-persistence over time, we use the Kaplan-Meier estimator [7]. This estimator uses non-parametric statistic to evaluate the survival function on a state takes. For example, it is used to estimate the amount of patients living for an amount of time after a treatment, the time-to-failure of machine parts,... Its force is to take into account the censored data, in particular by right censorship, each observation being weighted according to the number of observations censored previously. The four factors of censorship are: switch, death, palliative care and end of the extraction. The duration of 'survival' in the treatment phase is thus estimated by taking into account censorship factors such as legitimate end of treatment as well as censorship linked to the end of extraction (end of 2015).

The Fig. 1 shows the variations of the hazard function representing the treatment dropout rates as a function of time. There is a high drop-out rate at the beginning of the phase, during the first 150 days. During the first 5 months, the curve is significantly higher than the rest of the values. This period of high risk will therefore be the most beneficial period to help patients. Kaplan-Meier estimator allows us to analyze survival but we need to use a regression model to examine the factor influence of the different variables.

We use a Cox model [1] to identify the characteristics related to poor adherence. The Cox regression estimates a fixed effect of each variable in relation to the patients' average behavior. It is based on two strong assumptions:

(1) the expected effect of each variable is linear
(2) the effect of each variable does not vary over time. An example in our case is that, if the weight found for the *CMU-C* variable is 1.40, we assume that a person who benefits from *CMU-C* has 40% more risk to discontinue their treatment than someone who doesn't benefit from *CMU-C*

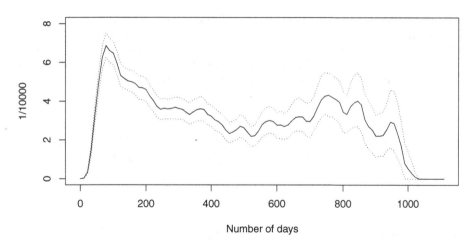

Fig. 1. Kaplan-Meier hazard function for Tamoxifen which represents the rate of failure (here drug drop-out) at time t. The plain curve represents the estimated value and the dotted ones represent the 95% confidence intervals (computed with bootstrapping).

The explanatory variables in the Cox model are characteristics of the phase, the patient pathway and patient profile. In order to extract the most significant variables and to robustly estimate the associated coefficient, the model was estimated with the following iterative process:

- estimation of the coefficients for the set of variables,
- selection of the variables having a p-value lower than threshold of 0.05
- new estimation of the coefficients for the model limited to the selected variables

The most influential coefficients are presented in Table 1. The characteristics highlighted by the literature are found to be influential to the patient's adherence to their treatment. We can then evaluate the impact of the age, social support, or previous illness (psychiatric, mastectomy, ...). We also underline that the treatment preceding the current phase has a major influence.

This prompted us to analyze this value in particular. The Fig. 2 shows the different lifelines depending on the treatment preceding the current Tamoxifen phase. We see three types of influences. First, the classic pathway: a hospitalization (here chemotherapy or radiotherapy) preceding the current phase shows the lowest risk of abandonment. Second, a hormonotherapy other than Tamoxifen was used, corresponds to a *switch* of treatment and shows a higher risk. Third a Tamoxifen phase was used before the current phase. This case suggests that an illegitimate stop has happened before the current phase, and could explain the highest risk this case has. Nevertheless, this underlines the interest of our model to find additional information to predict the evolution of Tamoxifen intake phases. As illustrated in the Fig. 3. We can use the background information of the patient to compute a score at the beginning of a *Tamoxifen* phase. Then, we

Table 1. Weights computed with the Cox-regression showing their different influence. The odd ratio indicates the impact of the variable on the average risk (1.5 means 50% more risk of non-adherence). The first ones are indicators of income (CMU-C (Supplementary universal health cover) and ACS (Assistance with the acquisition of supplementary health insurance) and their p-value show their influence.

	Cox computed coefficient	Odd ratio (exp(coefficient))	p-value
CMU-C	3.84e−01	1.47e+00	6.62e−04
ACS	4.16e−01	1.52e+00	1.87e−03
Time since ALD status (log)	7.88e−02	1.08e+00	3.91e−02
Number of medical consultation	−5.70e−03	9.94e−01	1.19e−02
Psychiatric illness	1.78e−01	1.19e+00	9.31e−03
Recent hospitalization with diagnostic C50: Malignant neoplasms of breast	−3.83e−01	6.82e−01	3.59e−07
Last treatment - tamoxifen	9.12e−01	2.49e+00	<1e−10
Last treatment - radiotherapy	−7.09e−01	4.92e−01	<1e−10
Last treatment - chemotherapy	−8.62e−01	4.22e−01	<1e−10
Menopause	1.17e−01	1.12e+00	2.76e−02

select the most accurate survival function which gives the probability of abandonment during the specific number of days of treatment, which allows us to predict the abandon risk over time.

Yet, we based our model on the strong assumption that the effect of each variable does not vary over time as explained in (2). This proportional hazard assumption can be checked with a Schoenfeld individual test and visualized with the log-log plot of survival displayed in the Fig. 4. Using Schenfeld residual, we obtain p-values that verify this hypothesis except for the assumption concerning the previous treatment. This indicates that the previous treatment has different

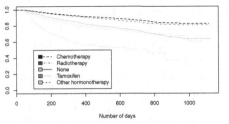
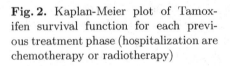
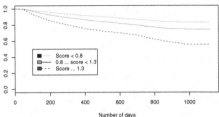

Fig. 2. Kaplan-Meier plot of Tamoxifen survival function for each previous treatment phase (hospitalization are chemotherapy or radiotherapy)

Fig. 3. Evolution of the different survival curves given a specific score computed at the beginning of the phase

influences over the duration of the current phase and that our assumption was too strong for this variable. However, the Fig. 4 illustrates whether the hazards are approximatively proportional throughout. We can see that this assumption remains valid after the 20 first days. This analysis gives us insights to improve our model with a special focus to put on the beginning of the phase.

The next step of this study is to challenge our model with machine-learning approaches and other statistical models to improve our predictions.

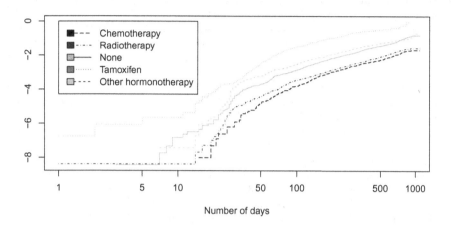

Fig. 4. Log-log plot of survival for each previous treatment. We observe a validation of our model after the 20 first days

5   Conclusion and Future Work

In this paper, we show the importance of the survival function analysis to predict the adherence of a patient to their treatment during of a phase of medication. The study of explanatory variables gives more insights about the different cases of patient courses. We applied this method to the study of *Tamoxifen*: we validates our approach by retrieving information in agreement with the literature. We also found other explanatory variables that we can use to compute more accurate risk estimations for patients. These risks could trigger alerts that indicate the patient's need of support. With an appropriate response, this could lead to improve the patient's adherence to their treatment.

This predictive model allows us to validate the possibility of evaluating the risk of abandonment during a phase of the treatment. We plan to challenge this approach with other algorithms, especially sequence-mining and deep-learning which are very suitable to the amount of data provided by SNIIRAM. One major advantage to our statistic-based approach is that they are less parameters to fine tune compare to machine-learning approaches. We are planning to survey these different kind of analysis to provide a meta-comparison of this tools to the community.

References

1. Cox, D.: Regression models and life-tables. J. Roy. Stat. Soc.: Ser. B (Methodol.) **34**(2) (1972)
2. DiMatteo, M.R.: Social support and patient adherence to medical treatment: a meta-analysis. Health Psychol. **23**(2), 207 (2004)
3. DiMatteo, M.R.: Variations in patients adherence to medical recommendations: a quantitative review of 50 years of research. Med. Care **42**(3), 200–209 (2004)
4. DiMatteo, M.R., Lepper, H.S., Croghan, T.W.: Depression is a risk factor for noncompliance with medical treatment: meta-analysis of the effects of anxiety and depression on patient adherence. Arch. Intern. Med. **160**(14), 2101–2107 (2000)
5. Fallowfield, L., et al.: Patients' preference for administration of endocrine treatments by injection or tablets: results from a study of women with breast cancer. Ann. Oncol. **17**(2), 205–210 (2005)
6. Franklin, J.M., et al.: Observing versus predicting: initial patterns of filling predict long-term adherence more accurately than high-dimensional modeling techniques. Health Serv. Res. **51**(1), 220–239 (2016)
7. Kaplan, E.L., Meier, P.: Nonparametric estimation from incomplete observations. J. Am. Stat. Assoc. **53**(282) (1958)
8. Krolop, L., Ko, Y.D., Schwindt, P.F., Schumacher, C., Fimmers, R., Jaehde, U.: Adherence management for patients with cancer taking capecitabine: a prospective two-arm cohort study. BMJ Open **3**(7), e003139 (2013)
9. Lo-Ciganic, W.H., et al.: Using machine learning to examine medication adherence thresholds and risk of hospitalization. Med. Care **53**(8), 720 (2015)
10. Mann, D.M., Woodward, M., Muntner, P., Falzon, L., Kronish, I.: Predictors of nonadherence to statins: a systematic review and meta-analysis. Ann. Pharmacother. **44**(9), 1410–1421 (2010)
11. Morel, M., Bacry, E., Gaïffas, S., Guilloux, A., Leroy, F.: ConvSCCS: convolutional self-controlled case series model for lagged adverse event detection. arXiv preprint arXiv:1712.08243 (2017)
12. Neumann, A., Weill, A., Ricordeau, P., Fagot, J., Alla, F., Allemand, H.: Pioglitazone and risk of bladder cancer among diabetic patients in france: a population-based cohort study. Diabetologia **55**(7), 1953–1962 (2012)
13. O'neill, V., Twelves, C.: Oral cancer treatment: developments in chemotherapy and beyond. Br. J. Cancer **87**(9), 933 (2002)
14. Osterberg, L., Blaschke, T.: Adherence to medication. N. Engl. J. Med. **353**(5), 487–497 (2005)
15. Spoelstra, S.L., et al.: An intervention to improve adherence and management of symptoms for patients prescribed oral chemotherapy agents: an exploratory study. Cancer Nurs. **36**(1), 18–28 (2013)
16. Tuppin, P., De Roquefeuil, L., Weill, A., Ricordeau, P., Merlière, Y.: French national health insurance information system and the permanent beneficiaries sample. Revue d'epidemiologie et de sante publique **58**(4), 286–290 (2010)

Joint Robust Imputation and Classification for Early Dementia Detection Using Incomplete Multi-modality Data

Kim-Han Thung, Pew-Thian Yap, and Dinggang Shen[✉]

Department of Radiology and BRIC,
University of North Carolina at Chapel Hill, Chapel Hill, USA
dgshen@med.unc.edu

Abstract. It is vital to identify Mild Cognitive Impairment (MCI) subjects who will progress to Alzheimer's Disease (AD), so that early treatment can be administered. Recent studies show that using complementary information from multi-modality data may improve the model performance of the above prediction problem. However, multi-modality data is often incomplete, causing the prediction models that rely on complete data unusable. One way to deal with this issue is by first imputing the missing values, and then building a classifier based on the completed data. This two-step approach, however, may generate non-optimal classifier output, as the errors of the imputation may propagate to the classifier during training. To address this issue, we propose a unified framework that jointly performs feature selection, data denoising, missing values imputation, and classifier learning. To this end, we use a low-rank constraint to impute the missing values and denoise the data simultaneously, while using a regression model for feature selection and classification. The feature weights learned by the regression model are integrated into the low rank formulation to focus on discriminative features when denoising and imputing data, while the resulting low-rank matrix is used for classifier learning. These two components interact and correct each other iteratively using Alternating Direction Method of Multiplier (ADMM). The experimental results using incomplete multi-modality ADNI dataset shows that our proposed method outperforms other comparison methods.

1 Introduction

Alzheimer's Disease (AD) is the most common type of dementia, where the brain neurons are degenerated progressively, causing the affected patients to gradually lose memory, cognitive and motor abilities. As AD is irreversible and has caused enormous economic and social burden to the community, it is therefore vital to

This work was supported in part by NIH grants AG053867, EB008374, AG041721, AG049371, and AG042599.

© Springer Nature Switzerland AG 2018
I. Rekik et al. (Eds.): PRIME 2018, LNCS 11121, pp. 51–59, 2018.
https://doi.org/10.1007/978-3-030-00320-3_7

detect its prodromal stage, called Mild Cognitive Impairment (MCI) as early as possible, so that the patients can be treated to potentially slow down or stop the disease progression. A lot of AD biomarkers have been developed, including measurements derived from neuroimaging data (i.e., magnetic resonance imaging (MRI) and flurodeoxglucose positron emission tomography (FDG-PET)), and from biological data like the cerebruspinal fluid (CSF). Recent studies have shown that the complementary information from different data modality can improve the accuracy of the multi-modality based AD prediction model [14]. Unfortunately, samples with complete multi-modality data are limited, e.g., in Alzheimer's Disease Neuroimaging Initiative (ADNI) dataset, only about $\frac{1}{4}$ of its total samples contains complete MRI, PET and CSF data at baseline.

The easiest way to deal with missing data perhaps is by discarding the samples with missing values in any of their modalities. Though convenient, this approach discards a huge amount of useful information and leaves a smaller subset of data for analysis. To use all the samples for analysis, we can impute the missing data [4,6,11] based on the available information from other samples, and subsequently perform classification based on the completed dataset. However, as shown in various studies [8,10,13], most imputation methods are not accurate for block-wise missing data as in our case, and this error may propagate to the subsequent classifier and cause unstable performance. In addition, as this is a 2-step approach, there is no way for the classification step to feedback to the imputation step for focusing on discriminative features.

To address the above issues, we propose a novel diagnostic model (using incomplete multi-modality data) that simultaneously imputes the missing values (while also denoises the data) and learns a classifier (while also selects discriminative features). To this end, we assume our data is low-rank (i.e., similar to previous works in [1,4,5,9,10]) and incorporate a low-rank matrix completion [4] algorithm to impute the missing values, while also denoising the features matrix. Furthermore, we use linear classification model to learn the mapping between the denoised feature matrix and their corresponding labels. These two processes are optimized intertwinely in a single optimization objective, so that they can correct each other to obtain a more robust prediction model. For instance, the missing values are imputed based not only on the peer samples, but also in a way that they can be classified properly, while the classifier weights will be corrected based on the denoised and imputed data. In addition, we also regularize the weight vector of the classifier (e.g., ℓ_1 or ℓ_2 norm regularization), to control how specific features contribute in building the classifier [1,13].

2   Method

2.1   Notation

Let $\mathbf{X} \in \mathbb{R}^{N \times d}$ denotes the feature matrix of N subjects (i.e., samples), each containing d-dimensional features from MRI, PET and clinical score data. As not all the subjects have complete multi-modality data, this matrix is incomplete, i.e., feature values of some modalities from some subjects are missing. We use

Ω to denote the index set of known (or observed) values, and $\bar{\Omega}$ to denote its complement, *i.e.*, index set of the missing values. The corresponding target output is given as $\mathbf{Y} \in \{1, -1\}^{N \times c}$, where c is the number of target outputs, *i.e.*, 1 in our case for pMCI/sMCI classification. We use $(\mathbf{x}_i \in \mathbb{R}^{1 \times d}, \mathbf{y}_i \in \mathbb{R}^{1 \times c})$ to denote the feature-target pair for the i-th sample.

2.2 Preliminaries

1. **Low-rank matrix completion** (LRMC) has been proposed to recover missing data from a limited number of samples. Assuming a noise-free incomplete data $\mathbf{X}$, its formulation is given as $\{\min_{\mathbf{Z}} \|\mathbf{Z}\|_*, \text{ s.t. } \mathcal{P}_\Omega(\mathbf{Z}) = \mathcal{P}_\Omega(\mathbf{X})\}$, where $\mathbf{Z}$ is the completed version of $\mathbf{X}$, and $\mathcal{P}$ is the orthogonal projection so that the (i, j)-th element of $\mathcal{P}_\Omega(\mathbf{Z})$ is equal to $\mathbf{Z}_{ij}$ if $(i, j) \in \Omega$ and zero otherwise. In the presence of noise, we relax the equality constraint, and modify the optimization problem to [4]

$$\min_{\mathbf{Z}} \|\mathbf{Z}\|_* + \lambda \|\mathcal{P}_\Omega(\mathbf{Z}) - \mathcal{P}_\Omega(\mathbf{X})\|_F^2, \tag{1}$$

where $\| \cdot \|_F$ denotes the Frobenius norm, and λ is a positive trade-off parameter that can be determined by the noise level in the data.

2. **Robust principal component analysis** (RPCA) assumes that the noisy data can be decomposed into two components – a low-rank component $\mathbf{Z}$, which represents the clean data, and the error component $\mathbf{E}$, which represents the data noise. Its formulation is given as $\{\min_{\mathbf{Z}, \mathbf{E}} \|\mathbf{Z}\|_* + \lambda \|E\|_1, \text{ s.t. } \mathbf{X} = \mathbf{Z} + \mathbf{E}\}$, where $\| \cdot \|_1$ denotes the ℓ_1-norm, assuming sparse noise in $\mathbf{X}$. With the presence of missing data, this formulation can be rewritten as [7]

$$\min_{\mathbf{Z}, \mathbf{E}} \|\mathbf{Z}\|_* + \lambda \|\mathcal{P}_\Omega(\mathbf{F})\|_1, \text{ s t } \mathcal{P}_\Omega(\mathbf{X}) - \mathcal{P}_\Omega(\mathbf{Z} + \mathbf{E}). \tag{2}$$

Note that if we use Frobenius norm for the error matrix (*i.e.*, assuming Gaussian noise in $\mathbf{X}$), and substitute $\mathbf{E} = \mathbf{Z} - \mathbf{X}$ in Eq. (2), it will be equivalent to Eq. (1). Thus, RPCA with missing data can be seen as a matrix completion problem, with more robustness to the data noise, as it explicitly models the noise as an error term. Without loss of generality, we can assume $\mathcal{P}_{\bar{\Omega}}(\mathbf{X}) = \mathbf{0}$, and make $\mathcal{P}_{\bar{\Omega}}(\mathbf{E})$ to be any value that satisfies $\mathcal{P}_{\bar{\Omega}}(\mathbf{X}) = \mathcal{P}_{\bar{\Omega}}(\mathbf{Z} + \mathbf{E})$. This will simplify Eq. (2) to an easier problem as

$$\min_{\mathbf{Z}, \mathbf{E}} \|\mathbf{Z}\|_* + \lambda \|\mathcal{P}_\Omega(\mathbf{E})\|_1, \text{ s.t. } \mathbf{X} = \mathbf{Z} + \mathbf{E}, \tag{3}$$

where we call this formulation as incomplete data version of RPCA (IRPCA).

3. **Classifier** can be trained to map data sample $\mathbf{x}_i$ to the target output $\mathbf{y}_i$ by learning a coefficient matrix $\mathbf{W} \in \mathbb{R}^{d x c}$. The general formulation for a classifier (e.g., linear regression model) is given as

$$\min_{\mathbf{W}} L(\mathbf{X}, \mathbf{Y}, \mathbf{W}) + \text{Reg}(\mathbf{W}), \tag{4}$$

where $L(\cdot)$ is the classifier loss function, and $\mathrm{Reg}(\cdot)$ is the regularizer for **W**, e.g., $\ell_{2,1}$-norm for joint sparse feature learning. We use least square loss function in this study, i.e., $L(\cdot) = \|\mathbf{Y} - \mathbf{XW}\|_F^2$. This classification formulation requires all values in **X** to be known, and becomes unusable if **X** is incomplete. Thus, we propose to combine Eqs. (3) and (4) to impute the missing values in the feature matrix, denoise the data, and learn the classifier jointly.

2.3 Proposed Method

Given an incomplete input matrix **X** and its corresponding target matrix **Y**, we propose to concurrently impute the missing values in **X** and learn a classifier coefficient matrix **W** based on the completed data. More specifically, we employ the IRPCA formulation (i.e., Eq. (3)) to decompose **X** into low-rank and error components, and learn the classifier based on the low-rank denoised data. We call our method "Joint Robust Imputation and Classification (JRIC)". Figure 1 shows the overview of our method. Note that $\mathbf{X} = [\mathbf{X}_{tr}; \mathbf{X}_{te}]$ is the concatenation of training input data $\mathbf{X}_{tr}$ and testing input data $\mathbf{X}_{te}$. **X** could be incomplete, as shown by the white boxes in **X**, and after applying IRPCA, it will be transformed into $\mathbf{Z} = [\mathbf{Z}_{tr}; \mathbf{Z}_{te}]$, where the data are denoised and the missing feature values are imputed. Then, we train a classifier using $(\mathbf{Z}_{tr}, \mathbf{Y}_{tr})$ by learning a classifier weight **W**, which could be sparse. Besides, we also feedback **W** to IRPCA to focus on reducing the reconstruction error of discriminative features, while relaxing the reconstruction error of redundant or noisy features. Note that the above learning are formulated in an unified framework, so that each component of the formulation can correct each other iteratively until the algorithm converges. Our proposed JRIC formulation is given as:

$$\min_{\mathbf{Z},\mathbf{E},\mathbf{W}} \mu\|\mathbf{Z}\|_* + \lambda_1\|\mathcal{P}_{\Omega_\mathbf{W}}(\mathbf{E})\|_p + L(\mathbf{Z}_{tr}, \mathbf{Y}_{tr}, \mathbf{W}) + \lambda_2\mathrm{Reg}(\mathbf{W}), \text{ s.t. } \mathbf{X} = \mathbf{Z} + \mathbf{E},$$
(5)

where $\mu, \lambda_1, \lambda_2$ are the regularization parameters. The first two terms in (5) together with the constraint term compose the IRPCA component (i.e., Eq. (3)), while the last two terms compose the classifier component (i.e., Eq. (4)). More specifically, the first term is a nuclear norm, which encourages **Z** to be low rank, assuming that the "clean" data is low rank. The second term is the reconstruction error term, to ensure that the low rank matrix **Z** not too much differs from the original matrix **X**. The third term is the classifier loss function, which could be linear regression loss, logistic loss, hinge loss, etc., to learn a classifier weight **W** (which is a vector if there is only one column in **Y**, and a matrix otherwise). The fourth term is the regularizer of **W**, to ensure that classifier is not overtrained, and to select discriminative features if sparse constraint (e.g., l_1 or l_{21}-norm) is used. Note that we have used $\Omega_\mathbf{W}$ instead of Ω in the second term of Eq. (5) to include the information from **W** when computing the reconstruction loss. We define $\Omega_\mathbf{W}$ as the index set of discriminative non-missing feature values in **X**, where the discriminative features are determined via detecting non-zero rows in **W**.

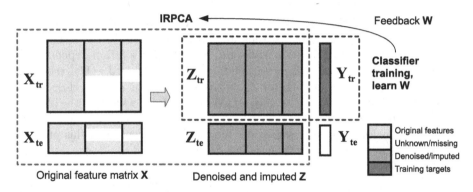

Fig. 1. Overview of the proposed JRIC framework, which denoises data, imputes missing feature values and learns a classifier jointly.

We use Alternating Direction Method of Multiplier (ADMM) [2] to solve (5). In ADMM, a complex optimization problem is simplified by introducing some auxiliary variables, so that it can be decomposed into several smaller convex optimization problems that can be solved efficiently. Specifically, we introduce an auxiliary variable J:

$$\min_{\mathbf{J},\mathbf{Z},\mathbf{E},\mathbf{W}} \mu\|\mathbf{J}\|_* + \lambda_1\|\mathcal{P}_{\Omega_{\mathbf{W}}}(\mathbf{E})\|_p + L(\mathbf{Z}_{tr}, \mathbf{Y}_{tr}, \mathbf{W}) + \lambda_2\mathrm{Reg}(\mathbf{W}), \qquad (6)$$

$$\text{s.t. } \mathbf{X} = \mathbf{Z} + \mathbf{E}, \quad \mathbf{Z} = \mathbf{J}.$$

The augmented Lagrangian function for (6) is given as:

$$\min_{\mathbf{J},\mathbf{Z},\mathbf{E},\mathbf{W},\mathbf{U}_1,\mathbf{U}_2} \mu\|\mathbf{J}\|_* + \lambda_1\|\mathcal{P}_{\Omega_{\mathbf{W}}}(\mathbf{E})\|_p + L(\mathbf{Z}_{tr}, \mathbf{Y}_{tr}, \mathbf{W}) + \lambda_2\mathrm{Reg}(\mathbf{W})$$
$$+ \frac{\rho}{2}\left(\|\mathbf{X} - \mathbf{Z} - \mathbf{E} + \mathbf{U}_1\|_F^2 + \|\mathbf{Z} - \mathbf{J} + \mathbf{U}_2\|_F^2\right), \qquad (7)$$

where $\mathbf{U}_1$ and $\mathbf{U}_2$ are the Lagrangian multipliers, and ρ is a trade-off parameter, controlling the rate of convergence. We then solve Eq. (7) by solving the following optimization subproblems iteratively, until one of the convergence criteria is met.

1. **Update J:**

$$\mathbf{J}^k = \arg\min_{\mathbf{J}} \lambda_1\|\mathbf{J}\|_* + \frac{\rho}{2}\left(\|(\mathbf{Z} + \mathbf{U}_2) - \mathbf{J}\|_F^2\right). \qquad (8)$$

The solution for this problem is given by singular value thresholding shrinkage operator [3], $\mathcal{S}_{\frac{\lambda_1}{\rho}}(\mathbf{Z} + \mathbf{U}_2) = \mathbf{G}\mathcal{R}_{\frac{\lambda_1}{\rho}}(\boldsymbol{\Sigma})\mathbf{H}^T$, where $\mathbf{G}\boldsymbol{\Sigma}\mathbf{H}^T$ is the singular value decomposition (SVD) of $(\mathbf{Z} + \mathbf{U}_2)$, and $\mathcal{R}_\tau(\cdot)$ is a shrinkage operator defined as $\mathcal{R}_\tau(x) = \mathrm{sign}(x)\max(|x| - \tau, 0)$.

2. **Update Z:**

$$\mathbf{Z}^k = \arg\min_{\mathbf{Z}} L(\mathbf{Z}_{tr}, \mathbf{Y}_{tr}, \mathbf{W}) + \frac{\rho}{2}\|\mathbf{Z} - (\mathbf{X} - \mathbf{E} + \mathbf{U}_1)\|_F^2 + \frac{\rho}{2}\|\mathbf{Z} - (\mathbf{J} - \mathbf{U}_2)\|_F^2, \qquad (9)$$

where we define $L(\mathbf{Z}_{tr}, \mathbf{Y}_{tr}, \mathbf{W}) = \|\mathbf{Y}_{tr} - \mathbf{Z}_{tr}\mathbf{W}\|_F^2$ as a linear regression loss function. We solve $\mathbf{Z}_{tr}$ and $\mathbf{Z}_{te}$ separately for this subproblem. To solve for $\mathbf{Z}_{te}$, the first term in Eq. (9) is irrelevant, and thus its solution depends only to the other two terms in Eq. (9). Let $\mathbf{S} = \mathbf{X} - \mathbf{E} + \mathbf{U}_1 + \mathbf{J} - \mathbf{U}_2$, then it is easy to show that the solution for $\mathbf{Z}_{te}$ is given as $\mathbf{S}_{te}$. For $\mathbf{Z}_{tr}$, the closed-form solution is given as $\left(\mathbf{Y}_{tr}\mathbf{W}^T + \frac{\rho}{2}(\mathbf{S}_{tr})\right)\left(\mathbf{W}\mathbf{W}^T + \rho\mathbf{I}\right)^{-1}$, where $\mathbf{I}$ is the identity matrix. Then, $\mathbf{Z}^k = [\mathbf{Z}_{tr}; \mathbf{Z}_{te}]$. Note that, other classifier loss functions can be used, and as long as the classifier loss function is differentiable, this problem can always be solved using subgradient descent method.

3. **Update $\mathbf{W}$**:

$$\mathbf{W}^k = \arg\min_{\mathbf{W}} L(\mathbf{Z}_{tr}, \mathbf{Y}_{tr}, \mathbf{W}) + \text{Reg}(\mathbf{W}), \tag{10}$$

where this problem can be solved using the current classifier solver.

4. **Update $\Omega_{\mathbf{W}}$**: Remove indices in Ω corresponding to zero-value rows in $\mathbf{W}$.
5. **Update $\mathbf{E}$**:

$$\mathbf{E}^k = \arg\min_{\mathbf{E}} \lambda_2 \|\mathcal{P}_{\Omega_{\mathbf{W}}}(\mathbf{E})\|_p + \frac{\rho}{2}\|(\mathbf{X} - \mathbf{Z} + \mathbf{U}_1) - \mathbf{E}\|_F^2. \tag{11}$$

When $p = 1$, we can use a shrinkage operator to solve for $\mathbf{E}$, given as $\mathcal{R}_{\frac{\lambda_2}{\rho}}(\mathbf{X} - \mathbf{Z} + \mathbf{U}_1)$, for $\Omega_{\mathbf{W}}$ locations of $\mathbf{E}$. For $\bar{\Omega}_{\mathbf{W}}$ locations of $\mathbf{E}$, the solution is given as $\mathbf{X} - \mathbf{Z} + \mathbf{U}_1$.

6. **Update $\mathbf{U}_1, \mathbf{U}_2$**: $\mathbf{U}_1^k = \mathbf{U}_1 + \mathbf{X} - \mathbf{Z} + \mathbf{E}, \quad \mathbf{U}_2^k = \mathbf{U}_2 + \mathbf{Z} - \mathbf{J}$.
7. **Stopping criteria**: Step 1 to 5 above are iterated until a convergence condition is achieved, e.g., when the changes of $\mathbf{Z}$ are negligible.

We summarize our algorithm in Algorithm 1. After the training we will obtain the denoised and imputed testing data and also the classifier weight $\mathbf{W}$. The prediction for the testing data is thus given by $\text{sign}(\mathbf{Z}_{te}.\mathbf{W})$

Data: $\mathbf{X} = [\mathbf{X}_{tr}; \mathbf{X}_{te}], \mathbf{Y} = [\mathbf{Y}_{tr}, \mathbf{Y}_{te}]$
1 Intialization: $\mathbf{X}_{\bar{\Omega}} = 0, \mathbf{Z} = \mathbf{X}, \mathbf{U}_1, \mathbf{U}_2 = 0, \Omega_{\mathbf{W}} = \Omega$;
2 for $k \leftarrow 1$ to *maxiter* do
3   Update $\mathbf{J}^k$ in Eq. (8) ;
4   Update $\mathbf{Z}^k$ in Eq. (9) ;
5   Update $\mathbf{W}^k$ in Eq. (10) ;
6   Update $\Omega_{\mathbf{W}}^k$;
7   Update $\mathbf{E}^k$ in Eq. (11) ;
8   Update $\mathbf{U}_1^k, \mathbf{U}_2^k$;
9   if *converges* then
10 | stop
11   end
12 end
13 return $W^*, \mathbf{Z}$

Algorithm 1: Joint Robust Imputation Classifier

3   Experiment

3.1   Data

In this study, we use multi-modality data (i.e., MRI, PET and clinical scores) from ADNI baseline dataset (http://adni.loni.ucla.edu). Only subjects that were categorized as MCI at baseline are used in this study, and we define progressive MCI (pMCI) subjects as MCI subjects that will progress to AD within 2 years, and define stable MCI (sMCI) subjects as otherwise. Based on this definition, we have 124 pMCI and 118 sMCI subjects. Each MRI image is processed using the following steps: AC-PC alignment, N3 intensity inhomogeneity correction, skull stripping, tissue segmentation, registration to a template with 93 ROIs [12], and used the normalized Gray matter (GM) volumes from the 93 ROIs as MRI features. We also affinely aligned each PET image to its corresponding MRI image, and used the mean ROI intensity values as a PET features. Besides, clinical scores (e.g., ADAS, CDR, MMSE, etc.) are also used in this study.

3.2   Experimental Results and Discussions

We compare our method with 2-step imputation-based classification methods, i.e., we first use IRPCA to impute and denoise the data, and then use sparse least-squared regression (IRPCA-sparse), and linear SVM (IRPCA-SVM) to classify the data. Besides, we also compare our method with two state-of-the-art methods that were designed for incomplete multi-modality dataset, i.e., low-rank matrix completion method (LRMC) [10], and incomplete data sparse feature learning (iMSF) method (that uses least-squared loss function) [13]. Besides, we conduct our experiments using different modality combinations of MRI, PET and clinical scores (Cli), to show the performance of each method for each modality combination. For more robust comparison, we also conduct our experiments using 10 repetitions of 10-fold cross validations and report the average accuracies as the performance measures. The hyper-parameters of all the methods are determined via nested cross validation using the training data. The classification results are shown in Fig. 2.

From Fig. 2, it can be seen that the proposed method JRIC outperforms other comparison methods for most of the modality combinations, i.e., MRI+PET, MRI+Cli and MRI+PET+Cli. The classification performance of our method using single modality (i.e., MRI) is comparable with IRPCA-SVM and LRMC. This is probably because we use a simple least square loss function to train our classifier, while IRPCA-SVM and LRMC use more advanced loss functions, i.e., hinge loss and logistic loss functions, respectively. This indicates that if the data is complete, as in single modality case, we should use more advanced classifiers to get the better classification performance. Nevertheless, comparing the results of IRPCA-sparse (which trains classifier using the denoised data) and iMSF (which trains classifier using the original data) also reveals that using the denoised data may have better chance of getting better classification accuracy.

The advantage of using our proposed method becomes more significant when using multi-modality data, especially when some data is missing, e.g., when using MRI+PET data. This is probably due to the use of intertwining the learning of IRPCA and sparse classifier in our proposed method, which enables both components to correct each other for better classifier performance. Besides, the feedback from the classifier also enables the IRPCA to have more low-rank smoothing on redundant and non-discriminative features, and lower reconstruction error for discriminative features. This will prevent the IRPCA from over smoothing (denoising) the data via low-rank constraint which may cause the loss of important information from discriminative features.

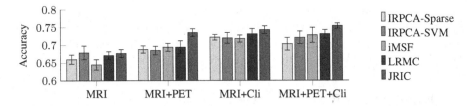

Fig. 2. Accuracy of pMCI/sMCI classification using MRI, PET and clinical scores data. Error bars: standard deviations.

4   Conclusion

In this paper, we introduce a robust classifier for dementia diagnostic problem using incomplete multi-modality data. Our proposed method JRIC jointly imputes the missing value, denoises the data and trains a classifier. We formulate our proposed framework in a general way, so that it can be adapted to different types of classifier easily. For fast implementation, we show case our proposed framework using sparse classifier with least-squared loss function. Our experimental results show that our proposed methods outperforms other comparison methods, implying the benefit of iterative learning of matrix completion and classification.

References

1. Adeli-Mosabbeb, E., Thung, K.H., An, L., Shi, F., Shen, D.: Robust feature-sample linear discriminant analysis for brain disorders diagnosis. In: NIPS (2015)
2. Boyd, S.P., Vandenberghe, L.: Convex Optimization. Cambridge University Press (2004)
3. Cai, J.F., Candès, E.J., Shen, Z.: A singular value thresholding algorithm for matrix completion. SIAM J. Optim. **20**(4), 1956–1982 (2010)
4. Candès, E.J., Recht, B.: Exact matrix completion via convex optimization. Found. Comput. Math. **9**(6), 717–772 (2009)

5. Goldberg, A., Zhu, X., et al.: Transduction with matrix completion: three birds with one stone. Adv. Neural Inf. Process. Syst. **23**, 757–765 (2010)
6. Schneider, T.: Analysis of incomplete climate data: estimation of mean values and covariance matrices and imputation of missing values. J. Clim. **14**(5), 853–871 (2001)
7. Shang, F., Liu, Y., et al.: Robust principal component analysis with missing data. In: Conference on Information and Knowledge Management, pp. 1149–1158. ACM (2014)
8. Thung, K.H., Wee, C.Y., Yap, P.T., Shen, D.: Identification of progressive mild cognitive impairment patients using incomplete longitudinal MRI scans. Brain Struct. Funct. **221**(8), 3979–3995 (2016)
9. Thung, K.H., Yap, P.T., et al.: Conversion and time-to-conversion predictions of mild cognitive impairment using low-rank affinity pursuit denoising and matrix completion. Med. Image Anal. **45**, 68–82 (2018)
10. Thung, K.H., et al.: Neurodegenerative disease diagnosis using incomplete multi-modality data via matrix shrinkage and completion. Neuroimage **91**, 386–400 (2014)
11. Troyanskaya, O., Cantor, M., et al.: Missing value estimation methods for DNA microarrays. Bioinformatics **17**(6), 520–525 (2001)
12. Wang, Y., Nie, J., Yap, P.-T., Shi, F., Guo, L., Shen, D.: Robust deformable-surface-based skull-stripping for large-scale studies. In: Fichtinger, G., Martel, A., Peters, T. (eds.) MICCAI 2011. LNCS, vol. 6893, pp. 635–642. Springer, Heidelberg (2011). https://doi.org/10.1007/978-3-642-23626-6_78
13. Yuan, L., Wang, Y., et al.: Multi-source feature learning for joint analysis of incomplete multiple heterogeneous neuroimaging data. Neuroimage **61**(3), 622–632 (2012)
14. Zhang, D., Shen, D.: Multi-modal multi-task learning for joint prediction of multiple regression and classification variables in Alzheimer's disease. Neuroimage **59**(2), 895–907 (2012)

Shared Latent Structures Between Imaging Features and Biomarkers in Early Stages of Alzheimer's Disease

Adrià Casamitjana[1]([✉]), Verónica Vilaplana[1]([✉]), Paula Petrone[2],
José Luis Molinuevo[2], and Juan Domingo Gispert[2]

[1] Universitat Politècnica de Catalunya (UPC BarcelonaTech), Barcelona, Spain
{adria.casamitjana,veronica.vilaplana}@upc.edu
[2] Fundació Pasqual Maragall, BarcelonaBeta Brain Research Center,
Barcelona, Spain

Abstract. In this work, we identify meaningful latent patterns in MR images for patients across the Alzheimer's disease (AD) continuum. For this purpose, we apply Projection to Latent Structures (PLS) method using cerebrospinal fluid (CSF) biomarkers (t-tau, p-tau, amyloid-beta) and age as response variables and imaging features as explanatory variables. Freesurfer pipeline is used to compute MRI surface and volumetric features resulting in 68 cortical ROIs and 84 cortical and subcortical ROIs, respectively. The main assumption of this work is that there are two main underlying processes governing brain morphology along the AD continuum: brain aging and dementia. We use two different and orthogonal PLS models to describe each process: PLS-aging and PLS-dementia. To define PLS-aging model we use normal aging subjects and age as predictor and response variables, respectively, while for PLS-dementia we only use demented subjects and biomarkers as response variables.

Keywords: PLS · Preclinical AD · Latent model

1 Introduction

Human brains are constantly evolving throughout life, changing their neurobiological structure according to an uncountable number of factors, ranging from genetics or hormonal to vascular factors [1,3]. Hence, we can define multiple interdependent processes occurring at the same time in each subject's brain. One key factor to describe brain's condition is subject's real age leading to *normal aging* processes that describe similar changes in groups of subjects with similar age. Often, in elderly subjects, other processes related to *dementia* occur in parallel and eventually result in cognitive or memory decline. The etiology of those processes is still unknown but a large literature of promising research can be found in the literature [2], specifically for the Alzheimer's disease, the most common type of dementia. In that sense, cerebrospinal fluid (CSF) biomarkers

© Springer Nature Switzerland AG 2018
I. Rekik et al. (Eds.): PRIME 2018, LNCS 11121, pp. 60–67, 2018.
https://doi.org/10.1007/978-3-030-00320-3_8

obtained by lumbar puncture (extracellular amyloid depositions and intracellular accumulation of t-tau and p-tau proteins) show an acceptable sensitivity and specificity for diagnostic purposes and can be used as a measure of progression along the AD continuum [4]. Moreover, the use of high-field MR imaging provide detailed brain anatomical information that could be used to analyze brain conditions related to each of these factors. In this work we relate brain morphometry measurements, to other factors from the same observations like age and CSF biomarkers describing brain aging and brain dementia processes, respectively.

Structural brain changes are heterogeneous among subjects and may not be uniform across the brain, specially if related to dementia. However, we hypothesize that these changes can be described by a small set of underlying processes that define common morphological patterns across all subjects and we build different latent models to find specific patterns for both processes (aging and dementia). Moreover, we constrain both subspaces to be orthogonal to each other in order to disentangle aging effects and gain better understanding of the dementia process. We use Projection to Latent Structures (PLS) to jointly model the variation of MRI measurements as predictor variables (X) and age and CSF biomarkers as response variables (Y).

Related to our work, PLS is used to model brain aging accounting for different sources of variability in [5], while in [6] it is used to jointly model age and clinical scores from brain shape features. A latent model for preclinical Alzheimer's disease stage using clinical and cognitive variables is shown in [7].

2   Methods

In this work, we aim to describe brain aging and brain dementia processes by means of few underlying latent structures. We use Projection to Latent Structures (PLS) for that purpose. Two different PLS models are built for aging and dementia processes, using imaging features as predictors and age and CSF biomarkers (amyloid-beta (Aβ), t-tau and p-tau proteins) as response variables for each process, respectively.

2.1   PLS: Projection to Latent Structures

PLS is a linear latent variable model that finds a set of components (called latent vectors) by performing a simultaneous decomposition of a predictor matrix $X \in \mathcal{R}^{NxK}$ and a response matrix $Y \in \mathcal{R}^{NxM}$ with the constraint of maximizing the covariance between X and Y [8]. Here N stands for the number of subjects, while K and M define the number of predictors and response variables, respectively. For a single latent dimension ($L = 1$) PLS finds the underlying representations $t = Xw$, $u = Yc$ such that

$$\text{maximize} \quad \text{cov}(Xw, Yc) = \mathcal{E}\left\{(t - t_0)(u - u_0)\right\} \tag{1}$$
$$\text{s.t} \quad w^T w = 1, c^T c = 1$$

where w, c are the weights for X, Y variables respectively. Rewriting Eq. 1, PLS can also be seen as looking for the latent space that best explains the variation in X-space and Y-space and the correlation between both spaces.

$$\text{maximize} \quad \text{cov}(Xw, Yc) = \sigma_t \cdot \text{corr}(t, u) \cdot \sigma_u \tag{2}$$
$$\text{s.t} \quad w^T w = 1, c^T c = 1$$

where $corr()$ is the correlation coefficient. Solving Eq. 2 using Lagrange multipliers, weight vectors have the following analytical expression:

$$w = \frac{1}{\sqrt{u^T X X^T u}} X^T u, \quad c = \frac{1}{\sqrt{t^T Y Y^T t}} Y^T t \tag{3}$$

For a latent space of dimension $L > 1$, each latent factor is computed by iterating over the same optimization process (i.e. Eq. 3). However, at each step PLS uses deflated versions of X and Y as new predictors and response variables, forcing successive latent directions to be orthogonal to previous ones and hence, maximizing the input variance explained.

$$X_d = X - tp^T = (I - \frac{tt^T}{t^T t})X, \quad \text{where} \quad p = \frac{X^T t}{t^T t} \tag{4}$$
$$Y_d = Y - tq^T = (I - \frac{tt^T}{t^T t})Y, \quad \text{where} \quad q = \frac{Y^T t}{t^T t}$$

Due to continuous deflation of input spaces, weight matrices (W,C) do not directly relate input (X,Y) and latent (T,U) spaces. Accounting for that, rotation matrices, R_x, R_y, are defined:

$$R_x = W \cdot (P^T \cdot W)^{-1}, \quad R_y = C \cdot (Q^T \cdot C)^{-1}, \quad T = X \cdot R_x, \quad U = Y \cdot R_y \tag{5}$$

where $T \in \mathcal{R}^{N x L}$, $U \in \mathcal{R}^{N x L}$ are the latent factors found at each iteration and $W \in \mathcal{R}^{K x L}$, $C \in \mathcal{R}^{M x L}$, $P \in \mathcal{R}^{K x L}$, $Q \in \mathcal{R}^{M x L}$ are the matrices containing weights and loadings. Finally, PLS modeling can also be used for linear regression using the coefficient matrix B:

$$B = R_x \cdot Q^T \rightarrow Y = TQ^T + E = X \cdot R_x \cdot Q^T + E = X \cdot B + E \tag{6}$$

2.2   PLS Orthogonalization and Coupling

In order to disentangle the effects of normal brain aging and dementia, a PLS orthogonalization method is proposed. To this purpose, separate models are estimated imposing an orthogonality constraint between them, similarly to [9]. For brain aging process it is sufficient to use only non-demented subjects (i.e. healthy control subjects). For dementia process, we use subjects in the AD pathophysiological path and constrain the underlying latent space to be orthogonal to the brain aging model. Finally, we need to merge both models in a single latent space. We first model brain aging using PLS-aging and thereafter use a deflated version of brain morphology features to model brain dementia using PLS-dementia. The final latent space is built by concatenating the latent factors of each model, as well as the coefficients and rotation matrices.

PLS-aging is found by solving Eq. 1 for L_{age}-dimensional subspace with weights w_{age_i} for $i = 1 : L_{age}$. The modified PLS dementia model is as follows:

$$\text{maximize} \quad cov(X_{d_0}w, Yc) = \mathcal{E}\left\{(t - t_0)(u - u_0)\right\} \tag{7}$$
$$\text{s.t} \quad w^T w = 1, c^T c = 1, w^T w_{age_i} = 0 \quad i = 1 : L_{age}$$

where w_{age_i} are the columns of the aging PLS rotation matrix $R_{x_{age}}$ and $X_{d_0} = X - TP^T$ the deflated version of X using PLS-aging. Using Lagrange multipliers, the resulting weights can be expressed as:

$$w_j = X_{d_j}^T u - \sum_{i=1}^{L_{age}} \frac{w_{age_i} X^T u}{w_{age_i}^T w_{age_i}} w_{age_i} \Rightarrow w = \frac{w}{||w||} \tag{8}$$

$$c_j = Y_{d_j}^T u \Rightarrow c = \frac{c}{||c||} \qquad j = 1 : L_{dementia} \tag{9}$$

where X_{d_j} and Y_{d_j} are the deflated version of X_{d_0} and Y_{d_j} at jth iteration. The full PLS model is build by concatenating latent scores and rotation matrices from both models: $t = concat(t_l)$ and $R = concat(R_l)$ where $l = 1, ..., L_{age}, ..., L_{age} + L_{dementia}$.

2.3   Outcome Measures

The outcome measures of interest using the aforementioned PLS model are: (i) the effect strength $\rho_{l(s)}$, defined as the pearson correlation of the lth latent factor and the response variable s (e.g. CSF biomarkers, age) and (ii) the effect type, ν_l defined as the projection from input X-space to its related latent space.

$$\rho_{l(s)} = \frac{cov(t_l, y_s)}{\sigma_{t_l} \cdot \sigma_{y_s}} = \frac{\nu_l^T \cdot X/(N-1)}{\sigma_{t_l} \cdot \sigma_{y_l}} \qquad \nu_l = R_l \tag{10}$$

3   Experimental Analysis

3.1   Data

In our experiments we use the publicly available dataset from the Alzheimer's Disease Neuroimaging Initiative[1]. We build a sample of $N = 802$ subjects: $N_{HC} = 189$ healthy controls, $N_{PC} = 136$ on the preclinical stage of AD, $N_{MCI} = 330$ subjects labeled as mild cognitive impairment (MCI) and $N_{AD} = 147$ subjects diagnosed with AD. MCI and AD subjects are diagnosed following the

---

[1] http://adni.loni.usc.edu.

standard criteria used in ADNI while for preclinical subjects we select asymptomatic subjects with positive amyloid-beta ($A\beta < 192$). All subjects have associated a T1-weighted MRI preprocessed using FreeSurfer[2] extracting region of interest (ROI) global averages of gray matter cortical thickness and cortical and subcortical volumetric information. Thus, ROI-level measurements are used as predictor variables X, while age and CSF biomarkers ($A\beta$, p-tau, t-tau) are used as response variables Y. A normalized CSF index as diagnostic metric for disease progression (AD-CSF, [4]) is also used in its two versions to assess the correlation with the latent factors: (i) AD-CSF1 that involves p-tau protein and $A\beta$ and (i) AD-CSF2 that involves t-tau and $A\beta$.

We use the linear regression model in Eq. 6 to define the dimension of each latent space by evaluating the total mean absolute error (MAE) of the predicted response variables in a cross-validation framework. To model brain aging we use only HC subjects ($L_{age} = 2$), while for modeling brain dementia ($L_{dem} = 4$) we use PC, MCI and AD subjects to build the latent space. We investigate the latent factors found and their correlation with the response variables as well as the brain patterns associated with the scores. Finally, we show the predictive power for each model.

3.2   Results and Discussion

Using a single model for all disease stages, we assume that the effect type of dementia is preserved throughout the AD continuum while the effect strength changes at each stage. To better understand the latent factors t_k at each stage we will first analyze their effect strength $\rho_{l(s)}$ with s = age, CSF biomarkers and the two AD-CSF indices. Afterwards, we show the effect type ν_l related to them.

Figure 1 shows the correlation between each latent variable and the respective indicators for different AD stages using volumetric and cortical thickness features. Brain aging factors are most correlated with HC subjects, even though they are relevant for early stages of AD (PC, MCI). On the other hand, the brain dementia model finds patterns (t_2, t_3) significantly correlated with t-tau and p-tau in early stages of AD, specially for the later during the preclinical stage. The relationship between $A\beta$ and the latent model is higher for volumetric data and t_2. On the other hand, disease related factors at AD stage seem to be more correlated with age rather than CSF biomarkers and have low effect strength in HC subjects.

Interesting patterns are found for the brain aging model. We observe that the first latent variable involves global volume atrophy (Fig. 2) or cortical thickness reduction (Fig. 3) except for choroid plexus and most of the cingulate regions, respectively. Interestingly, when using a combination of both volume and cortical thickness, the second latent variable of the aging model describes a global cortical thickness increase together with global volume atrophy except for a few insignificant regions.

---

[2] https://surfer.nmr.mgh.harvard.edu/.

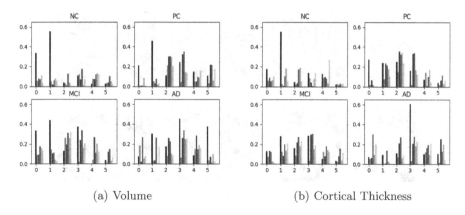

(a) Volume   (b) Cortical Thickness

Fig. 1. Absolute correlation with several indicators: age (black), amyloid-beta (red), p-tau (green), t-tau (blue), AD-CSF-1 (magenta), AD-CSF-2 (cyan). Latent variables are shown in the x-axis: brain aging (0,1) and brain dementia (2,3,4,5). (color figure online)

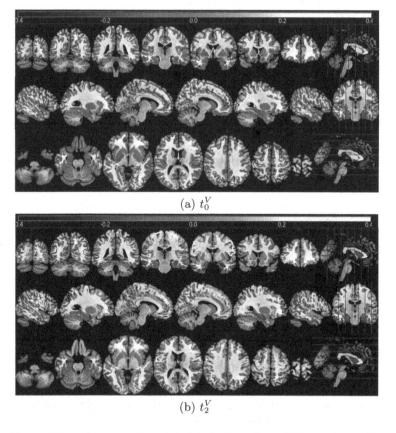

(a) t_0^V

(b) t_2^V

Fig. 2. Volumetric patterns (a, b) related to brain aging and brain dementia models, respectively.

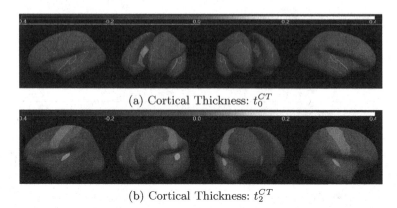

(a) Cortical Thickness: t_0^{CT}

(b) Cortical Thickness: t_2^{CT}

Fig. 3. Cortical thickness patterns (a, b) related to the brain aging and brain dementia models, respectively.

Table 1. Predictive error of response variables for each diagnosis label and feature type using a single model for all AD continuum.

Features	Diagnosis	Age	Aβ	p-tau	t-tau
Volume	HC	0.49 ($\pm$ 0.05)	1.91 ($\pm$ 0.16)	0.74 ($\pm$ 0.09)	0.71 ($\pm$ 0.07)
	PC	0.68 ($\pm$0.11)	0.46 ($\pm$0.06)	0.72 ($\pm$0.13)	0.63 ($\pm$0.09)
	MCI	0.67 ($\pm$0.09)	0.4 ($\pm$0.04)	0.7 ($\pm$0.05)	0.72 ($\pm$0.08)
	AD	0.85 ($\pm$0.09)	0.37 ($\pm$0.05)	0.88 ($\pm$0.18)	0.94 ($\pm$0.08)
Cortical Th	HC	0.55 ($\pm$0.06)	1.94 ($\pm$0.16)	0.7 ($\pm$0.08)	0.63 ($\pm$0.08)
	PC	0.76 ($\pm$0.16)	0.48 ($\pm$0.07)	0.68 ($\pm$0.12)	0.66 ($\pm$0.11)
	MCI	0.77 ($\pm$0.06)	0.42 ($\pm$0.03)	0.69 ($\pm$0.04)	0.72 ($\pm$0.08)
	AD	0.91 ($\pm$0.06)	0.38 ($\pm$0.04)	0.87 ($\pm$0.19)	0.88 ($\pm$0.19

On the other hand, effect types of brain dementia model are positively correlated with t-tau and p-tau (t_2, t_3) and consist of a combination of different effects in each ROI, mostly characterized by a reduction of the enthorinal cortex (t_2^{CT}), shrinkage of the parahippocampal combined with an increase of the precuneus thickness (t_3^{CT}), atrophy in the hippocampus, fusiform and inferior temporal combined with increasing volume for the precentral region (t_2^V) and a volume increase in the choroid plexus regions combined with atrophy in the temporal pole (t_3^V).

Finally, we evaluate the predictive power of the latent factors found for both real age and CSF biomarkers. Table 1 shows the normalized predictive error for each class using cortical thickness and volumetric data. High Aβ errors are due to the initial difference in mean between HC and other stages of the continuum: PC, MCI and AD. Volumetric data better fits real age while both behave similarly for predicting biomarkers. The combination of both features provides similar performance.

4   Conclusions

We present a multivariate analysis that finds a shared latent space between imaging features and relevant factors (age and CSF biomarkers) and describes two different processes that may occur simultaneously in elderly subjects: brain aging and brain dementia. Relevant and specific patterns related to neuropathological conditions are found for different stages of the AD continuum by imposing orthogonality constraints between both processes. One limitation of the model is that localized interpretations of condition effects (e.g. aging, dementia) in independent ROIs is not possible and the only conclusion that can be drawn is related to the overall morphometric patterns found. Future work may involve modeling separately each stage of AD to study their different characteristics, with special focus on preclinical stage. Other imaging modalities can be incorporated in the study.

References

1. Peters, R.: Aging and the brain. Postgrad. Med. J. **82**(964), 84–88 (2006)
2. Aisen, P.S., et al.: On the path to 2025: understanding the Alzheimer's disease continuum. Alzheimer's Res. Therapy **9**(1), 60 (2017)
3. Dubois, B., et al.: Preclinical Alzheimer's disease: definition, natural history, and diagnostic criteria. Alzheimer's Dementia **12**(3), 292–323 (2016)
4. Molinuevo, J.L., et al.: The AD-CSF-index discriminates Alzheimer's disease patients from healthy controls: a validation study. J. Alzheimer's Dis. **36**(1), 67–77 (2013)
5. Ziegler, G., Dahnke, R., Gaser, C.: Models of the aging brain structure and individual decline. Front. Neuroinformatics **6**, 3 (2012)
6. Wachinger, C., Rieckmann, A., Reuter, M.: Latent processes governing neuroanatomical change in Aging and Dementia. In: Descoteaux, M., Maier-Hein, L., Franz, A., Jannin, P., Collins, D.L., Duchesne, S. (eds.) MICCAI 2017. LNCS, vol. 10435, pp. 30–37. Springer, Cham (2017). https://doi.org/10.1007/978-3-319-66179-7_4
7. Hayden, K., et al. : Preclinical cognitive phenotypes for Alzheimer's disease: a latent profile approach. Alzheimer's Dementia J. Alzheimer's Assoc. **8**(4), P363 (2012)
8. Abdi, H.: Partial least squares regression and projection on latent structure regression (PLS Regression). Wiley Interdisc. Rev. Comput. Stat. **2**(1), 97–106 (2010)
9. Konukoglu, E., et al.: Multivariate statistical analysis of diffusion imaging parameters using partial least squares: application to white matter variations in Alzheimer's disease. Neuroimage **134**, 573–586 (2016)

Predicting Nucleus Basalis of Meynert Volume from Compartmental Brain Segmentations

Hennadii Madan[1(✉)], Rok Berlot[2], Nicola J. Ray[3], Franjo Pernuš[1],
and Žiga Špiclin[1]

[1] Faculty of Electrical Engineering, Laboratory of Imaging Technologies,
University of Ljubljana, Tržaška 25, 1000 Ljubljana, Slovenia
{hennadii.madan,franjo.pernus,ziga.spiclin}@fe.uni-lj.si
[2] Department of Neurology, University Medical Centre Ljubljana,
Zaloška 2, 1000 Ljubljana, Slovenia
[3] Department of Psychology, Manchester Metropolitan University,
53 Bonsall Street, Manchester M15 6GX, UK

Abstract. In clinical practice one often encounters a situation when
a quantity of interest cannot be measured routinely, for reasons such as
invasiveness, high costs, the need for special equipment, etc. For instance,
research showed that early cognitive decline can be predicted from volume (atrophy) of the nucleus basalis of Meynert (NBM), however its
small size makes it difficult to measure from brain magnetic resonance
(MR) scans. We treat NBM volume as an unobservable quantity in a statistical model, exploiting the structural integrity of the brain, and aim to
estimate it indirectly based on one or more interdependent, but possibly
more accurate and reliable compartmental brain volume measurements
that are easily accessible. We propose a Bayesian approach based on the
previously published reference-free error estimation framework to achieve
this aim. The main contribution is a novel prior distribution parametriza-
tion encoding the scale of the distribution of the unobservable quantity.
The proposed prior is more general and better interpretable than the
original. In addition to unobservable quantity estimates, for each observable we calculate a figure of merit as an individual predictor of the unobservable quantity. The framework was successfully validated on synthetic
data and on a clinical dataset, predicting the NBM volume from volumes
of the whole-brain and hippocampal subfields, based on compartmental
segmentations of structural brain MR images.

Keywords: Bayesian inference · Markov Chain Monte Carlo
Validation · Brain segmentation · Clinical dataset
Magnetic resonance imaging

1 Introduction

Computational analysis of medical images is increasingly used for extracting
quantitative imaging biomarker (QIBs)—scalar measurements that characterize

© Springer Nature Switzerland AG 2018
I. Rekik et al. (Eds.): PRIME 2018, LNCS 11121, pp. 68–75, 2018.
https://doi.org/10.1007/978-3-030-00320-3_9

a certain morphological or functional aspect of the anatomy of interest. In certain diseases there exist QIBs that allow for disease diagnosis at an early stage, well before clinical symptoms appear. For instance, recent research showed that early cognitive decline can be predicted by measuring volume (atrophy) of nucleus basalis of Meynert (NBM)[4], however its small size makes it a difficult target for computational or even manual segmentation on resolution–limited magnetic resonance (MR) brain images.

Based on the integrity of the brain, one may treat the difficult to measure NBM as an unobservable quantity and model it in terms of one or several inter-dependent observed routine compartmental brain volume measurements. Two questions are then of interest: (a) which observed quantities are the best "pre-dictors" of the unobservable quantity and (b) what are the likely values of the unobservable quantity given the observed ones?

To answer these questions we propose a novel Bayesian approach based on the reference-free error estimation framework [3]. The original framework was designed to compare measurement method (MMs) for the same quantity and has assumptions specific to MMs that are necessary for model identification (see Sect. 2.1). We lift these assumptions by using additional information about the distribution of the unobservable quantity (Sect. 2.2) and use the reference-free estimates to answer the questions (a) and (b) for a synthetic and a clinical dataset (Sect. 3).

2   Reference-Free Error Estimation

Let q denote the unobservable quantity in patient p, $p = 1..N$. Assume that we have M easy-to-measure observables, indexed with m, $m = 1..M$. Let y_{pm} be the value of m-th observable in patient p defined by the value of a certain deterministic function $g_m(q_p)$, corrupted by random noise ϵ:

$$y_{pm} = g_m(q_p) + \epsilon_{pm} \tag{1}$$

Assuming that g_m are analytic and we are dealing with values of q_p from a finite interval $[\underline{q_p}, \overline{q_p}]$, we may approximate g_m with a $K - th$ degree polynomial representing truncated Taylor series about a point $q_o \in [\underline{q_p}, \overline{q_p}]$:

$$y_{pm} = \sum_{k=0}^{K} b_{km}(q_p - q_0)^k + \epsilon_{pm} = \sum_{k=0}^{K} b_{km}x_p^k + \epsilon_{pm} \tag{2}$$

where notation $x_p \triangleq q_p - q_0$ is introduced for brevity. Multivariate Gaussian(MVG) distribution is assumed for random errors:

$$\epsilon_p \sim \mathcal{N}(0, \Sigma) \tag{3}$$

where $\epsilon_p = (\epsilon_{p1}, ..., \epsilon_{pM})^\top$ and Σ is a covariance matrix.

From (2) and (3) the likelihood of observing $\boldsymbol{y_p} \triangleq [y_{p1}, ..., y_{pM}]$ is:

$$l_p \triangleq f(\boldsymbol{y_p} \mid B, \Sigma, x_p) = \mathcal{N}(B\boldsymbol{\chi}, \Sigma) \tag{4}$$

where f denotes probability density, $B \triangleq [b_{km}] \in \mathbb{R}^{KM}$ and $\chi \triangleq [1, x_p, x_p^2, \ldots, x_p^K]$. The likelihood for the entire set of observations is then:

$$l \triangleq f(Y \mid \theta) = \prod_{p=1}^{N} l_p \qquad (5)$$

where $Y = [y_{pm}] \in \mathbb{R}^{N \times M}$, $\theta = \{B, \Sigma, x\}$, $x = [x_1, ..., x_N]$. By Bayes' Theorem the posterior probability density of θ given the observed values Y is:

$$f(\theta \mid Y) \propto l \cdot f(\theta) \qquad (6)$$

where $f(\theta)$ is the prior probability density of model parameters. When both l and $f(\theta)$ are specified, one can draw samples from $f(\theta \mid Y)$ using Markov chain Monte-Carlo (MCMC). The samples allow estimation of marginal posterior expectations of quantities of interest with associated uncertainties. For instance the quantity

$$F_m \triangleq \max_{q \in [\underline{q_p}, \overline{q_p}]} \frac{\mid g_m'(q) \mid}{\sigma_m} \qquad (7)$$

can be shown to be equal to the reciprocal of the smallest possible (over $q \in [\underline{q_p}, \overline{q_p}]$) root mean square error (RMSE) of q_p estimates, obtained from y_{pm} for a particular m by inversion of g_m. In other words, it is the reciprocal value of the smallest error one would make if one used only the m-th observable (with known g_m) to estimate q. Quantity in (7) can be interpreted as a figure of merit of the m-th observable as a predictor of q, thereby providing an answer to the question (a), while the estimates of q_p provide an answer to the question (b), as posed in the Introduction.

2.1 Priors in Previous Works

The likelihood l can be shown to be degenerate. This means that, in order to identify the model, the priors must be sufficiently informative. In previous research, uniform priors on q_p were used in conjunction with peaked informative priors on b_{km}:

$$q_p \sim \mathcal{U}(\underline{q_p}, \overline{q_p}), \quad \forall p, \qquad (8)$$

$$b_{1m} \sim \mathcal{N}(1, \sigma_{b1}), \quad \forall m, \qquad (9)$$

$$b_{km} \sim \mathcal{N}(0, \sigma_{bk}), \quad \forall m, k \neq 1, \qquad (10)$$

where $\underline{q_p}$ and $\overline{q_p}$ are either physical or physiological bounds on q_p and $\sigma_{bk} = c_k(\overline{q_p} - \underline{q_p})^{-k}$, $c_k \approx 1$. Such priors are based on the assumption that y_{mp} are (imperfect) measurements of q_p and therefore g_m are close to identity at least in the vicinity of q_0. To parametrize the covariance matrix a noise variance-correlation separation strategy [1] based on the following decomposition was applied:

$$\Sigma = SRS \qquad (11)$$

where $S = diag([\sigma_1, ..., \sigma_M])$ is a diagonal matrix of random error standard deviation (STDs) and $R = [r_{ij}]$ a symmetric correlation matrix. Then, STDs were assigned truncated Jeffreys priors:

$$f(\sigma_m) = \begin{cases} \frac{1}{\sigma_m}, & \underline{\sigma_m} < \sigma_m < \overline{\sigma_m} \\ 0, & \text{otherwise} \end{cases} \quad (12)$$

Truncation guaranteed that the posterior was proper, $\underline{\sigma_m}$ was set to measurement resolution, while $\overline{\sigma_m}$ was set to $(\max\limits_p y_{pm} - \min\limits_p y_{pm})$. The correlation matrix was assigned LKJ priors [2] with $\eta = 1$.

This approach was successfully validated on a clinical in vivo dataset and several synthetic datasets [3]. Despite the usefulness of informative priors on b_{km} in the context of MM comparison, these priors are not applicable for general $g_m(q)$.

2.2 Proposed Prior

The main contribution in this paper is a novel encoding of prior distribution that lifts assumptions on b_{km} that constrain g_m to be close to identity. Instead, the novel prior draws on additional information about the scale of q_p distribution to identify the model. The additional information required is (i) an interval of likely values of the minimum and maximum (over p) points in the x_p sample encoded as the following conditions:

$$\min\limits_p q_p \leq \underline{q_p} + \underline{\epsilon}$$
$$\max\limits_p q_p \geq \overline{q_p} - \overline{\epsilon} \quad (13)$$

where $\overline{\epsilon}, \underline{\epsilon} > 0$ are a priori limits on how far the minimum and the maximum values of q_p might reside from the boundaries of the specified uniform prior on q_p, defining the *magnitude* of the scale of q_p distribution; and (ii) a pair of indices $(\underline{p}, \overline{p})$ for which it is known that $q_{\overline{p}} > q_{\underline{p}}$, disambiguating the *sign* of the scale of q_p distribution and determining the order of q_p estimates w.r.t. their true values. The points $\underline{p}$ and $\overline{p}$ need not coincide with the minimum and maximum points. Polynomial coefficients b_{km} are assigned flat priors, while the priors on Σ are left unchanged as per (11) and (12).

3   Validation

The capability of the proposed framework to estimate the values of an unobservable quantity based on several related and interdependent quantities was validated on datasets of synthetic and clinical scalar measurements.

We focus on the ability of the framework to estimate F_m in (7) and q_p. Each plot of F_m also reports correlation coefficient ρ w.r.t. the reference values:

$$\rho \triangleq \frac{\sum_{m=1}^{M}(\tilde{F}_m - \langle\tilde{F}_m\rangle)(F_m^* - \langle F_m^*\rangle)}{\sum_{m=1}^{M}(\tilde{F}_m - \langle\tilde{F}_m\rangle)^2(F_m^* - \langle F_m^*\rangle)^2}, \quad (14)$$

where $\tilde{F}_m$ is the posterior estimate and F_m^* is the value obtained by least squares regression against *known* reference values of q, used in validation. Plots for q_p also provide the RMSE of the estimates:

$$A \triangleq \sqrt{\sum_{p=1}^{n} q_p^2/N} \tag{15}$$

and the smallest RMSE one would obtain if he or she used only the best predictor with known polynomial coefficients:

$$A_1 \triangleq \min_{m} 1/F_m^*. \tag{16}$$

3.1   Synthetic Data

Experiment with synthetic data was conducted to demonstrate the ability of the framework to estimate the model parameters with highly non-linear g_m that would otherwise have invalidated the assumptions of the original reference-free error estimation scheme [3]. We have generated $N = 30$ points from $\mathcal{U}(0, 55)$ and, at those points, evaluated polynomials with coefficients given in table 1. The obtained values were then perturbed with MVG noise with standard deviations σ_m and correlation matrix R from table 1.

Table 1. Parameters used to generate synthetic data.

m	b_{0m}	b_{1m}	b_{2m}	σ_m
1	80	−4.0	0.01	7.0
2	−80	4.0	−0.02	6.2
3	−80	12.0	−0.20	4.3
4	40	−3.5	0.04	2.2

$$R = \begin{pmatrix} 1 & 0.9 & 0 & 0 \\ 0.9 & 1 & 0 & 0 \\ 0 & 0 & 1 & 0 \\ 0 & 0 & 0 & 1 \end{pmatrix}$$

The parameters of the prior were setup as follows: $\underline{q_p} = 0$, $\overline{q_p} = 55$, $\underline{\epsilon} = \overline{\epsilon} = 5$, $\underline{\sigma_m} = 0.001$, $\overline{\sigma_m} = 55$, indices $\overline{p}$ and $\underline{p}$ were picked at random. K was set to 2, q_0 was set to 0.

Results are given in Fig. 1. Figure of merit estimates are in agreement with the true values and as such allow to answer the question (a). The unobservable quantity estimates are very close to the known true values and can thus be used to answer the question (b). Although $A > A_1$, it must be understood that A is actual RMSE calculated over $[\underline{q_p}, \overline{q_p}]$, while A_1 assumes that q is in the optimal region for the particular predictor that produces the smallest value of this quantity.

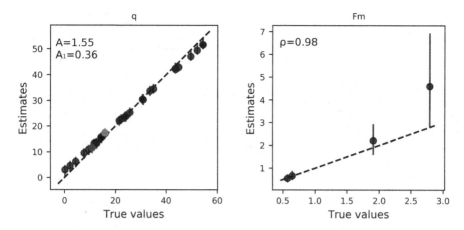

Fig. 1. Reference-free estimates of the unobservable variable q and the figure of merit F_m compared to corresponding known true values for the synthetic dataset. *Red and green points* were used to disambiguate the slope sign in regression model (see Sect. 2.2). See Sect. 3 for definitions of A, A_1 and ρ. *Dashed* identity lines correspond to a perfect match between the estimates and the true values. (Color figure online)

3.2 Clinical Data

Structural T1-weighted MR scans of a group of 40 patients, including 20 healthy elderly and 20 with mild cognitive impairment, the prodromal stage of Alzheimer's disease were analysed. Data for analysis consisted of volumetric measurements of whole-brain, hippocampus and its subfields, obtained using Freesurfer and DARTEL segmentation tools. These data were used to attempt to predict the NBM volume.

The NBM is a small region that is not routinely measured, yet it is associated with cognitive health and implicated in various neurodegenerative disorders. For validation purposes, the NBM volume was extracted using a detailed stereotactic atlas. All volumetric measurements were normalized to the total intracranial volume to account for the differences in head size between subjects.

The minimum and the maximum points were determined from normalized reference NBM volumes and provided indices $\underline{p}$ and $\overline{p}$, based on which the remaining parameters of the prior were setup: $\underline{\epsilon}$ and $\overline{\epsilon}$ were set to 0.02, while q_p and $\overline{q_p}$ were set so that the respective minimum and maximum values were approximately at $q_p + \underline{\epsilon}/2$ and $\overline{q_p} + \overline{\epsilon}/2$. K was set to 1, q_0 was set to $(q_p + \overline{q_p})/2$.

The resulting estimates in Fig. 2 show good agreement with the reference. The RMSE was slightly lower as compared to the RMSE obtainable from a single predictor, thus successfully answering the question (b). Generally, estimates of F_m were in good agreement with those obtained using least squares on reference values, taking into account the associated uncertainty, and therefore enable one to answer question (a).

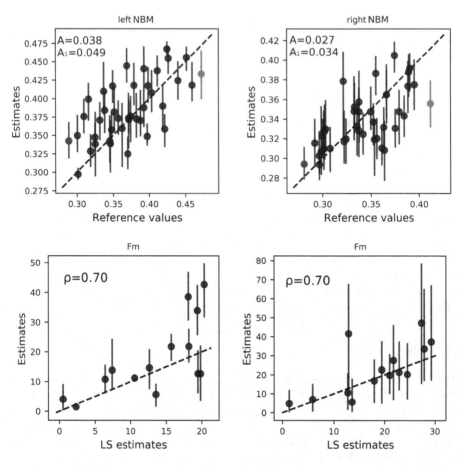

Fig. 2. *Top:* estimates of normalized NBM volume from volumes of hippocampal sub-fields for each hemisphere plotted against reference values. *Green and red points* denote $\underline{p}$ and $\overline{p}$ (Sect. 2.2). *Bottom:* figure of merit F_m estimates of hippocampal subfields as predictors for MBM volume plotted against the estimates obtained by least squares regression with respect to reference values. See Sect. 3 for definitions of A, A_1 and ρ. *Dashed* identity lines correspond to the perfect match between the estimates and the reference. (Color figure online)

4   Discussion

Results show that the proposed priors for the reference-free error estimation framework produce valid estimates of the unobservable quantity (NBM) and identify best easy-to-measure predictors of this quantity. The proposed priors are more general, but at the same time are more practical and objective than the original ones [3]. Instead of vague guesses about coefficients of Taylor expansion one has to provide interpretable, clearly defined parameters: span of the unobservable quantity, its uncertainty in the form of tolerance parameters and a pair of point indices with known value ordering.

For many biomarkers these parameters can be measured or inferred. For example, lower bound of the biomarker distribution may be defined exactly by including a healthy control subject into the dataset. If the patient with the highest value of the biomarker can be identified, then by a single application of a (possibly expensive) gold standard MM, the uncertainty of the upper bound can be reduced to the level of the method's nominal accuracy. To specify the pair of order-defining indices one may again use controls: for a large class of biomarkers a healthy control subject will have the value of the biomarker equal to zero, which is guaranteed to be less than that of a patient who has the relevant medical condition. Another possibility is to use up to two applications of a gold standard MM.

Whenever applicable, reference-free error estimation provides significant savings of time and costs normally associated with reference measurements: those of human operators, non-standard protocols, high-end acquisition equipment, material costs (e.g. contrast agents, materials of phantoms), instrumentation (frames, fiducial markers), administrative overhead, patient recovery and side effects from invasive measurements, making it an invaluable analytical tool.

Acknowledgments. The authors acknowledge the financial support from the Slovenian Research Agency (research core funding No. P2-0232, research grant funding Nos. J7-6781, J2-7211, J2-7118, and J2-8173).

References

1. Barnard, J., McCulloch, R., Meng, X.L.: Modeling covariance matrices in terms of standard deviations and correlations, with application to shrinkage. Statistica Sinica, pp. 1281–1311 (2000)
2. Lewandowski, D., Kurowicka, D., Joe, H.: Generating random correlation matrices based on vines and extended onion method. J. Multivariate Anal. **100**(9), 1989–2001 (2009)
3. Madan, H., Pernuš F., Špiclin, Ž.: Reference-free error estimation for multiple measurement methods. Stat. Methods Med. Res., 0962280217754231 (2018). https://doi.org/10.1177/0962280217754231, pMID: 29384043
4. Ray, N.J., et al.: In vivo cholinergic basal forebrain atrophy predicts cognitive decline in de novo Parkinson's disease. Brain **141**(1), 165–176 (2018)

Multi-modal Neuroimaging Data Fusion via Latent Space Learning for Alzheimer's Disease Diagnosis

Tao Zhou[1], Kim-Han Thung[1], Mingxia Liu[1], Feng Shi[2], Changqing Zhang[1,3], and Dinggang Shen[1(✉)]

[1] Department of Radiology and BRIC, University of North Carolina, Chapel Hill, USA
dgshen@med.unc.edu
[2] Shanghai United Imaging Intelligence Co., Ltd., Shanghai, China
[3] School of Computer Science and Technology, Tianjin University, Tianjin, China

Abstract. Recent studies have shown that fusing multi-modal neuroimaging data can improve the performance of Alzheimer's Disease (AD) diagnosis. However, most existing methods simply concatenate features from each modality without appropriate consideration of the correlations among multi-modalities. Besides, existing methods often employ feature selection (or fusion) and classifier training in two independent steps without consideration of the fact that the two pipelined steps are highly related to each other. Furthermore, existing methods that make prediction based on a single classifier may not be able to address the heterogeneity of the AD progression. To address these issues, we propose a novel AD diagnosis framework based on latent space learning with ensemble classifiers, by integrating the latent representation learning and ensemble of multiple diversified classifiers learning into a unified framework. To this end, we first project the neuroimaging data from different modalities into a common latent space, and impose a joint sparsity constraint on the concatenated projection matrices. Then, we map the learned latent representations into the label space to learn multiple diversified classifiers and aggregate their predictions to obtain the final classification result. Experimental results on the Alzheimer's Disease Neuroimaging Initiative (ADNI) dataset show that our method outperforms other state-of-the-art methods.

1 Introduction

Alzheimer's disease (AD) impairs patients' memory and other cognitive functions and is often found in people over 65 years old [1]. As there is no cure for AD, timely and accurate diagnosis of AD and its prodromal stage (i.e., Mild Cognitive Impairment (MCI)) is highly desirable in clinical practices.

Neuroimaging techniques including Magnetic Resonance Imaging (MRI) and Positr-on Emission Topography (PET) have been widely used to investigate the neurophysiological characteristics of AD [15,18]. As neuroimaging data are very

© Springer Nature Switzerland AG 2018
I. Rekik et al. (Eds.): PRIME 2018, LNCS 11121, pp. 76–84, 2018.
https://doi.org/10.1007/978-3-030-00320-3_10

high-dimensional, existing methods often use Region-Of-Interest (ROI) based features instead of the original voxel based features for analysis [4,17]. Recently, many studies have been proposed to fuse the complementary information from multi-modality data for accurate AD diagnosis [10,14,19]. For example, Zhu et al. [19] use Canonical Correlation Analysis (CCA) to first transform multi-modality data into a common CCA space, and then use the transformed features for classification. Hinrichs et al. [8] use Multiple Kernel Learning (MKL) to fuse multi-modality data by learning an optimal linearly combined kernels for classification.

Most of the multi-modality data based AD studies in the literature are based on the 2-step strategy, where feature selection or fusion is first performed, and then a classifier (e.g., Support Vector Machine (SVM)) is learned [10,19]. Because the features selected in the first step may not be best to the classifier in the second step, which will degrade the final classification performance. Further, most methods [10,19] also focus on learning a single classifier for AD diagnosis, which is difficult to address the heterogeneity of complex brain disorder. To deal with this disease heterogeneity issue, it is more reasonable to train a set of diversified classifiers and ensemble them (instead of training a single classifier), which has been shown effective in previous studies [2,5].

To this end, we propose a novel multi-modal neuroimaging data fusion via latent space learning with ensemble classifier for AD diagnosis framework, which can seamlessly perform latent space learning and ensemble of diversified classifiers learning in a unified framework. Specifically, we first project neuroimaging data from different modalities (i.e., MRI and PET) into a common latent space, to exploit the correlation between MRI and PET features, and learn the latent representations. Concurrently, we also select a subset of discriminative ROI-based features from both modalities jointly, by imposing a cross-modality joint sparsity constraint on the concatenated projection matrices (as shown in Fig. 1). This is based on the assumption that, both the structure and function of an ROI could be affected by the disease progression, hence it is intuitive to select the same ROI based features for MRI and PET data in the latent space. Further, we learn multiple diversified classifiers by mapping the latent representations into the label space, and use an ensemble strategy to obtain the final result. Note that we integrate all the above learning tasks into a unified framework, so that all components can work together to achieve a better AD diagnostic model. We have verified the effectiveness of our method on the Alzheimer's Disease Neuroimaging Initiative (ADNI) dataset.

2   Methodology

Latent Space Learning with Cross-Modality Joint Sparsity. Given a multi-modality data set $\mathbf{X} = \{\mathbf{X}_1, \cdots, \mathbf{X}_M\}$, where $\mathbf{X}_m \in \mathbb{R}^{d_m \times n}$ denotes the feature matrix for the m-th modality with d_m features and n subjects, and M is

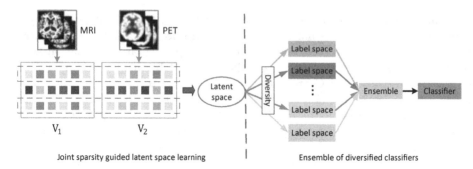

Fig. 1. A flow diagram of our proposed AD diagnosis framework. We project multi-modality data (i.e., MRI and PET in our case) into a common latent space to exploit the correlation among multi-modal neuroimaging data. Besides, a joint sparsity constraint (denoted by the dashed red rectangles) is imposed on different modalities, to encourage the selection of same ROIs from MRI and PET data. Furthermore, multiple classifiers with diversity constraint are trained and an ensemble strategy is used to obtain the final classification result.

the number of modalities. To exploit the correlations among different modalities, we project different modalities into a common latent space as follows:

$$\min_{\mathbf{V}_m, \mathbf{H}} \sum\nolimits_{m=1}^{M} \left(\|\mathbf{V}_m^T \mathbf{X}_m - \mathbf{H}\|_F^2 + \gamma \|\mathbf{V}_m\|_{2,1} \right), \tag{1}$$

where $\mathbf{V}_m \in \mathbb{R}^{d_m \times h}$ is a projection matrix, $\mathbf{H} \in \mathbb{R}^{h \times n}$ is a matrix of latent representation, γ is the regularization parameter, and h is the dimension of the latent space. We use $\ell_{2,1}$-norm regularizer (i.e., $\|\mathbf{V}\|_{2,1} = \sum_{i=1}^{d} \sqrt{\sum_{j=1}^{h} \mathbf{v}_{ij}^2}$, where $\mathbf{V} \in \mathbb{R}^{d \times h}$) in Eq. (1) to enforce row-wise sparsity in $\mathbf{V}_m$, by penalizing the coefficients in each row of $\mathbf{V}_m$ together. In other words, the $\ell_{2,1}$-norm encourages the selection of useful (ROI-based) features from $\mathbf{X}_m$ during the latent space learning. To encourage cross-modality joint sparsity, assuming the features from different modalities are related, the objective function in Eq. (1) is extended to the following formulation:

$$\min_{\mathbf{V}_m, \mathbf{H}} \sum\nolimits_{m=1}^{M} \|\mathbf{V}_m^T \mathbf{X}_m - \mathbf{H}\|_F^2 + \gamma \|[\mathbf{V}_1 \cdots \mathbf{V}_M]\|_{2,1}, \tag{2}$$

where a joint sparsity constraint is imposed on the concatenated projection matrices. In our case, ROI-based features are used for both the MRI and PET data, thus Eq. (2) will enforce the features from the same ROI to be selected for multi-modalities. This is based on the assumption that both the brain structure (quantified by MRI features) and function (quantified by the PET features) will be degraded for the same AD-affected ROIs. In this way, the correlations among multi-modality data can effectively be exploited.

It is worth noting that the Frobenius norm in Eq. (2) is sensitive to sample outliers. To address this issue, we reformulate Eq. (2) as:

$$\min_{\mathbf{V}_m, \mathbf{E}_m, \mathbf{H}} \sum_{m=1}^{M} \|\mathbf{E}_m\|_1 + \gamma \|[\mathbf{V}_1 \cdots \mathbf{V}_M]\|_{2,1},$$
$$s.t. \ \ \mathbf{H} = \mathbf{V}_m^T \mathbf{X}_m + \mathbf{E}_m, m = 1, \ldots, M, \tag{3}$$

where an error term $\mathbf{E}_m \in \mathbb{R}^{h \times n}$ is introduce to model the reconstruction error (i.e., the first term in Eq. (2)), and use ℓ_1-norm to penalize $\mathbf{E}_m$.

Ensemble of Diversified Classifiers Learning. After obtaining the latent representations from multi-modality data, we regard the new representations in the latent space as input to train a classifier. As SVM is a widely used classifier due to its promising performance in many applications [13], we incorporate the latent space learning and classifier learning into a unified framework as follows:

$$\min_{\mathbf{V}_m, \mathbf{E}_m, \mathbf{w}, \mathbf{H}, b} \sum_{i=1}^{n} f(y_i, \mathbf{h}_i^T \mathbf{w} + b) + \lambda \Psi(\mathbf{w})$$
$$+ \beta \sum_{m=1}^{M} \|\mathbf{E}_m\|_1 + \gamma \|[\mathbf{V}_1 \cdots \mathbf{V}_M]\|_{2,1} \tag{4}$$
$$s.t. \ \ \mathbf{H} = \mathbf{V}_m^T \mathbf{X}_m + \mathbf{E}_m, m = 1, \ldots, M,$$

where $\mathbf{h}_i \in \mathbb{R}^{h \times 1}$ is the latent representation of the i-th sample (i.e., i-th column of $\mathbf{H}$), $y_i \in \{-1, 1\}$ is the corresponding label, and $\mathbf{w}$ and b denote the weight vector and bias of the classifier, respectively. Besides, $f(\cdot)$ in Eq. (4) is the classifier loss function, while the second term in Eq. (4) is the regularizer for $\mathbf{w}$ (e.g., ℓ_1 or ℓ_2-norm of $\mathbf{w}$). If we use hinge loss function for $f(\cdot)$, the first term in Eq. (4) can be given as:

$$\sum_{i=1}^{n} f(y_i, \mathbf{h}_i^T \mathbf{w} + b) = \sum_{i=1}^{n} (1 - (\mathbf{h}_i^T \mathbf{w} + b) y_i)_+^p, \tag{5}$$

where the operation $(x)_+ := max(x, 0)$ keeps x unchanged if it is non-negative, and returns zero otherwise, and p is a constant with either value 1 or 2 to have physical meaning. In Eq. (4), only a classifier is trained, which may not be able to address the heterogeneity of AD progression. In addition, some studies have also indicated that ensembling multiple classifiers may result in a more robust and accurate classifier. Thus, following the work in [6], we replace the loss function in Eq. (4) with the loss functions from multiple classifiers, as follows:

$$\min_{\mathbf{V}_m, \mathbf{E}_m, \mathbf{W}, \mathbf{H}, \mathbf{b}} \sum_{c=1}^{C} \sum_{i=1}^{n} (1 - (\mathbf{h}_i^T \mathbf{w}_c + b_c) y_i)_+^p + \lambda \Psi(\mathbf{W})$$
$$+ \beta \sum_{m=1}^{M} \|\mathbf{E}_m\|_1 + \gamma \|[\mathbf{V}_1 \cdots \mathbf{V}_M]\|_{2,1}, \tag{6}$$
$$s.t. \ \ \mathbf{H} = \mathbf{V}_m^T \mathbf{X}_m + \mathbf{E}_m, m = 1, \ldots, M,$$

where $\mathbf{W} = [\mathbf{w}_1 \cdots \mathbf{w}_C] \in \mathbb{R}^{h \times C}$ is a matrix with each of its column denoting the weight vector for one classifier, $\mathbf{b} = [b_1 \cdots b_C] \in \mathbb{R}^{C \times 1}$ is the corresponding bias vector, and C is the number of classifiers. To ensure that we have a diversity of classifiers rather than redundant classifiers, we minimize the exclusivity function between each pair of classifier weight vectors, given as $\{\min \|\mathbf{w}_i \circ \mathbf{w}_j\|_0, i \neq j\}$ [6], where $\circ$ denotes Hadamard product, and $\|\cdot\|_0$ denotes ℓ_0-norm. This constraint will ensure the column weight vectors in $\mathbf{W}$ be exclusive and orthogonal to each other, thus giving us diversified classifiers.

However, as this constraint is too strong and difficult to optimize, we choose to minimize the relaxed exclusivity function instead, i.e., given by $\{\min \|\mathbf{w}_i \circ \mathbf{w}_j\|_1 = \min \sum_k |\mathbf{w}_i(k)| \cdot |\mathbf{w}_j(k)|, i \neq j\}$, where $\mathbf{w}_i(k)$ denotes the k-th element in $\mathbf{w}_i$, and $|\cdot|$ denotes the absolute operator. Following the work in [6], we use the following regularizer as a diversity constraint to encourage the learning of diversified classifiers. The regularizer is given as:

$$
\begin{aligned}
\Psi(\mathbf{W}) &= \frac{1}{2}\|\mathbf{W}\|_F^2 + \sum_{i,j \neq i} \|\mathbf{w}_i \circ \mathbf{w}_j\|_1 \\
&= \frac{1}{2}\sum_{k=1}^{K}\left(\sum_{c=1}^{C}|\mathbf{w}_c(k)|\right)^2 = \frac{1}{2}\|\mathbf{W}^T\|_{1,2}^2.
\end{aligned}
\tag{7}
$$

The derivation details for the above equation can be found in [6].

Unified AD Diagnosis Framework. By integrating the latent space learning and ensemble learning of diversified classifiers into a unified framework, the final objective function of our proposed model is given as:

$$
\begin{aligned}
\min_{\mathbf{V}_m, \mathbf{E}_m, \mathbf{W}, \mathbf{H}, \mathbf{b}} &\sum_{c=1}^{C}\sum_{i=1}^{n}(1 - (\mathbf{h}_i^T \mathbf{w}_c + b_c)y_i)_+^p + \frac{\lambda}{2}\|\mathbf{W}^T\|_{1,2}^2 \\
&+ \beta \sum_{m=1}^{M}\|\mathbf{E}_m\|_1 + \gamma\|[\mathbf{V}_1 \cdots \mathbf{V}_M]\|_{2,1}, \\
s.t. \quad &\mathbf{H} = \mathbf{V}_m^T \mathbf{X}_m + \mathbf{E}_m, m = 1, \ldots, M.
\end{aligned}
\tag{8}
$$

2.1 Optimization and Prediction

The objective function in Eq. (8) is not jointly convex with respect to all variables. Therefore, we utilize the Augmented Lagrange Multiplier (ALM) [11] algorithm to solve Eq. (8) efficiently and effectively. After we train our model and obtain $\mathbf{W}$ and $\mathbf{b}$, we can obtain the ensemble classifier weight and bias via $\mathbf{w} = \frac{1}{C}\sum_{c=1}^{C}\mathbf{w}_c$, and $b = \frac{1}{C}\sum_{c=1}^{C}b_c$. Then, for a testing sample $\mathbf{X}^{test} = \{\mathbf{X}_1^{test}, \ldots, \mathbf{X}_M^{test}\}$, the corresponding testing label $\mathbf{y}_{test}$ is estimated by using $\mathbf{y}_{test} = \text{sign}(\mathbf{h}_{test}^T \mathbf{w} + b)$, where $\mathbf{h}_{test} = \frac{1}{M}\sum_{m=1}^{M}\mathbf{V}_m^T \mathbf{X}_m^{test}$, denoting the latent representation of the testing sample.

3 Experiments

3.1 Subjects and Neuroimage Preprocessing

In this study, we select 379 subjects from the ADNI cohort (www.adni-info.org) with complete MRI and PET data at baseline scan, including 101 Normal Control (NC), 185 MCI, and 93 AD. In our experiments, we used ROI-based features from both MRI and PET images (i.e., $M=2$ in our study). Then, we further processed the MR images using a standard pipeline including the following steps: (1) intensity inhomogeneity correction, (2) brain extraction, (3) cerebellum removal, (4) tissues segmentation, and (5) template registration. After that, the processed MR images were divided into 93 pre-defined ROIs [9], and the gray matter volumes in these ROIs were computed as MRI features. For PET data, we aligned the PET images to their corresponding MR images by using affine registration, and calculated the average intensity value of each ROI as PET features. Thus, we have 93 ROI-based features from both the MRI and PET data, respectively.

3.2   Experimental Setup

We evaluated the effectiveness of the proposed model by conducting the following two binary classification experiments: i.e., AD vs. NC and MCI vs. NC classifications. We used classification accuracy (ACC) and Area Under Curve (AUC) as evaluation metrics.

We compared our proposed framework with the following comparison methods: (1) baseline method ("ORI"), which concatenates MRI and PET ROI-based features into a long vector for SVM classification, (2) Lasso based feature selection method [16], which selects features from both modalities using ℓ_1-norm, (3) CCA [7] and MKL [8] based multi-modality fusion methods; and (4) Deep learning based feature representation method, i.e., Stacked Auto-encoder (SAE) [12].

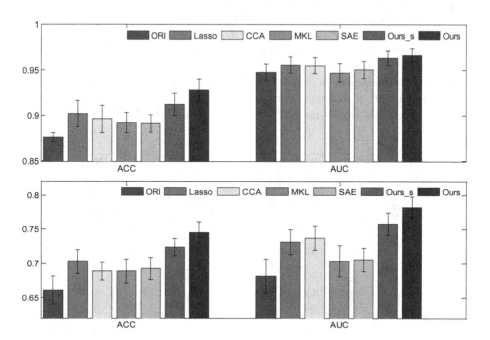

Fig. 2. Comparison of classification results using two evaluation metrics (i.e., ACC and AUC) for two classification tasks: AD/NC (top) and MCI/NC (bottom).

Note that all the above comparison methods are based on 2-step strategy, where feature selection and feature fusion (or feature learning) are first performed, before using SVM (from LIBSVM toolbox [3]) for classification. We performed 10-fold cross validation for all the methods under comparison, and reported the means and standard deviations of the experimental results. For parameter setting of our method, we determined the regularization parameter values (i.e., $\{\lambda, \beta, \gamma\} \in \{10^{-5}, \ldots, 10^2\}$) and the dimension of the latent space (i.e., $h \in \{10, \ldots, 60\}$) via an inner cross-validation search on the training data, and searched the number of classifiers C in the range $\{5, 10, 15, 20\}$. We also used inner cross-validation to select hyper-parameter values for all the comparison methods. Besides, we further determined the soft margin parameter of SVM classifier via grid search in the range of $\{10^{-4}, \ldots, 10^4\}$.

Figure 2 shows the classification performance of all the competing methods. From Fig. 2, it can be clearly seen that our proposed method performs consistently better than all the comparison methods in terms of ACC and AUC. Compared with the Lasso based feature selection method, which fuses multi-modality data without effective consideration of the correlation between MRI and PET, our method performs significantly better. In addition, our method also outperforms SAE, which uses high-level features learned from auto encoder for classification. This is probably due to the fact the SAE is an unsupervised feature learning method that does not consider label information. In addition, to verify the effectiveness of ensemble of diversified classifiers, we also compare the performance of our proposed method for the cases of using single classifier and multi-classifiers, with "Ours_s" denoting the results of our proposed method using a single classifier. From the results shown in Fig. 2, our proposed method using the ensemble of diversified classifiers performs better than the case of using only a single classifier.

To analyze the benefit of multi-modalities fusion, Fig. 3 illustrates the performance comparison of different methods using independent modality (i.e., MRI or PET). Note that, multi-modality fusion methods (i.e., CCA and MKL) are

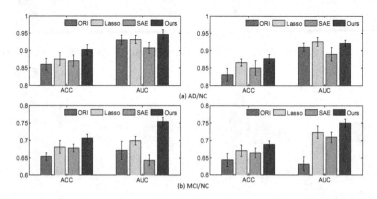

Fig. 3. Comparison of results for two classification tasks (i.e., (a) AD/NC and (b) MCI/NC) using two different modalities: MRI (left) and PET (right).

excluded in this comparison. From Fig. 3, it can be seen that our method still outperforms other comparison methods. Besides, comparing Figs. 2 and 3, we can see that all the methods perform better when using multi-modality data, compared to the use of just the single modality data.

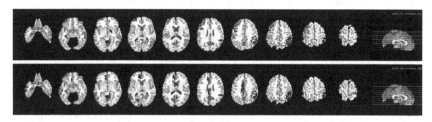

Fig. 4. Top selected regions for two classification tasks: AD/NC (top) and MCI/NC (bottom).

Furthermore, we also identified the potential brain regions that can be used as AD biomarkers. We ranked the ROIs based on their average weight values. Figure 4 shows the top ranked ROIs by using our proposed method for different tasks. Specifically, for AD/NC task, the top selected ROIs (common to both MRI and PET data) are globus palladus right, precuneus right, precuneus left, entorhinal cortex left, hippocampal formation left, middle temporal gyrus right, and amygdala right. For MCI/NC task, the top selected ROIs are angular gyrus right, precuneus right, precuneus left, middle temporal gyrus left, hippocampal formation left, postcentral gyrus right, and amygdala right. These regions are consistent with some previous studies [10, 19] and can be used as potential biomarkers for AD diagnosis.

4   Conclusion

In this paper, we have proposed an AD diagnosis model based on latent space learning with diversified classifiers. This is different from the conventional AD diagnosis models that often perform feature selection (or fusion) and classifier training separately. Specifically, we project the original ROIs-based features into a latent space to effectively exploit the correlations among multi-modality data. Besides, we impose a cross-modality joint sparsity constraint to encourage the selection of same ROIs for MRI and PET data, based on the assumption that the degenerated brain regions would affect both brain structure and function. Then, using the learned latent representations as input, we learn multiple diversified classifiers and further use an ensemble strategy to obtain the final result, so that the ensemble classifier is more robust to disease heterogeneity. Experimental results on ADNI dataset have demonstrated the effectiveness of the proposed method against other methods.

Acknowledgment. This research was supported in part by NIH grants EB006733, EB008374, MH100217, AG041721 and AG042599.

References

1. Alzheimer's Association: 2013 Alzheimer's disease facts and figures. Alzheimer's Dement. **9**(2), 208–245 (2013)
2. Brown, G., Wyatt, J., Harris, R., Yao, X.: Diversity creation methods: a survey and categorisation. Inf. Fusion **6**(1), 5–20 (2005)
3. Chang, C.C., Lin, C.J.: LIBSVM: a library for support vector machines. ACM Trans. Intell. Syst. Tech. (TIST) **2**(3), 27 (2011)
4. Chaves, R., Ramírez, J.: SVM-based computer-aided diagnosis of the Alzheimer's disease using t-test nmse feature selection with feature correlation weighting. Neurosci. Lett. **461**(3), 293–297 (2009)
5. Freund, Y., Schapire, R.E.: A decision-theoretic generalization of on-line learning and an application to boosting. J. Comput. Syst. Sci. **55**(1), 119–139 (1997)
6. Guo, X., Wang, X., Ling, H.: Exclusivity regularized machine: a new ensemble SVM classifier. In: IJCAI, pp. 1739–1745 (2017)
7. Hardoon, D.R., Szedmak, S., Shawe-Taylor, J.: Canonical correlation analysis: an overview with application to learning methods. Neural Comput. **16**(12), 2639–2664 (2004)
8. Hinrichs, C., Singh, V., Xu, G., Johnson, S.: MKL for robust multi-modality AD classification. In: Yang, G.-Z., Hawkes, D., Rueckert, D., Noble, A., Taylor, C. (eds.) MICCAI 2009. LNCS, vol. 5762, pp. 786–794. Springer, Heidelberg (2009). https://doi.org/10.1007/978-3-642-04271-3_95
9. Kabani, N.J.: 3D anatomical atlas of the human brain. NeuroImage **7**, P-0717 (1998)
10. Lei, B., Yang, P.: Relational-regularized discriminative sparse learning for Alzheimer's disease diagnosis. IEEE Trans. Cybern. **47**(4), 1102–1113 (2017)
11. Lin, Z., Liu, R., Su, Z.: Linearized alternating direction method with adaptive penalty for low-rank representation. In: NIPS, pp. 612–620 (2011)
12. Suk, H.: Latent feature representation with stacked auto-encoder for AD/MCI diagnosis. Brain Struct. Funct. **220**(2), 841–859 (2015)
13. Suykens, J.A., Vandewalle, J.: Least squares support vector machine classifiers. Neural Process. Lett. **9**(3), 293–300 (1999)
14. Thung, K.H.: Conversion and time-to-conversion predictions of mild cognitive impairment using low-rank affinity pursuit denoising and matrix completion. Med. Image Anal. **45**, 68–82 (2018)
15. Thung, K.H., Wee, C.Y., Yap, P.T., Shen, D., Initiative, A.D.N., et al.: Neurodegenerative disease diagnosis using incomplete multi-modality data via matrix shrinkage and completion. NeuroImage **91**, 386–400 (2014)
16. Tibshirani, R.: Regression shrinkage and selection via the Lasso. J. R. Stat. Soc. Ser. B, **58**, 267–288 (1996)
17. Zhou, T., Thung, K.H., Liu, M., Shen, D.: Brain-wide genome-wide association study for Alzheimer's disease via joint projection learning and sparse regression model. IEEE Trans. Biomed. Eng. (2018, in press)
18. Zhou, T., Thung, K.-H., Zhu, X., Shen, D.: Feature learning and fusion of multi-modality neuroimaging and genetic data for multi-status dementia diagnosis. In: Wang, Q., Shi, Y., Suk, H.-I., Suzuki, K. (eds.) MLMI 2017. LNCS, vol. 10541, pp. 132–140. Springer, Cham (2017). https://doi.org/10.1007/978-3-319-67389-9_16
19. Zhu, X.: Canonical feature selection for joint regression and multi-class identification in Alzheimer's disease diagnosis. Brain Imaging Behav. **10**(3), 818–828 (2016)

Transfer Learning for Task Adaptation of Brain Lesion Assessment and Prediction of Brain Abnormalities Progression/Regression Using Irregularity Age Map in Brain MRI

Muhammad Febrian Rachmadi[1,2]([envelope]) [ID], Maria del C. Valdés-Hernández[2][ID], and Taku Komura[1]

[1] School of Informatics, University of Edinburgh, Edinburgh, UK
febrian.rachmadi@ed.ac.uk
[2] Centre for Clinical Brain Sciences, University of Edinburgh, Edinburgh, UK

Abstract. The Irregularity Age Map (IAM) for the unsupervised assessment of brain white matter hyperintensities (WMH) opens several opportunities in machine learning-based MRI analysis, including transfer task adaptation learning in the segmentation and prediction of brain lesion progression and regression. The lack of need for manual labels is useful for transfer learning. Whereas the nature of IAM itself can be exploited for predicting lesion progression/regression. In this study, we propose the use of task adaptation transfer learning for WMH segmentation using CNN through weakly-training UNet and UResNet using the output from IAM and the use of IAM for predicting patterns of WMH progression and regression.

Keywords: Brain lesion's progression/regression prediction
Brain MRI analysis · Task adaptation
Weakly supervised deep neural networks

1 Introduction

Magnetic Resonance Imaging (MRI) facilitates identifying brain pathologies. However, variations in MRI acquisition protocols and scanner manufacturer's parameters lead to differences in the appearance of the clinical MRI features making their automatic detection challenging. Although the widespread use of MRI has produced large amount of datasets to be used in machine learning approaches, the lack of expert labelled data limits their applicability.

A new method named Irregularity Age Map (IAM) has been recently proposed for detecting irregular textures in T2-FLAIR MRI without requiring manual labels for training [5]. The IAM indicates the degree in which the texture of the neighbourhood around each pixel/voxel differs from the texture of the tissue considered normal. Differently, most machine learning algorithms generate

© Springer Nature Switzerland AG 2018
I. Rekik et al. (Eds.): PRIME 2018, LNCS 11121, pp. 85–93, 2018.
https://doi.org/10.1007/978-3-030-00320-3_11

a map indicating the probability of each pixel/voxel of belonging to a particular class (*e.g.*, normal white and grey matter, cerebrospinal fluid, lesions, etc.). We believe that the unsupervised nature and the concept of IAM itself are useful for: (1) task adaptation learning in assessing MRI abnormalities and (2) generation of progression/regression patterns that can be used to predict the evolution of these abnormalities. These two topics are the main contributions in this study.

2   Task Adaptation Transfer Learning in MRI

2.1   Current Approaches of Transfer Learning in MRI

Deep neural networks (DNN) architectures are considered the state-of-art machine learning models in MRI data classification and segmentation as they exhibit or surpass human-level performance on the task and domain they are trained. However, when the domain changes (e.g. imaging protocol or sequence type differ), or they are asked to perform tasks that are related to but not the same task they were trained for (e.g. lesion segmentation vs. lesion assessment), they suffer a significant loss in performance.

Transfer learning (TL) helps dealing with these novel scenarios, as enables a model trained on one task to be re-purposed on a second related task. In DNN the first few layers learn the general visual building of the image, such as edges and corners, while the deeper layers of network learn more complex task-dependent features [1]. Using TL, domain, task or distribution in training and target processes can differ and be adjusted to fit the final purpose better.

Domain adaptation TL, where data domains in training and testing processes differ, has been proven useful. In one study, TL improved Support Vector Machine's performance in MRI segmentation using different distribution of training data [9]. Another study pre-trained DNN using natural images for segmentation of neonatal to adult brain images [10], and another study pre-trained a DNN for brain lesion segmentation using MRI data from other protocols [1].

However, task adaptation TL, where tasks in training and testing processes are different, has not been widely explored in medical image analysis. The newly proposed unsupervised method of Limited One Time Sampling IAM (LOTS-IAM) [5] has been reported to serve the purpose of white matter hyperintensities (WMH) segmentation performing at the level of DNN architectures trained for this specific purpose while executing a different task *i.e.*, extracting irregular brain tissue texture in the form of irregularity age map (IAM).

2.2   Weakly-Training CNN in MRI Using Age Map

In this study, we explore the use of adapting the task of WMH segmentation on DNN, by using the IAM produced by LOTS-IAM as target instead of binary mask of WMH manually generated by an expert. We evaluate how the DNN recognition capabilities are preserved during the task adaptation TL process.

For our experiments we selected UNet [8] and UResNet [2] architectures used in various natural/medical image segmentation studies. In this study we made two modifications to allow UNet and UResNet to learn IAM: (1) no non-linear activation function (*e.g.*, sigmoid, softmax or ReLU) is used in the last layer of both architectures and (2) mean squared error loss function is used instead of Dice similarity coefficient or binary cross entropy in both architectures. Detailed flowchart of the proposed method is available on the GitHub page[1].

3   Brain Lesion's Progression and Regression

3.1   Prediction of Brain Lesion's Progression/Regression

Brain lesion's evolution over time is very important in medical image analysis because it not only helps estimating the pathology's level of severity but also selecting the 'best' treatment for each patient [7]. However, predicting brain lesion's evolution is challenging because it is influenced by various hidden parameters unique to each individual. Hence, brain lesions can appear and disappear at any point in time [7] and the reasons behind it are still unknown.

Previous studies that have modelled brain lesion progression/regression, use longitudinal (*i.e.*, time-series) data to formulate lesion's metamorphosis [3,7] by estimating direction and speed of the lesion evolution over time. Hence, multiple scans are necessary to simulate the evolution of the lesion.

In this study, we propose the use of IAM for simulating brain lesion evolution (*i.e.*, progression and regression) by using one MRI scan at one time point. This is possible thanks to the nature of IAM which retains original T2-FLAIR MRI's complex textures while indicating WMH's irregular textures. Compared to manually produced WMH binary mask by experts or automatically produced probability masks by machine learning algorithms, information contained/retained in IAM is much richer (see Fig. 1).

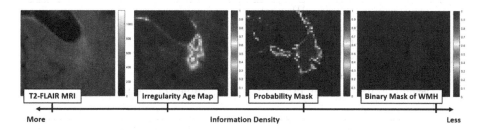

Fig. 1. Information density retained in each domain of the original T2-FLAIR, irregularity age map (IAM), probability mask and binary mask of WMH.

---

[1] https://github.com/febrianrachmadi/iam-tl-progression.

3.2   Proposed Brain Lesions' Regression (Shrinkage) Algorithm

We predict the regression pattern of brain lesions by lowering the threshold value of the IAM. This is possible as each IAM voxel contains different age value. It can be observed in Fig. 1 where age values of brain lesion decrease gradually from the border to the centre of each brain lesion. This is not possible using probability masks produced by most machine learning algorithms or binary masks of WMH produced manually by expert where most lesion voxels have flat value of 1.

The algorithm for predicting brain lesions' regression is detailed in Algorithm 1. To predict the brain lesions' regression pattern, we generate pseudo-healthy tissue of T2-FLAIR MRI first calculating the age map (Algorithm 2). In IAM, the nearest neighbour patches of the original patches are decided based on a distance value calculated using the distance function as per Eq. 1.

Algorithm 1. Brain lesions regression (shrinkage) prediction algorithm

---

    input   : Original T2-FLAIR MRI
    output: Age map and sequential time points of "healthier" T2-FLAIR
1 $t = 1$;
2 $age(t) = age_{IAM} = \text{LOTS-IAM(T2-FLAIR)}$;
3 load/make pseudo-healthy of T2-FLAIR (see Algorithm 2);
4 **while** $t > 0$ **do**
5     $t = t - 0.05$;
6     $age(t) = age_{IAM} - (1 - t)$;
7     $flair(t) = \text{blend } age(t)$ with pseudo-healthy T2-FLAIR;
8   save $age(t)$ and $flair(t)$;
9 **end**

Algorithm 2. Pseudo-healthy MRI generation algorithm

---

    input   : Original T2-FLAIR MRI
    output: Pseudo-healthy T2-FLAIR MRI
1 $age_{IAM} = \text{LOTS-IAM(T2-FLAIR)}$;
2 **for** *each patch that has age value* > 0.20 **do**
3   replace the original patch with the nearest neighbour brain's normal tissue patch (*i.e.*, based on MSE of age values of the patch);
4 **end**

3.3   Proposed Brain Lesions' Progression (Growth) Algorithm

Compared to the previous algorithm for predicting regression, the algorithm for predicting brain lesions' progression is more complex as it involves nearest neighbour searching and patch replacement processes. The idea is simple; we need to find similar (*i.e.*, nearest neighbour) IAM patches for each original IAM patch while the nearest IAM patch needs to have slightly higher age values than the original IAM patch. Once the nearest IAM patch is found, the original

IAM patch is then replaced. Once all patches are replaced by their nearest IAM patches, a new T2-FLAIR MRI showing brain lesion progression can be produced by blending the new IAM with the pseudo-healthy T2-FLAIR MRI.

The algorithm for predicting brain lesion progression is detailed in Algorithm 3. It uses the pseudo-healthy T2-FLAIR MRI produced by Algorithm 2. The distance function used in Algorithms 2 and 3 is defined below. Let $\mathbf{s}$ be the original IAM patch and $\mathbf{t}$ be the candidate of nearest neighbour patch, the distance d between the two patches is:

$$d = \alpha \cdot |\max(\mathbf{s} - \mathbf{t})| + (1 - \alpha) \cdot |\text{mean}(\mathbf{s} - \mathbf{t})| . \tag{1}$$

where $\alpha = 0.5$. Whereas, the patch's size used in this study is 4×4.

Algorithm 3. Brain lesions progression (growth) prediction algorithm

---

    input : Irregularity age map of T2-FLAIR (age_{IAM}) and pseudo-healthy
          of T2-FLAIR (see Algorithm 2).
    output: Generated age map and T2-FLAIR in each next time steps.
1 $\gamma = 0.05$;   /* maximum increase of age value */
2 **for** $t = 1.05 : 0.05 : 2.00$ **do** /* progression by 0.05 at a step   */
3      $[patches] = find(age_{IAM} \geq 0.16)$;   /* patch's size is 4×4 */
4   **for** $patch$ **in** $[patches]$ **do**
5           $[patchs_{temp}] = find(age_{IAM} > patch + 0.05$ **and**
              $age_{IAM} \leq patch + 0.05 + \gamma))$;
6   select 128 random $patches$ from $[patchs_{temp}]$ **as** $[candidates]$;
7   **for** $candidate$ **in** $[candidates]$ **do**
8   rotate $candidate$ by 90° four times /* data augmentation */
9   **end**
10   calculate distance values between $patch$ and $[candidates]$ using
           distance function (Equation 1);
11   select a nearest neighbour $patch$;
12   **if** $age\ value$ **in** $nearest\ neighbour > age\ value$ **in** $patch$ **then**
13   replace $age\ value$;
14   **end**
15   **end**
16   save the new generated age map;
17   blend T2-FLAIR with the new generated age map and save;
18 **end**

---

4   MRI Data and Experiment Setup

A set of 60 T2-Fluid Attenuation Inversion Recovery (T2-FLAIR) MRI data from 20 subjects was used. Each T2-FLAIR MRI volume has dimension of $256 \times 256 \times 35$. Data used in this study were obtained from the ADNI [4] public database[2]. Training/testing and pre-processing steps are the same as in [6]. The Dice similarity coefficient (DSC) was used to evaluate performance of UNet and UResNet segmenting WMH weakly-trained using IAM.

5 Results

5.1 Weakly-Training of UNet and UResNet Using IAM

Figure 2 shows the performance of the two algorithms evaluated in this study: UNet(1) and UResNet(2) segmenting WMH in our sample. Figure 2A shows distribution of results (DSC) by both algorithms trained without TL(Aa) (*i.e.*, manual WMH labels) and with TL(Ab) where IAM from LOTS-IAM was thresholded[3] at 0.18 (see [5]). Both DNN schemes could yield better results if task-adaptation TL using IAM is performed. However, the IAM's dependence on pre-processing poses a risk for their use in TL, as it can also worsen DNN's performance.

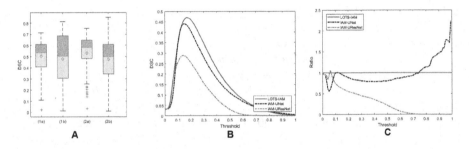

Fig. 2. Performance of UNet(A1) and UResNet(A2) in WMH segmentation without transfer learning(Aa) and using transfer learning(Ab, B and C).

In another experiment where UNet and UResNet are directly trained using IAM as target[3] (Fig. 2B), the peak mean performances are 0.2888 (0.0990) for IAM-UResNet, 0.4409 (0.1410) for IAM-UNet and 0.4704 (0.1587) for the LOTS-IAM. The UNet performs 15.21% better than the UResNet, which is quite opposite to when TL is not used (see [5] and Fig. 2A). Our guess is that residual blocks in UResNet perform poorly if it has to learn from real values of IAM. Whereas, UNet learned IAM with minimal performance drops (*i.e.*, 2.95% from the LOTS-IAM and 6.21% from manual WMH labels as per [5]). Although the performance of IAM-UResNet and IAM-UNet apparently follow the LOTS-IAM's performance at different thresholds in terms of DSC, a closer look at the learning process shows these relationships are not linear. Figure 2C

---

[2] Database can be accessed at http://adni.loni.usc.edu. A complete listing of ADNI investigators can be found at http://adni.loni.usc.edu/wp-content/uploads/how_to_apply/ADNI_Acknowledgement_List.pdf.

shows the ratio between the mean DSC values of these DNN schemes and LOTS-IAM output. The peak DSC performance is not achieved using exactly the same threshold.

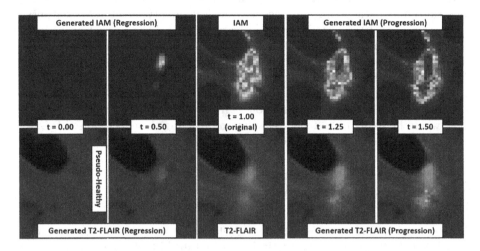

Fig. 3. Visualisation of brain lesion's progression and regression prediction by manipulating age values of IAM.

5.2 Results on Prediction of Brain Lesions' Progression/Regression

Figure 3 shows an example of IAM and T2-FLAIR generated by using Algorithms 1, 2 and 3, from the original IAM and T2-FLAIR (centre with $t = 1.00$)(also shown). The regression step of IAM and T2-FLAIR (2nd column with $t = 0.50$) was generated by using Algorithm 1 whereas the progression steps of IAM and T2-FLAIR (4th and 5th column with $t = 1.25$ and $t = 1.50$) were generated by using Algorithm 3. On the other hand, the pseudo-healthy T2-FLAIR (1st column with $t = 0.00$) was generated using Algorithm 2.

As Fig. 3 shows, prediction of brain lesions' regression works really well for WMH, but prediction of brain lesions' progression shows a small unmatched tessellation problem. This problem is common in computer graphics and should be easy to fix as there have been many studies that have proposed different solutions to this problem. Nevertheless, this experiment shows the suitability of IAM for predicting brain lesions' progression/regression.

6 Discussion

In this study, we have presented the use of a publicly available unsupervised method (i.e. IAM produced by LOTS-IAM[3]) as target for weakly-training two

---

[3] https://github.com/febrianrachmadi/lots-iam-gpu.

DNN schemes, *i.e.*, UResNet and UNet, and predicting brain lesions' progression/regression. Performance of UNet weakly-trained using IAM was close to the LOTS-IAM and UNet trained by using manual label of WMH and can sometimes be improved. In the future, we will widen our sample and investigate the conditions under which TL improves/worsens the quality of the DNN outputs.

Furthermore, IAM has shown to be very useful for the prediction of brain lesions progression/regression. There are still some problems in the prediction of progression such as unmatched tessellation, T2-FLAIR contrast changes and slightly higher computation time compared to predicting regression. However, it does not change the fact that the use of IAM facilitates the prediction and modelling of brain lesions' progression/regression. Next steps in this research topic would be fixing unmatched tessellation, avoiding the effect caused by contrast differences and the use of pre-trained DNN (*e.g.*, UNet) for predicting brain lesions' progression/regression.

Acknowledgement. Funds from Indonesia Endowment Fund for Education (LPDP) of Ministry of Finance, Republic of Indonesia and Row Fogo Charitable Trust (Grant No. BRO-D.FID3668413) (MCVH) are gratefully acknowledged. Data collection and sharing for this project was funded by the Alzheimer's Disease Neuroimaging Initiative (ADNI) (National Institutes of Health Grant U01 AG024904) and DOD ADNI (Department of Defense W81XWH-12-2-0012).

References

1. Ghafoorian, M., et al.: Transfer learning for domain adaptation in MRI: application in brain lesion segmentation. In: Descoteaux, M., Maier-Hein, L., Franz, A., Jannin, P., Collins, D.L., Duchesne, S. (eds.) MICCAI 2017. LNCS, vol. 10435, pp. 516–524. Springer, Cham (2017). https://doi.org/10.1007/978-3-319-66179-7_59
2. Guerrero, R.: White matter hyperintensity and stroke lesion segmentation and differentiation using convolutional neural networks. NeuroImage Clin. **17**, 918–934 (2018)
3. Hong, Y., Joshi, S., Sanchez, M., Styner, M., Niethammer, M.: Metamorphic geodesic regression. In: Ayache, N., Delingette, H., Golland, P., Mori, K. (eds.) MICCAI 2012. LNCS, vol. 7512, pp. 197–205. Springer, Heidelberg (2012). https://doi.org/10.1007/978-3-642-33454-2_25
4. Mueller, S.G.: The alzheimer's disease neuroimaging initiative. Neuroimaging Clin. North Am. **15**(4), 869–877 (2005). https://doi.org/10.1016/j.nic.2005.09.008
5. Rachmadi, M.F., et al.: Limited one-time sampling irregularity age map (LOTS-IAM): Automatic unsupervised detection of brain white matter abnormalities in structural magnetic resonance images. bioRxiv p. 334292 (2018)
6. Rachmadi, M.F., Valdés-Hernández, M.d.C., Agan, M.L.F., Di Perri, C., Komura, T., Initiative, A.D.N., et al.: Segmentation of white matter hyperintensities using convolutional neural networks with global spatial information in routine clinical brain MRI with none or mild vascular pathology. Comput. Med. Imaging Graph. **66**, 28–43 (2018)
7. Rekik, I., Allassonnière, S., Carpenter, T.K., Wardlaw, J.M.: Using longitudinal metamorphosis to examine ischemic stroke lesion dynamics on perfusion-weighted images and in relation to final outcome on T2-w images. NeuroImage Clin. **5**, 332–340 (2014)

8. Ronneberger, O., Fischer, P., Brox, T.: U-Net: convolutional networks for biomedical image segmentation. In: Navab, N., Hornegger, J., Wells, W.M., Frangi, A.F. (eds.) MICCAI 2015. LNCS, vol. 9351, pp. 234–241. Springer, Cham (2015). https://doi.org/10.1007/978-3-319-24574-4_28
9. Van Opbroek, A., Ikram, M.A., Vernooij, M.W., De Bruijne, M.: Transfer learning improves supervised image segmentation across imaging protocols. IEEE Trans. Med. Imaging **34**(5), 1018–1030 (2015)
10. Xu, Y., Géraud, T., Bloch, I.: From neonatal to adult brain MR image segmentation in a few seconds using 3D-like fully convolutional network and transfer learning. In: IEEE International Conference on Image Processing (ICIP) 2017, pp. 4417–4421. IEEE (2017)

Multi-view Brain Network Prediction from a Source View Using Sample Selection via CCA-Based Multi-kernel Connectomic Manifold Learning

Minghui Zhu and Islem Rekik[✉]

BASIRA Lab, CVIP Group, School of Science and Engineering, Computing,
University of Dundee, Dundee, UK
irekik@dundee.ac.uk
http://www.basira-lab.com

Abstract. Several challenges emerged from the dataclysm of neuroimaging datasets spanning both healthy and disordered brain spectrum. In particular, samples with missing data views (e.g., functional imaging modality) constitute a hurdle to conventional big data learning techniques which ideally would be trained using a maximum number of samples across all views. Existing works on predicting target data views from a source data view mainly used brain images such as predicting PET image from MRI image. However, to the best of our knowledge, predicting a set of target brain networks from a source network remains unexplored. To fill this gap, a multi-kernel manifold learning (MKML) framework is proposed to learn how to predict multi-view brain networks from a source network to impute missing views in a connectomic dataset. Prior to performing multiple kernel learning of multi-view data, it is typically assumed that the source and target data come from the same distribution. However, multi-view connectomic data can be drawn from different distributions. In order to build robust predictors for predicting target multi-view networks from a source network view, it is necessary to take into account the shift between the source and target domains. Hence, we first estimate a mapping function that transforms the source and the target domains into a shared space where their correlation is maximized using canonical correlation analysis (CCA). Next, we nest the projected training and testing source samples into a connectomic manifold using multiple kernel learning, where we identify the most similar training samples to the testing source network. Given a testing subject, we introduce a cross-domain trust score to assess the reliability of each selected training sample for the target prediction task. Our model outperformed both conventional MKML technique and the proposed CCA-based MKML technique without enhancement by trust scores.

1 Introduction

Neurological disorders, such as Alzheimer's disease and Schizophrenia, alter brain connections in various ways across different brain views. Leveraging

© Springer Nature Switzerland AG 2018
I. Rekik et al. (Eds.): PRIME 2018, LNCS 11121, pp. 94–102, 2018.
https://doi.org/10.1007/978-3-030-00320-3_12

multi-view connectomic data can provide complementary information on a disorder mechanism. These connectomic multi-view data can be derived from functional magnetic resonance imaging (fMRI) or diffusion tensor imaging (DTI). Recent works introduced multi-view morphological brain networks which quantify changes in brain morphology using various morphological metrics across pairs of anatomical brain regions. These showed promise in diagnosis and brain connectional fingerprint identification [1–3] using multi-view brain network data compared to single network views.

However, due to various reasons including high clinical costs, it is common that in real medical practices, a subject does not complete all the scans and thus have missing data points or missing modalities or brain views. For many existing models, these incomplete subjects will have to be discarded. Moreover, it can be difficult to handle cross-domain prediction, since all views come from different distributions. To address this issue, several works focused on designing methods for data imputation. For instance, the Cascaded Residual Autoencoder (CRA) algorithm developed by [4] stacks autoencoders and grows iteratively to model the residual between prediction and original data. Another study on fMRI imputation is based on available case analysis, neighbor replacement and regression [5]. However, all these papers were not applied to connectomic data, i.e., brain networks.

To fill this gap, we design a prediction framework that maps a source brain network into a target brain network. We base our method on a simple hypothesis: if one can identify *the best* neighbors to a given testing subject in the source domain, one can use a weighted average of their corresponding views in the target domain to predict the missing target network. To account for the domain shift between the source and target domains, we use canonical correlation analysis to find a *coupled source-target subspace* where one assumes the existence of a performing linear classifier on the two domains [6]. We bridge the distribution shift by looking for the best coupled space that would nest projected source and target data samples. Next, we learn a subject-to-subject similarity matrix using multi-kernel connectomic manifold learning which models the relationships between all training and testing samples in the coupled space. We then identify the most similar training samples to the testing subject in the source domain for prediction in the target domain. We further prune the selected closest training samples by introducing a trust score which quantifies the cross-domain consistency of selected samples. In essence, the trust score decides if a neighbor is 'trustworthy' by examining whether the nearest neighbors of a training subject in source and target views highly overlap. To the best of our knowledge, this is the first work to predict multiple brain views from a single source view using connectomic data.

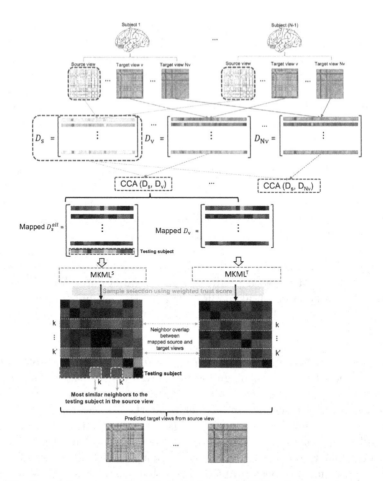

Fig. 1. *Pipeline of the proposed multi-view network predicting from input source network view.* Each training subject has a source network view (outlined in dashed view) and target network views. We represent each view by a feature vector extracted by vectorizing the off-diagonal upper triangular part of each network matrix. We stack training source feature vectors in a training source matrix $\mathbf{D}_s$ and target feature vectors in different training target matrices. Next, by fixing the training source matrix $\mathbf{D}_s$ and pairing it with a particular training target matrix $\mathbf{D}_v$, we learn a coupled source-target subspace using Canonical Correlation Analysis (CCA), where the correlation between both domains is maximized. For a given testing subject, we used the trained CCA model to map its source view onto the shared subspace. We then use multiple kernel manifold learning (MKML) to learn a similarity matrix that models the relationship between all *mapped* training and testing subjects in the shared subspace. For a specific target domain, we also learn a target manifold that nests only *mapped* training subjects. To assess the reliability of the identified most similar training samples in the shared domain, we introduce a trust score which quantifies the cross-domain consistency of selected samples, thereby filtering out 'untrustworthy' samples. Ultimately, we used weighted averaging of the corresponding target networks of the selected source training networks to predict the missing target views for a new testing subject. (Color figure online)

2   CCA-Based Multi-kernel Manifold Learning for Predicting Multi-view Brain Networks from a Source View

In this section, we present the key components of our proposed target multi-view brain network prediction from a single network view using a multi-kernel connectomic manifold learning in a learned coupled source-target subspace. We denote matrices by boldface capital letters, e.g., $\mathbf{X}$, and scalars by lowercase letters, e.g., x. We denote the transpose operator and the trace operator as $\mathbf{X}^T$ and $tr(\mathbf{X})$, respectively. We illustrate in Fig. 1 the key components of the proposed pipeline, and which we detail below.

- **Step 1: Feature extraction.** Each brain is represented by a set of connectivity matrices defined in the source and target domains (Fig. 1). Each element in a single matrix captures the relationship between two anatomical regions of interest (ROIs) using a specific metric (e.g., correlation between neural activity or similarity in brain morphology). We then vectorize each connectivity matrix i to define a feature vector $\mathbf{f}_s^i$ (resp. $\mathbf{f}_t^i$) for a particular source (resp. target) brain network view by concatenating the off-diagonal elements in the upper triangular part of the input matrix. Hence, each brain network view of size $n \times n$ is represented by a feature vector of size $(n \times (n-1)/2)$.

- **Step 2: Source to multi-target CCA mappings.** Given a set of target brain network views, each capturing a unique and complex relationship between different brain network regions, we aim to learn how to predict these networks from a source brain network view (outlined in dashed blue in Fig. 1). Since multi-view brain connectomic data might be drawn from different distributions, investigating associations between these data samples without mapping them onto a space where their distributions are 'aligned' and where they become comparable might mislead any learning method trained in original source and target spaces. To solve this issue and motivated by the fact that canonical correlation analysis is efficient in analyzing and mapping two sets of variables onto a shared space [7,8], we fix the training source network data and pair it with a particular training target network data. By multiple source-target pairings, we generate multiple CCA mappings that align the source data with target multi-view data, respectively. Given a training source matrix $\mathbf{D}_s \in \mathbb{R}^{(N-1) \times d}$ comprising $N-1$ training feature vectors, each of size d, and a training target matrix $\mathbf{D}_k \in \mathbb{R}^{(N-1) \times d}$, we estimate a source transformation $\mathbf{W}_s$ and a target transformation $\mathbf{W}_k$ that map both onto the couple source-target subspace. In the testing stage, we use the learned canonical transformation matrices to map the source feature vector of a testing subject onto the shared space, where we learn how to identify the most similar training source feature vectors to the testing subject using multi-kernel manifold learning (MKML).

- **Step 3: Multi kernel learning of source and target manifolds.** Following the CCA-based mapping of both *source* training and testing samples, we learn how to nest all N samples into a manifold using the recent work of

[9] where multiple kernels are learned to handle different data sample distributions.

Each kernel $\mathbf{K}$ is Gaussian defined as The Gaussian kernel is expressed as follows: $\mathbf{K}(\mathbf{f}^i, \mathbf{f}^j) = \frac{1}{\epsilon_{ij}\sqrt{2\pi}} e^{\left(-\frac{|\mathbf{f}^i - \mathbf{f}^j|^2}{2\epsilon_{ij}^2}\right)}$, where $\mathbf{f}^i$ and $\mathbf{f}^j$ denote the feature vectors of the i-th and j-th subjects respectively and ϵ_{ij} is defined as: $\epsilon_{ij} = \sigma(\mu_i + \mu_j)/2$, where σ is a tuning parameter and $\mu_i = \frac{\sum_{l \in KNN(\mathbf{f}^i)} |\mathbf{f}^i - \mathbf{f}^j|}{k}$, where $KNN(\mathbf{f}^i)$ represents the top k neighboring subjects of subject i. The learned similarity matrix $\mathbf{S_s}$ is estimated by optimizing the following energy functional:

$\min_{\mathbf{S},\mathbf{L},\mathbf{w}} \sum_{i,j} -w_l \mathbf{K}_l(\mathbf{f}^i, \mathbf{f}^j)\mathbf{S}_{ij} + \beta||\mathbf{S}||_F^2 + \gamma \mathbf{tr}(\mathbf{L}^T(\mathbf{I}_n - \mathbf{S})\mathbf{L}) + \rho \sum_l w_l log w_l$

Subject to: $\sum_l w_l = 1$, $w_l \geq 0$, $\mathbf{L}^T\mathbf{L} = \mathbf{I}_c$, $\sum_j \mathbf{S}_{ij} = 1$, and $\mathbf{S}_{ij} \geq 0$ for all (i,j), where:

1. $\sum_{i,j} -w_l \mathbf{K}_l(\mathbf{f}^i, \mathbf{f}^j)\mathbf{S}_{ij}$ refers to the relation between the similarity and the kernel distance with weights w_l between two subjects. The learned similarity should be small if the distance between a pair of subjects is large.

2. $\beta||\mathbf{S}||_F^2$ denotes a regularization term that avoids over-fitting the model to the data.

3, $\gamma \mathbf{tr}(\mathbf{L}^T(\mathbf{I}_n - \mathbf{S})\mathbf{L})$: $\mathbf{L}$ is the latent matrix of size $n \times c$ where n is the number of subjects and c is the number of clusters. The matrix $(\mathbf{I}_n - \mathbf{S})$ denotes the graph Laplacian.

4. $\rho \sum_l w_l log w_l$ imposes constraints on the kernel weights to avoid selection of a single kernel.

To solve this problem, we adopt alternating convex optimization where each variable is optimized while fixing the other variables until convergence [9].

- *Step 4: Predicting multi-target views using trust score weighting (TSW) strategy for training samples.* In our designed prediction pipeline, once the most similar source training samples to the testing sample of the source view are identified, we identify their corresponding views in the target domain, then use weighted average to predict the missing target views. However, relying on the learned similarity matrix based on the mapped source network data is disentangled from the target domain where most similar training subjects to the 'ground truth' missing target view might be different from those identified using the source MKML. Hence, we define a 'trust score' for each training sample i similar to the testing subject j based on the overlap of their local neighborhoods in mapped source and target domains, respectively. Following the learning of $\mathbf{S}_s$ using all samples in the mapped source domain using Step **3**, we identify the top K-closest training subjects to a given testing subject. Next, for each training sample, we find its nearest neighbors using $\mathbf{S}_s$ and $\mathbf{S}_t$, learned in the mapped target domain using only training subjects (Fig. 1).

The intuition behind this is that for a training subject k, the more shared neighbors k has across views, the more reliable it is in predicting the target view from the source view, and thus k is considered as 'trustworthy'. We compute a normalized trust score (TS) for each closest training subject k by (i) first identifying the list of its top m closest neighbors $\mathcal{N}_s$ in $\mathbf{S}_s$ and $\mathcal{N}_t$ in $\mathbf{S}_t$, then (ii) computing the normalized overlap between both lists as $TS(k) = \frac{\mathcal{N}_s \bigcap \mathcal{N}_t}{m}$. The ultimate $TSW(k)$ score is thus calculated as a soft overlap between $\mathcal{N}_t$ and $\mathbf{S}_t$ weighted by $\mathbf{S}_s$.

3   Results and Discussion

Multi-view Connectomic Dataset and Method Parameters. We used leave-one-out cross-validation to evaluate the proposed prediction framework on 186 normal controls (NC) from Autism Brain Imaging Data Exchange (ABIDE I)[1] public dataset, each with structural T1w MR image. We used FreeSurfer [10] to reconstruct both right and left cortical hemispheres for each subject from T1-w MRI, and then parcellated each cortical hemisphere into 35 cortical regions using Desikan-Killiany Atlas. For each subject, we generated $N_v = 3$ cortical morphological brain networks using the technique proposed in [2]: $\mathbf{D}_1$ denotes the maximum principal curvature brain view, $\mathbf{D}_2$ denotes the mean sulcal depth brain view, and $\mathbf{D}_3$ denotes the mean of average curvature. For MKML, we used a nested grid search on all views respectfully, fixing the number of clusters c ($1 \leq c \leq 5$) and the number of top neighbors n_b ($3 \leq n_b \leq 50$). We used 10 kernels. For prediction, we set the number of training source neighbors to select to $m = 5$.

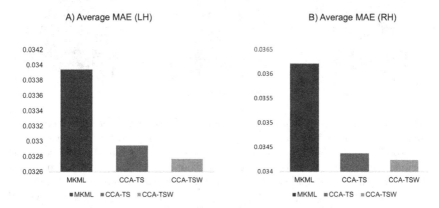

Fig. 2. *Evaluating the prediction performance of our proposed CCA-based multi-kernel manifold learning framework among all brain views applied on left and right hemisphere respectively using Mean absolute error (MAE).* MKML: multi-kernel learning. CCA-TS: CCA-based MKML using only Trust Score (TS) for training sample selections. CCA-TSW: CCA-based MKML combining our Trust Score Weighting strategy.

---

[1] http://fcon_1000.projects.nitrc.org/indi/abide/.

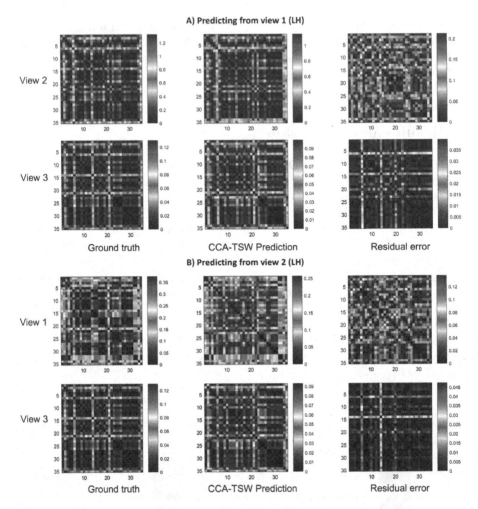

Fig. 3. *Comparison between the ground truth and predicted target networks from respectively source views 1 and 2 of the left hemisphere for a representative testing subject by the proposed CCA-based MKML framework.* We display the residual matrices computed using element-wise absolute difference between ground truth and predicted networks. View 1: the maximum principal curvature. View 2: mean sulcal depth. View 3: average curvature. Ground truth: the ground truth target view of a testing subject. CCA-TSW prediction: prediction of target views using our purposed framework. Note that each graph is scaled differently for the best display effect.

Evaluation and Comparison Methods. To compare the performance of our multi-target view prediction framework, we benchmark our framework against the baseline multi-kernel similarity learning method [9] using leave-one-out cross-validation. We further evaluated the contribution of the proposed trust score weighting strategy by comparing our results with those generated using TS with no additional weight derived from the learned source similarity learning. Our CCA-based MKML integrating TSW strategy significantly outperformed both conventional MKML and CCA-based MKML using TS for training sample selection ($p - value < 0.001$ using two tailed sample t-test) in left and right hemispheres (LH and RH). Figure 2 shows the mean absolute error (MAE) for all methods. Figure 3 displays the predicted target views from a source view along with the residuals in both left and the right hemispheres for a representative testing subject using the proposed method. Best result is given when predicting LH View 2 (mean sulcal depth) from LH View 1 (the maximum principal curvature) prediction, achieving the lowest MAE.

4   Conclusion

This paper presents a multi-view brain network prediction framework from a source framework, which first bridges the gap between source and target domains, then learns how to select the best training samples using a cross-domain trust score weighting strategy. Specifically, for handling differences across brain views, we performed canonical correlation analysis to map the data onto coupled source-target correlated subspace. We then applied multi-kernel manifold learning combined with the trust score weighting for prediction. Our method achieved the best prediction performance in comparison with the baseline methods. In our future work, we will learn how to *jointly* map all target views into a shared space using tensor CCA [11]. We will also evaluate our seminal pipeline on larger datasets to predict other types of brain networks (e.g., functional brain connectivity from structural connectivity).

References

1. Soussia, M., Rekik, I.: High-order connectomic manifold learning for autistic brain state identification. In: Wu, G., Laurienti, P., Bonilha, L., Munsell, B.C. (eds.) CNI 2017. LNCS, vol. 10511, pp. 51–59. Springer, Cham (2017). https://doi.org/10.1007/978-3-319-67159-8_7
2. Mahjoub, I., Mahjoub, M.A., Rekik, I.: Brain multiplexes reveal morphological connectional biomarkers fingerprinting late brain dementia states. Sci. Rep. **8**, 4103 (2018)
3. Lisowska, A., Rekik, I.: Joint pairing and structured mapping of convolutional brain morphological multiplexes for early dementia diagnosis. Brain Connect. (2018)
4. Tran, L., Liu, X., Zhou, J., Jin, R.: Missing modalities imputation via cascaded residual autoencoder. In: Proceedings of the IEEE Conference on Computer Vision and Pattern Recognition, pp. 1405–1414 (2017)
5. Vaden Jr., K.I., Gebregziabher, M., Kuchinsky, S.E., Eckert, M.A.: Multiple imputation of missing fMRI data in whole brain analysis. Neuroimage **60**, 1843–1855 (2012)
6. Blitzer, J., Kakade, S., Foster, D.: Domain adaptation with coupled subspaces. In: Proceedings of the Fourteenth International Conference on Artificial Intelligence and Statistics, pp. 173–181 (2011)

7. Zhu, X., Suk, H.I., Lee, S.W., Shen, D.: Canonical feature selection for joint regression and multi-class identification in Alzheimer's disease diagnosis. Brain Imaging Behav. **10**, 818–828 (2016)
8. Haghighat, M., Abdel-Mottaleb, M., Alhalabi, W.: Fully automatic face normalization and single sample face recognition in unconstrained environments. Expert Syst. Appl. **47**, 23–34 (2016)
9. Wang, B., Zhu, J., Pierson, E., Ramazzotti, D., Batzoglou, S.: Visualization and analysis of single-cell RNA-seq data by kernel-based similarity learning. Nat. Methods **14**, 414 (2017)
10. Fischl, B.: FreeSurfer. Neuroimage **62**, 774–781 (2012)
11. Luo, Y., Tao, D., Ramamohanarao, K., Xu, C., Wen, Y.: Tensor canonical correlation analysis for multi-view dimension reduction. IEEE Trans. Knowl. Data Eng. **27**, 3111–3124 (2015)

Predicting Emotional Intelligence Scores from Multi-session Functional Brain Connectomes

Anna Lisowska[1] and Islem Rekik[2(✉)]

[1] Department of Computer Science, University of Warwick, Coventry, UK
[2] BASIRA Lab, CVIP Group, School of Science and Engineering, Computing, University of Dundee, Dundee, UK
irekik@dundee.ac.uk
http://www.basira-lab.com/

Abstract. In this study, we aim to predict emotional intelligence scores from functional connectivity data acquired at different timepoints. To enhance the generalizability of the proposed predictive model to new data and accurate identification of most relevant neural correlates with different facets of the human intelligence, we propose a joint support vector machine and support vector regression (SVM+SVR) model. Specifically, we first identify most discriminative connections between subjects with high vs low emotional intelligence scores in the SVM step and then perform a multi-variate linear regression using these connections to predict the target emotional intelligence score in the SVR step. Our method outperformed existing methods including the Connectome-based Predictive Model (CPM) using functional connectivity data simultaneously acquired with the intelligence scores. The most predictive connections of intelligence included brain regions involved in processing of emotions and social behaviour.

1 Introduction

Understanding how intelligence is encoded in the human brain wiring can help boost the brain cognitive ability in solving new problems and build a more resilient cognitive reserve to neurological disorders. Recently, there has been an increasing interest in the emotional intelligence, which is defined as the ability to monitor emotions (in self and others) to guide one's thinking and behaviour [1]. Emotional intelligence was also associated with job-related, academic and life performance [2].

However, characterising the underlying brain connectivity associated with emotional intelligence remains challenging. Some attempts have been made to identify differences in the brain wiring based on statistical comparison between groups of individuals with dissimilar behavioural scores. While typical correlation and regression analyses are able to model the given dataset well, they lack generalizability. In other words, neural correlates discovered to be significant

© Springer Nature Switzerland AG 2018
I. Rekik et al. (Eds.): PRIME 2018, LNCS 11121, pp. 103–111, 2018.
https://doi.org/10.1007/978-3-030-00320-3_13

in predicting intelligence from the connectomic data may not be universal, i.e. applicable to the general population. [3] proposed a Connectome-based Predictive Model (CPM); a cross-validated predictive model, which infers the presence of brain-behaviour relationship on a training data and evaluates its performance on the test data, leading to a more robust and generalizable approach.

In their proposed framework, first, the functional connections that are significantly correlated with the behavioural score are identified using training data. These connections are divided into positively and negatively correlated with the behavioural score. Then, the strengths of significantly correlated connections are summed up for the positively and negatively correlated data, obtaining scalar values for each subject. Finally, a linear regression model is built for positively and negatively correlated features and for the combination of the two. These models are then applied to the test subjects to infer their behavioural scores. The main limitation of this work is that it sums up all positively (resp. negatively) correlated connections with the target behavioral score to create a positive (resp. negative) model. However, each sum may derive from brain connection strengths of different signs (i.e., negative or positive functional connectivity), thereby loosing interpretability of *signed* functional brain connectivitivies that might be associated with the target score.

To address the above limitations, we propose a joint SVM+SVR method to predict behaviour scores from connectomic data by first using a Support Vector Machine (SVM) to identify features which maximally separate the training data into subsets with high and low behavioural scores, thereby enabling a better representation of subjects with extreme scores. Next, we use these features to build a multi-variate regression model using Support Vector Regressor (SVR), which encourages model simplicity for a better generalizability on new data and easy utilizabiliy by clinicians. Further, we identify the top most relevant connections that are associated with different intelligence scores. Additionally, we consider multi-session (or longitudinal) connectomic data for our analysis to investigate the importance of gathering neuroimaging and behavioural data in close time proximity.

2   Methods

In this section we introduce our proposed framework to predict multiple emotional intelligence scores based on the multi-session functional connectivity data (Fig. 1). Each subject s is represented by a functional connectivity matrix $\mathbf{X}$ estimated from functional magnetic resonance (fMRI) scans performed at t different timepoints and an intelligence score vector $\mathbf{b} = \{b_1, \ldots, b_N\}$ recorded at a single timepoint t. We first build our model using functional connectivity data obtained at $t = t_1$. Since the functional brain connectivity matrices are symmetric (Fig. 1-A), we extract features from each connectivity matrix by directly concatenating the weights of all connectivities in each off-diagonal upper triangular matrix. For each network of size $n \times n$, we extract a feature vector of size $(n \times (n-1)/2)$, where each entry represents the strength of functional connection between two brain regions. This creates a high dimensional feature vector for

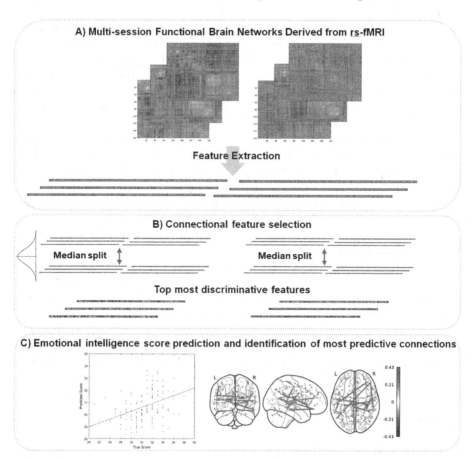

Fig. 1. *Pipeline of the proposed joint SVM+SVR framework to predict emotional intelligence scores from the functional brain connectivity* (A) Functional brain network construction using multi-session fMRI. (B) In the feature selection step, features are ranked according to their contribution to class separability between subjects with high emotional intelligence score and subjects with low emotional intelligence score using training data split at median value of the behavioural score. (C) We use these features to predict the emotional intelligence score of the left-out testing subject within a leave-one-out cross-validation and identify the most predictive functional connections.

each subject, which is particularly problematic in training a model that aims to map a high-dimensional feature vector into a single score. To address this issue, a feature selection method is required for dimensionality reduction, that would preserve the most informative features, while avoiding underrepresentation of subjects with behavioural scores at both tails of sample distribution.

Therefore, in our joint SVM+SVR framework, the features which maximise the separation of subjects with low scores from subjects with high scores are first identified. In the SVM step, a feature selection is used, which ranks features according to their contribution to class separability (Fig. 1-B). As a class separability criterion, we use the area under the ROC curve and identify the features which contribute most to maximising the area. Since this approach requires data to be divided into 2 classes, we define a class with low intelligence scores and high intelligence scores based on median split of the training data ($\leq median$ or $< median$, whichever gives a more balanced split) based on each behavioural score b in **b** separately (Fig. 1-B).

Once the top most discriminative features are identified in the SVM step using training data, these features can be used to build a predictive model by training the SVR. As the performance of the regression model heavily depends on the number of features used, we vary the number of input features for the SVR model, i.e. multiple models are built, each using different number of input features previously identified in the SVM step.

In the test step, the top features identified in the SVM step are used for the test data and then the intelligence score of the test subjects is predicted using multiple SVR models, each using a different number of input features. At the end of the test stage, the performance of the joint SVM+SVR model is assessed by computing the correlation between the predicted scores and the true emotional intelligence scores of all the test subjects (Fig. 1-C). Connections most predictive of the emotional intelligence are identified based on features identified in the model with the best predictive performance. We applied the same steps for each emotional intelligence score in **b** using functional connectivity data at each available timepoint t.

3   Results and Discussion

Evaluation Dataset. We used leave-one-out (LOO) cross validation to evaluate our proposed framework on 149 subjects (74 males, and 75 females, all within 17–27 age range) with structural and functional MRIs using SLIM Dataset [4]. Each MRI is parcellated into 160 regions of interest (ROIs) using Dosenbach Atlas [5]. For each subject, a 160×160 functional connectivity matrix is constructed from fMRI scans at 2 different timepoints: session 1 taking place at the same time as the behavioural assessment and session 2 after 304 days interval on average. Each entry in the connectivity matrix denotes the correlation between mean blood oxygenation level-dependent (BOLD) signals measured in two ROIs. For each subject four emotional intelligence scores are measured: (1) Monitor of Emotions, (2) Social Ability, (3) Appraisal of Emotions, and (4) Utilization of Emotions, as assessed by Schutte Self-Report Emotional Intelligence Scale [6].

Comparison Methods and Evaluation. For the regression task, we benchmarked our joint SVM+SVR method against: (1) CPM [3] and (2) Correlational SVR, which performs multi-variate linear regression using SVR on features having the most statistically significant correlation with the emotional intelligence score.

For evaluation, we report the R-score, representing the strength of the correlation between the predicted score and the true intelligence score. Since, the

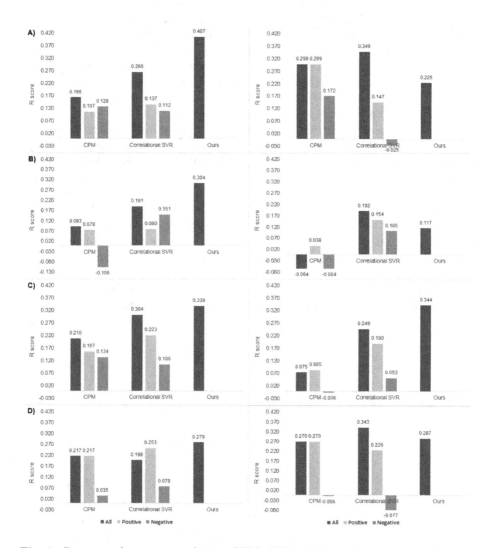

Fig. 2. *R-scores of our proposed joint SVM+SVR model and comparison regression models.* Left: Session 1. Right: Session 2. (A) Monitor of Emotions. (B) Social Ability. (C) Appraisal of Emotions. (D) Utilization of Emotions. Ours: joint SVM+SVR model. Correlational SVR: SVR using features, which are the most significantly correlated with the target emotional intelligence score. CPM [3]: univariate regression model using the sum of all the connections that are significantly correlated with the target emotional intelligence score. All: the model is build using connections that are positively and negatively correlated with the target emotional intelligence score. Positive: only connections that are positively correlated. Negative: Only connections that are negatively correlated.

performance of regression models heavily depends on the number of input features, for the joint SVR+SVR method and for the correlational SVR, we chose a range of input features 5, 10, 15, 20, 25, 30, 35, 40, 45, 50, 60, 70, 80, 90, 100, 125, 150, 175, 200, 300, 400, 500, 600, 700, 800, 900, 1000 to train the model. For the joint SVM+SVR, the identified features were ranked highest based on their contribution to the area under the ROC curve in the SVM classification task. For the correlational SVR method, features that were most significantly correlated with the target behavioural score were selected. Since CPM [3] used all features significantly correlated with the target score instead of choosing different number of features, we addressed this limitation by exploring the range of statistical significance thresholds in $\{0.1, 0.05, 0.01, 0.005, 0.001, 0.0005, 0.0001\}$ and used all significant features *at a given threshold* for the regression analysis using CPM model [3]. For evaluation, we report the top R-score obtained across different feature numbers (for joint SVM+SVR and correlational SVR) or significance thresholds (for CPM [3]). Figure 2 shows the comparison between R-scores obtained using our method and the benchmark methods for the four different emotional intelligence scores using functional connectome data from sessions 1 and 2.

Our method outperformed benchmark methods in predicting all the emotional intelligence scores using functional connectivity data from Session 1 of fMRI acquisition (Fig. 2). This was not the case for Session 2, where the

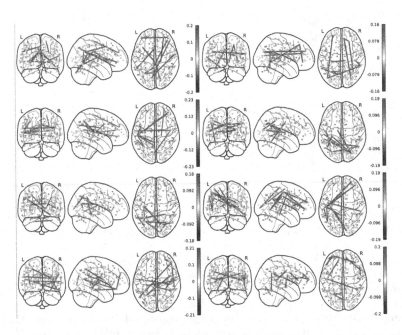

Fig. 3. *The top 10 connections disentangling subjects with high emotional intelligence scores and subjects with low scores.* Left: Session 1. Right: Session 2. (A) Utilization of Emotions. (B) Appraisal of Emotions. (C) Social Ability. (D) Monitor of Emotions.

correlational SVR performed best for the Utilization of Emotions Fig. 2-D, Social Ability Fig. 2-B and Monitor of Emotions Fig. 2-A, but not the Appraisal of Emotions Fig. 2-C, for which our method still performed best. Our method generally gave better results using a lower number of features as compared to the benchmark methods. It should be noted that the performance of the joint SVM+SVR heavily depends on the training data distribution and the way the data is split into classes. The more separable the subjects with high intelligence scores are from the subjects with low intelligence scores, the bigger is the area under the ROC curve obtained in the SVM classfication step. Hence, the more separable the data is in the SVM step, the better is the SVR prediction performance.

Identified Functional Brain Connections Fingerprinting Intelligence.
Our Findings. For each emotional intelligence score using functional connectivity from Session 1 and Session 2, we identified the top 10 features with the highest average rank across subjects. The most predictive connections were identified based on the features used for predicting the emotional intelligence score resulting in the best R-score. Figure 3 displays the top 10 features identified by the joint SVM+SVR for each emotional intelligence score. Top most predictive connections, that involved common brain regions across all the emotional intelligence scores, included mid insula, basal ganglia, post cingulate, ventral anterior prefrontal cortex and occipital lobe.

Insular cortex was proposed to facilitate social interaction and decision-making by integrating information about uncertainty with sensory, affective and bodily information [7]. Consistent with our findings, studies on insular lesion found that insula plays role in emotional intelligence [8]. Further, basal ganglia is involved in reward-stimulus processing and goal-directed bahaviour, specifically the subthalamic nucleus was suggested to integrate motor, congnitive and emotional aspects of behaviour [9]. While the cingulate gyrus plays a role in pain and emotion processing and a lesion study by [10] found decreased social interactions and time spent with other individuals, showing role of cingulate in emotion and social behaviour. The anterior prefrontal cortex is important for emotional control during social interactions. In their study, [11] showed that the anterior prefrontal cortex is required for coordination of action selection, emotional conflict detection and inhibition of emotionally-driven responses.

Furthermore, connections to the occipital cortex were found to be a significant predictor in case of all the emotional intelligence scores. This could be explained by aspects uncontrolled for in the rs-fMRI data acquisition step, such as low-frequency fluctuations occurring synchronously in functionally connected brain regions, present especially in auditory, visual and motor areas [12]. However, some evidence exist for occipital lobe's role in emotional information processing [13].

Variability of Discovered Intelligence Connectivity Trends Across Scores and Sessions. In our analysis, we found that the connections that are most predictive of the emotional inteligence scores are largely inconsistent between the two sessions (Fig. 3). Given that fMRI for Session 2 was performed on average 304 days after Session 1, one could expect some changes in the individual's functional connectivity. One explanation could be the difference in the conditions under which the fMRI was aquired and the general instability of the functional data [14].

In Fig. 2 the performance of the joint SVM+SVR model in predicting different emotional intelligence scores using a subset of connecions identified from the functional connectivity data aquired during Session 1 and Session 2 can be seen. While using a subset of connections from the functional connectivity data from Session 1, collected at the same time as the intelligence scores, gave better predictions for Monitor of Emotions and Social Ability, the connections chosen by the joint SVM+SVR to predict the Appraisal of Emotions and Utilization of Emotions perform similarly well using the functional data from Session 1 and Session 2. It is possible that the Monitor of Emotions and the Social Ability and their underlying neural correlates are more prone to changes over time than the Appraisal of Emotions and Utilization of Emotions, which emphasises the need to acquire fMRI data at the same time as intelligence scores for accurate predictions. This should be further investigated. Since a reasonable predictive power is obtained for the majority of intelligence scores using functional connectivity data from both Session 1 and Session 2, it is possible that the longitudinal data contains complementary information. Further studies could combine the functional data from different timepoints to predict the target intelligence scores as in [15], where a multi-task multi-linear regression model was proposed to predict infant cognitive scores from longitudinal neuroimaging data. For a more holistic investigation of the brain intelligence construct, we will include morphological brain networks [16,17] and structural networks [18,19] into our future brain-intelligence analyses.

4   Conclusion

We proposed a joint SVM+SVR model to predict emotional intelligence of individuals from their functional connectomic data. Our method outperformed the benchmark methods using functional data acquired at the same time as the target scores. The joint SVM+SVR benefits from model simplicity and interpretability, which is of particular interest for clinicians. Functional brain connections associated with intelligence identified by our model belonged to brain regions involved in emotion processing and social behaviour, consistent with previous research. Further studies could combine functional data acquired at different timepoints for improved emotional intelligence predictions.

References

1. Salovey, P., Mayer, J.D.: Emotional intelligence. Imagin. Cogn. Pers. **9**, 185–211 (1990)
2. Van Rooy, D.L., Viswesvaran, C.: Emotional intelligence: a meta-analytic investigation of predictive validity and nomological net. J. Vocat. Behav. **65**, 71–95 (2004)

3. Shen, X., Finn, E.S., Scheinost, D., Rosenberg, M.D., Chun, M.M., Papademetris, X., Constable, R.T.: Using connectome-based predictive modeling to predict individual behavior from brain connectivity. Nat. Protoc. **12**, 506 (2017)
4. Liu, W., et al.: Longitudinal test-retest neuroimaging data from healthy young adults in Southwest China. Sci. Data **4**, 170017 (2017)
5. Dosenbach, N.U., et al.: Prediction of individual brain maturity using fMRI. Science **329**, 1358–1361 (2010)
6. Schutte, N.S., et al.: Development and validation of a measure of emotional intelligence. Pers. Individ. Differ. **25**, 167–177 (1998)
7. Singer, T., Critchley, H.D., Preuschoff, K.: A common role of insula in feelings, empathy and uncertainty. Trends Cogn. Sci. **13**, 334–340 (2009)
8. Bar-On, R., Tranel, D., Denburg, N.L., Bechara, A.: Exploring the neurological substrate of emotional and social intelligence. Brain **126**, 1790–1800 (2003)
9. Mallet, L., et al.: Stimulation of subterritories of the subthalamic nucleus reveals its role in the integration of the emotional and motor aspects of behavior. Proc. Natl. Acad. Sci. **104**, 10661–10666 (2007)
10. Hadland, K., Rushworth, M.F., Gaffan, D., Passingham, R.: The effect of cingulate lesions on social behaviour and emotion. Neuropsychologia **41**, 919–931 (2003)
11. Volman, I., Roelofs, K., Koch, S., Verhagen, L., Toni, I.: Anterior prefrontal cortex inhibition impairs control over social emotional actions. Curr. Biol. **21**, 1766–1770 (2011)
12. Cordes, D., et al.: Frequencies contributing to functional connectivity in the cerebral cortex in "resting-state" data. Am. J. Neuroradiol. **22**, 1326–1333 (2001)
13. Chao, L.L., Lenoci, M., Neylan, T.C.: Effects of post-traumatic stress disorder on occipital lobe function and structure. Neuroreport **23**, 412–419 (2012)
14. Honey, C., et al.: Predicting human resting-state functional connectivity from structural connectivity. Proc. Natl. Acad. Sci. **106**, 2035–2040 (2009)
15. Adeli, E., Meng, Y., Li, G., Lin, W., Shen, D.: Multi-task prediction of infant cognitive scores from longitudinal incomplete neuroimaging data. NeuroImage (2018)
16. Mahjoub, I., Mahjoub, M.A., Rekik, I.: Brain multiplexes reveal morphological connectional biomarkers fingerprinting late brain dementia states. Sci. Rep. **8**, 4103 (2018)
17. Lisowska, A., Rekik, I.: Joint pairing and structured mapping of convolutional brain morphological multiplexes for early dementia diagnosis. Brain connectivity (2018)
18. Abdelnour, F., Voss, H.U., Raj, A.: Network diffusion accurately models the relationship between structural and functional brain connectivity networks. Neuroimage **90**, 335–347 (2014)
19. Bassett, D.S., Sporns, O.: Network neuroscience. Nat. Neurosci. **20**, 353 (2017)

Predictive Modeling of Longitudinal Data for Alzheimer's Disease Diagnosis Using RNNs

Maryamossadat Aghili[1]($\boxtimes$), Solale Tabarestani[1],
Malek Adjouadi[1], and Ehsan Adeli[2]

[1] Florida International University, Miami, USA
maghi001@fiu.edu
[2] Stanford University, Stanford, USA

Abstract. In this paper, we study the application of Recurrent Neural Networks (RNNs) to discriminate Alzheimer's disease patients from healthy control individuals using longitudinal neuroimaging data. Distinctions between Alzheimer's Disease (AD), Mild Cognitive Impairment (MCI), and healthy subjects in a multi-modal heterogeneous longitudinal dataset is a challenging problem due to high similarity between brain patterns, high portions of missing data from different modalities and time points, and inconsistent number of test intervals between different subjects. Due to these challenges, to distinguish AD patients from healthy subjects, conventionally researchers use cross-sectional data when applying deep learning methods in neuroimaging applications. Whereas we propose a method based on RNNS to analyze the longitudinal data. After carefully preprocessing the data to alleviate the inconsistency due to different data sources and various protocols of capturing modalities, we arrange the data and feed it into variations of RNNs, i.e., vanilla Long Short Term Memory (LSTM) and Gated Recurrent Unit (GRU). The accuracy, *F*-score, sensitivity, and specificity of our models are reported and are compared with the most immediate baseline method, multi-layer perceptron (MLP).

Keywords: Long Short Term Memory (LSTM) · Gated Recurrent Unit (GRU)
Recurrent Neural Networks (RNNs) · Alzheimer's Disease (AD)
Longitudinal data · Prognosis · Diagnosis

1 Introduction

Alzheimer's disease (AD) is one of the most frequent types of dementia, which leads to memory loss and other cognitive disabilities. As the majority cases of dementia fall in the Alzheimer's category, diagnosis and prognosis of this disease, especially in the early stage, has exceptional importance [1–3]. Early diagnosis, before the occurrence of the irreversible brain deformation, enables early treatment and plays a significant role in patient care, prediction of the progression risks, and severity recognition [3–5]. However, regardless of enormous efforts, pinpointing the prodromal stage of mild cognitive impairment is remained an open research field. Having incomplete samples in the longitudinal medical studies is a common phenomenon, as many patients may miss some of the tests and modalities in a time step or miss a complete visit within the

© Springer Nature Switzerland AG 2018
I. Rekik et al. (Eds.): PRIME 2018, LNCS 11121, pp. 112–119, 2018.
https://doi.org/10.1007/978-3-030-00320-3_14

study's lifespan. Generally, missing values occur for a variety of reasons including drop out of subjects from the study, insufficient resolution, image corruption, budget limitation, etc. [5–7]. Many algorithms simply discard subjects with missing modalities from further experiments, which indeed results in a considerable loss of valuable information. Disease diagnosis accuracy might be improved if the missing parameters could be estimated correctly from the rest of the available data or modalities. Furthermore, to have a better understanding of the disease progression and to correctly label a subject as Normal Control (NC), Mild Cognitive Impairment (MCI), or dementia (i.e., AD), data from every visit should not be scrutinized independently from the earlier steps. Currently, a majority of the classification algorithms focus on the cross-sectional data and only analyze a specific interval's biomarkers for the diagnosis and disregard the former patient's status for the decision making process. To address this shortcoming, recent studies moved toward longitudinal data analysis and proposed new methods to leverage valuable temporal data by considering the inherent correlations of such data [6–8].

Effectively mining AD longitudinal data is a challenging task, owing to its heterogeneous measurements, varying length of samples, missing modalities and tests, and small sample size. In this study, for the first time (to the best of our knowledge), we employ two RNN models, namely the Long Short Term Memory (LSTM) and the Gated Recurrent Unit (GRU), to discover the regression patterns of the subjects from the longitudinal data with missing variables and intervals, especially for the task of classifying AD/MCI *vs.* NC, which is a challenging task only depending on the cross-sectional dataset. The progression of the patients during time should be studied carefully to capture the correct status of the patient through the passage of time. Accordingly, in this study, we conduct several experiments to investigate the effectiveness of the RNNs in AD diagnosis. We compare the outcomes of the LSTM and GRU model with Multi-Layer Perceptron (MLP) to evaluate the efficacy of the sequential models.

2   Dataset

The data used in this study is obtained from the Alzheimer's Disease Neuroimaging Initiative (ADNI) database (http://adni.loni.usc.edu/). ADNI was launched in 2003 as a public-private partnership, led by Principal Investigator Michael W. Weiner, MD. The primary goal of ADNI has been to test whether structural magnetic resonance imaging (MRI), positron emission tomography (PET), other biological markers, and clinical and neuropsychological assessment can be combined to measure the progression of MCI and early AD. Recently the largest longitudinal dataset, which is a subset of ADNI 1/Go/2 cohorts, has been extracted from ADNI by Bruno M. Jedynak and Michael Donohue to make a baseline for researchers in the field to propose and apply quantitative templates for the progression of Alzheimer's disease. This is an invaluable baseline for accurate evaluation of the proposed algorithms.

The database has 1721 distinct subjects (521 NC, 864 MCI, and 336 AD) examined every 6 months during 11 years' period making 23 time points for a patient in the case of performing all the test regularly every six month (i.e., baseline, 6 months, 12 months, ..., 132 months). For every visit multiple outcomes provided including

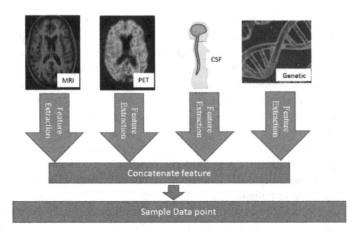

Fig. 1. Sample data point curation

ADAS13, CDRSB, RAVLT.learning MMSE, FAQ, FDG PET, Amyloid PET, CSF, ABETA, CSF TAU, CSF PTAU, FS WholeBrain, FS Hippocampus, FS Entorhinal, FS Ventricles, FS MidTemp, FS Fusiform and the covariates: age, APOE4 (yes/no), Gender, Education. The primary phenotype is the diagnostic group and Mini-Mental State Examination (MMSE). Sample data-point curation pipeline in our work is presented in Fig. 1. This figure shows that the samples are composed of features extracted from volumetric magnetic resonance imaging (MRI) including cortical thickness, hippocampal volume and shape along with fluoro-2-Deoxy-D-glucose, florbetapir F18, and PIB (which is radiotracer capable of highlighting deposits of beta-amyloid) from PET imaging, and some other Cerebrospinal fluid (CSF) features, such as TAU, PTAU and ABETA. Around 12 functional and behavioral assessment results such as Rey's Auditory Verbal Learning Test and Montreal Cognitive Assessment (MoCA) scores are also measured and used as features in this dataset.

The volumetric MRI measurements provide the cortical thickness, volume and shape of hippocampal or voxel-wise tissue probability [1–4] to measure the brain atrophy; 18-Fluoro-DeoxyGlucose PET imaging (FDG-PET) estimates the glucose hypometabolism in bilateral temporal, temporal, occipital areas or posterior cingulated brain regions [5–7]. Furthermore, global cognitive impairment tests are used by clinicians for screening and measuring individuals who are at the risk of AD; or cerebrospinal fluid (CSF) to measure the increase in t-tau, p-tau, or the decrease of amyloid-β, which is a sign of cognitive declination. Therefore, in total 47 features are used to represent each subject at each time point.

3　Models

In this section, we briefly overview the LSTM and GRU models used in our model and then explain our model design using these architectures for classifying the subjects into one of the AD, MCI, or NC categories from longitudinal data.

3.1   Long Short Term Memory Unit (LSTM)

RNNs with internal memory and feedback loop have previously been adopted mostly for processing arbitrary input sequences, like in handwriting recognition, speech recognition, natural language processing, and time series prediction applications. One of the main challenges in applying RNNs to long sequential data is that the gradient of some learnable weights become too small or too large if the network is unfolded for too many time steps. These phenomena are called the exploding and vanishing gradients problem [9]. LSTM was, hence, proposed by Hochreiter et al. for the first time in 1997 to solve the vanishing gradient problem through a gating mechanism [10]. An LSTM has three gates. The first gate determines whether the information should be forgotten or not. The second gate decides about updating the cell state, and the last gate is responsible for the cell output. Since then, several variations of LSTM architecture have been implemented especially with the utilization of Graphics Processing Units (GPUs).

3.2   Gated Recurrent Unit (GRU)

To adaptively capture dependencies of different time scales in each recurrent unit, Cho et al. [11] introduced a gated recurrent unit (GRU). Similar but not the same as LSTM design, GRU has two gates, a reset gate r, and an update gate z. Intuitively, the reset gate determines how to combine the new input with the previous memory, and the update gate defines how much of the past memory to keep around. Having simpler architecture than LSTM with a smaller number of parameters, GRU provides better results in some applications [12] and is less prone to overfitting, especially in cases that there are not enough training data.

3.3   Our Model

RNN models have achieved popularity due to their power in pattern recognition for the time series and sequential data. While there are plenty of research papers on regression and classification modeling of AD data with well-established and novel machine learning techniques, along with many deep convolutional neural networks for 2D and 3D brain MRI classification, number of research works exploiting RNNs for finding the patterns in the AD longitudinal data sets is limited [13–18]. Only a few papers recently adopted them for regression analysis on the clinical medical data [19]. Here, we employ RNN deep learning techniques for the classification of the subjects. All features are normalized by subtracting the mean value of each feature and dividing the result by the standard deviation of that feature in all samples (i.e., using their z-scores), before the analysis. To deal with missing modalities, we simply replace them with zero values. Since our goal is to showcase the usage of RNNs for longitudinal predictive analysis, we leave extensive data imputation experiments for future works. A recent work also models AD progression with RNN models [20]; however our work is different from that in multiple aspects. We use not only MRI features but also PET, Cognitive tests, and genetic features for modeling the disease. We also propose multiple approaches for handling the missing intervals and compare the potential RNN models with each other.

As described in Sect. 2, the dataset contains $N = 1721$ subjects each scanned in 24 different time points. Data from each time point is represented by $n = 47$ features. Figure 2 overviews the data arrangement. A challenge in analyzing longitudinal data sets is dealing with missing data at different time steps for some of the subjects. To address this inconsistency in the data points and to be able to input the data to RNNs, we define three settings: (1) In our first attempt, we fill the missing intervals with zero to create a same input size data for all the subjects and compose a stack of 1721, 2D matrices that all have a set of 47 biomarkers in the columns as features and all the possible time steps in the rows as time steps. We refer to this arrangement as *zero fill*. (2) In the second attempt, we buffer the data at every time point and replicate it in its next missing interval. This scheme is named as *replicate fill*. (3) In the last configuration we change the orientation of the input data and stack all the available intervals on top of each other, disregarding the missing intervals and pad them to the maximum size of the possible time steps, this is called *padding*.

One LSTM and GRU model with the memory of the maximum size of the available time steps, which is 24, are designed to process this stack of data. Each subject's time point data is fed to the corresponding cell along with its final diagnosis label (i.e., AD, MCI, or NC) allowing the model to learn the pattern of the change in the features for each subject. Figure 3 represents this pipeline. In two different sets of experiments, we replace the cells in this figure with LSTM and GRU sets and report the results.

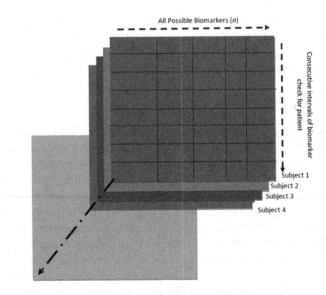

Fig. 2. Data arrangement for the RRN model

4 Experiments

In all the experiments, we train and tune the RNN model with different configurations of the hidden layers, percentages of drop out, various activation functions, loss, optimizers and different combination of other hyperparameters to find the best setting of the model through a grid search. We knowingly made the models as small as possible to avoid overfitting, which can easily mislead the comparison. Data has been split into 70% training, 15% validation set and the rest for the testing set. The best configuration of the LSTM and GRU is represented in Table 1.

For evaluations, we calculate the Accuracy, Sensitivity, Specificity, and F-score of all models. The results of LSTM and GRU models for all arrangements of the data are compared in Table 2, along with the results of their counterpart from non-recurrent networks, i.e., Multi-Layer Perceptron (MLP). The data is flattened to a 1D long vector and fed into the MLP once for each patient.

According to Table 2, LSTM and GRU models are superior to the MLP network in most of the cases as they result in the highest accuracy and F-score. Our LSTM model yields nearly 1% accuracy improvements over MLP in classifying AD patients from NC subjects. Interestingly, the RNN models with the *zero fill* data arrangement for the missing data yields consistently better results. The superiority is not significant, which can be mainly due to the limited amount of data in this domain, besides the high portion of the missing time points and modalities. These challenges prevented the vanilla RNNs to find the appropriate patterns despite various input data arrangement. Second, RNNs, especially the LSTM models, have a large number of trainable parameters, which necessitate the model to be trained in a great corpse of sequential data and despite having drop out layers in the architecture, they are still prone to overfitting to the training data in this relatively small dataset. The third is the limited hand engineered and structured feature set, used in this experiment. One of the main superiority of the RNNs is their power in automatic feature learning from the raw data, which can be further explored in the future.

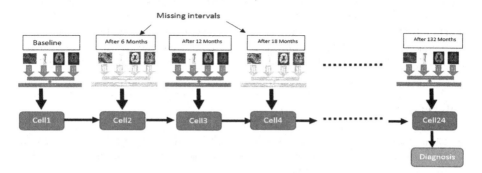

Fig. 3. RNN model used in this study.

Table 1. Model hyperparameters

	Hidden units	Activation function	Layers	Drop out
GRU	32	Softmax	1	0.3
LSTM	30	Softmax	1	0.4
MLP	20	Softmax	2	0.3

Table 2. Performance of the proposed models with three different data arrangements in classification of ADNI subjects. Best results for each data arrangement are underlined, and the best overall results of each column are in bold.

		AD - NC				AD - MCI				NC - MCI			
	Method	Accuracy	F-score	Sensitivity	Specificity	Accuracy	F-score	Sensitivity	Specificity	Accuracy	F-score	Sensitivity	Specificity
ZERO FILL	MLP	0.9467	0.9581	0.9626	0.9194	0.8474	0.8449	0.9405	0.7736	0.7729	0.7539	0.6207	**0.9670**
	LSTM	0.9526	0.9622	0.9532	**0.9516**	**0.8579**	0.8492	0.9048	0.8208	0.7729	**0.7793**	**0.7155**	0.8462
	GRU	**0.9527**	**0.9630**	**0.9720**	0.9194	0.8368	0.8360	0.9405	0.7547	0.7536	0.7536	0.6724	0.8571
REPLICATE FILL	MLP	0.9467	0.9577	0.9533	0.9345	0.8529	0.8492	0.9048	0.8208	0.7005	0.6667	0.5345	0.9121
	LSTM	**0.9586**	**0.9674**	**0.9720**	0.9355	0.8576	**0.8498**	0.9286	**0.8225**	0.7681	0.7757	**0.7155**	0.9352
	GRU	0.9527	0.9626	0.9626	0.9345	0.8211	0.8211	0.9286	0.7358	0.7101	0.7000	0.6034	0.8462
PADDING	MLP	0.9467	0.9577	0.9531	0.9355	0.8421	0.8295	0.8690	0.8208	0.7101	0.7609	0.6877	0.8423
	LSTM	0.9527	0.9623	0.9533	0.9516	0.8468	0.8298	0.8810	0.8219	0.7585	0.7619	0.6897	0.8462
	GRU	0.9408	0.9528	0.9439	0.9355	0.8158	0.8108	0.8929	0.7547	0.7101	0.7000	0.6034	0.8462

5   Conclusion

In this paper, we introduced the applications of LSTM and GRUs to model prediction tasks over the longitudinal data from the ADNI dataset. The proposed models can be used for the diagnosis of Alzheimer's disease. We also incorporated three different strategies to deal with the incomplete and missing data (from time points and modalities). Trying different variations of RNNs (i.e., LSTM and GRU), we found slightly better performance using the LSTM model. Our model can classify AD *vs.* NC with an accuracy of 95.9%, even with simple replicate and zero filling of the missing data. It also performs better classification of AD *vs.* MCI and NC *vs.* MCI patients. As a direction for future works, designing an end-to-end convolutional and LSTM model for this longitudinal dataset can be of great interest, to accurately learn powerful image features (from MRI and PET) and simultaneously learn the classifier parameters.

References

1. Glenner, G.G., Wong, C.W.: Alzheimer's disease: initial report of the purification and characterization of a novel cerebrovascular amyloid protein. Biochem. Biophys. Res. Commun. **120**(3), 885–890 (1984)
2. McKhann, G., Drachman, D., Folstein, M., Katzman, R.: Views & reviews clinical diagnosis of Alzheimer's disease. Neurology **34**(7), 939 (1984)

3. Cuingnet, R., et al.: Automatic classification of patients with Alzheimer's disease from structural MRI: a comparison of ten methods using the ADNI database. Neuroimage **56**(2), 766–781 (2011)
4. Petersen, R.C.: Mild cognitive impairment as a clinical entity and treatment target. Arch. Neurol. **62**(7), 1160–1163 (2004). Discussion 1167
5. Moradi, E., Pepe, A., Gaser, C., Huttunen, H., Tohka, J.: Machine learning framework for early MRI-based Alzheimer's conversion prediction in MCI subjects. Neuroimage **104**, 398–412 (2015)
6. Nie, L., Zhang, L., Meng, L., Song, X., Chang, X., Li, X.: Modeling disease progression via multisource multitask learners: a case study with Alzheimer's disease. IEEE Trans. Neural Netw. Learn. Syst. **28**(7), 1508–1519 (2017)
7. Zhou, J., Yuan, L., Liu, J., Ye, J.: A multi-task learning formulation for predicting disease progression. In: Proceedings of the 17th ACM SIGKDD KDD, p. 814 (2011)
8. Zhang, D., Shen, D.: Multi modal multi task learning for joint prediction of multiple regression and classification variables in Alzheimer's disease. Neuroimage **59**(2), 895–907 (2013)
9. Bengio, Y., Simard, P., Frasconi, P.: Learning long-term dependencies with gradient descent is difficult. IEEE Trans. Neural Nets **5**(2), 157–166 (1994)
10. Hochreiter, S., Schmidhuber, J.: Long short-term memory. Neural Comput. **9**(8), 1735–1780 (1997)
11. Cho, K., et al.: Learning phrase representations using RNN encoder-decoder for statistical machine translation. arXiv:1406.1078 (2014)
12. Che, Z., Purushotham, S., Cho, K., Sontag, D., Liu, Y.: Recurrent neural networks for multivariate time series with missing values, pp. 1–14 (2016)
13. Chen, Y., Shi, B., Smith, C.D., Liu, J.: Nonlinear feature transformation and deep fusion for Alzheimer's disease staging analysis. In: Zhou, L., Wang, L., Wang, Q., Shi, Y. (eds.) MLMI 2015. LNCS, vol. 9352, pp. 304–312. Springer, Cham (2015). https://doi.org/10.1007/978-3-319-24888-2_37
14. Fang, C., Li, C., Cabrerizo, M., Barreto, A., Andrian, J., Loewenstein, D.: A novel Gaussian discriminant analysis-based computer aided diagnosis system for screening different stages of Alzheimer's Disease. In: BIBE, pp. 279–284 (2017)
15. Shi, J., Zheng, X., Li, Y., Zhang, Q., Ying, S.: Multimodal neuroimaging feature learning with multimodal stacked deep polynomial networks for diagnosis of Alzheimer's disease. IEEE J. Biomed. Heal. Inform. **2194** (2017)
16. Chaves, R., et al.: SVM-based computer-aided diagnosis of the Alzheimer's disease using t-test NMSE feature selection with feature correlation weighting. Neurosci. Lett. **461**(3), 293–297 (2009)
17. Zhu, X., Il Suk, H., Wang, L., Lee, S.W., Shen, D.: A novel relational regularization feature selection method for joint regression and classification in AD diagnosis. Med. Image Anal. **38**, 205–214 (2017)
18. Lebedev, A.V., et al.: Random Forest ensembles for detection and prediction of Alzheimer's disease with a good between-cohort robustness. Neuroimage (Amst) **6**, 115–125 (2014)
19. Bange, S.-J., Wange, Y., Yange, Y.: Phased-LSTM based predictive model for longitudinal EHR data with missing values (2016)
20. Cui, R., Liu, M., Li, G.: Longitudinal analysis for Alzheimer's Disease diagnosis using RNN. In: 2018 IEEE 15th International Symposium on Biomedical Imaging (ISBI 2018), Washington, DC, pp. 1398–1401 (2018)

Towards Continuous Health Diagnosis from Faces with Deep Learning

Victor Martin[1,2](✉) [ID], Renaud Séguier[1], Aurélie Porcheron[2],
and Frédérique Morizot[2]

[1] CentraleSupelec, Avenue de la Boulaie, 35510 Cesson-Sévigné, France
victor@vmartin.fr
[2] CHANEL Parfums Beauté, 8 Rue du Cheval Blanc, 93500 Pantin, France

Abstract. Recent studies show that health perception from faces by humans is a good predictor of good health and healthy behaviors. We aimed to automatize human health perception by training a Convolutional Neural Network on a related task (age estimation) combined with a Ridge Regression to rate faces. Indeed, contrary to health ratings, large datasets with labels of biological age exist. The results show that our system outperforms average human judgments for health. The system could be used on a daily basis to detect early signs of sickness or a declining state. We are convinced that such a system will contribute to more extensively explore the use of holistic, fast, and non-invasive measures to improve the speed of diagnosis.

Keywords: Health estimation · Non-invasive diagnosis
Convolutional Neural Network · Facial features

1 Introduction

Judgments of a person's health based on facial appearance are a daily occurrence in social interactions. Understanding how we perceive health from a face is important because this judgment drive a wide array of social behaviors. Looking healthy has many positive real-life outcomes such as preferential treatment in the professional context, in the justice system or in dating interactions [1–4]. Inversely, looking unhealthy is associated to lower self-esteem [5] and may lead to a risk of social stigmatization and isolation [6]. A better understanding of how health is perceived and which facial cues alter this perception is likely to help reducing the negative social consequences which can follow.

Scientific recent evidences also show that facial healthy appearance is a good predictor of healthy behaviors [7] and good health [8–10]. Faces with an increase of oxygenated blood skin coloration are perceived healthier, and blood oxygenation level is known to be associated with cardiovascular fitness [10]. People with a healthy diet, such as daily consumption of fruits and vegetables, have a more attractive skin color and are perceived healthier [7]. Sleep deprived people appear less healthy compared with when they are well rested [11]. And people would

© Springer Nature Switzerland AG 2018
I. Rekik et al. (Eds.): PRIME 2018, LNCS 11121, pp. 120–128, 2018.
https://doi.org/10.1007/978-3-030-00320-3_15

acutely detect signs of sickness from the face in an early phase after exposure to infectious stimuli and potentially contagious people [12]. Figure 1 shows two average faces of people perceived in good health and people perceived in bad health. As health perception and age are known to be correlated [13], health ratings are decorrelated with age.

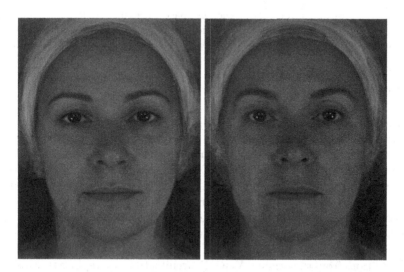

Fig. 1. Average face of the 10 faces with the greatest perceived health to the left, and with the lowest perceived health at right. Health ratings have been decorrelated from age.

We aim to develop an automatic system able to imitate human judgments of health. Such a technology, when used over the long term, could enable fast and non-invasive detection of a declining state of a person. That's why we introduce the first system able to estimate health scores from faces.

To the best of our knowledge, we introduce in this paper the first work on automatic health estimation from face. Lots of works have been made to estimate age from faces [14–17].

More recently, some researchers have begun to study whether it is possible to estimate less common attributes from the face such as intelligence [18], attractiveness [19–22] or social relation traits [23].

In view of the current state of art and our constraints, we use a Convolutional Neural Network trained on biological age combined with a Ridge Regression to assess health perception from faces (Sec. 2). Thereafter, we evaluate the system performance on our database and we compare it with human performance on the same database (Sec. 3).

54   22   46   31   11   80

Fig. 2. An excerpt of the Internet Movie Database with their corresponding biological age. As we see it above, the database contains faces with large variations in pose, illumination and color distribution. Pictures are resized to 224×224 before training.

2   Health Estimation

Based on the age estimation method of [17], we employ the Convolutional Neural Network VGG-16 pre-trained on the ImageNet database [24] to detect 1,000 classes of objects, and trained it on the Internet Movie Database (IMDb) of celebrities (Fig. 2). We filtered the $\approx 500K$ images to keep only those containing faces with resolution greater than 120×120 pixels, no more than one face detected in each image, and only picture depicting people from 11 to 85 years old. For each picture, we have the date of birth of the celebrity pictured and the date of the photo acquisition, thus we can deduce the biological age of the depicted person.

In addition, from the original VGG-16 architecture, we replace the final Multi Layer Perceptron containing a large part of the parameters, by a lighter one with one layer of 1024 units (Fig. 4) and an output layer of 120 units. The objective of doing so is to shift the learning effort onto the convolutional layers because the final Multi Layer Perceptron will be dropped as we want to estimate health and not biological age – thus, having the fastest training with the lowest score is not the main goal here.

Thus, the last 3 convolutional blocks and the fully connected layers has been trained on IMDb with Stochastic Gradient Descent with a Learning Rate of 10^{-4} on 1000 epochs with 10 steps per epoch and a batch size of 16. The decrease of the Mean Absolute Error for the training set and validation set can be seen in Fig. 3.

After that, we have to develop our system of health estimation with only 140 images annotated with health scores (Fig. 5). We want to compute a representation of our faces from the newly trained ConvNet using only the convolutions and pooling blocks, and use a regression to estimate health scores from representations. The question remains, at which epoch can we stop the training for health estimation? If we take the weights at an early epoch, the system will be underfitted. In the same way, as we do not want to predict biological age, taking the weights corresponding to an advanced epoch with a low MAE is not the go-to choice to make.

We evaluate the suitability of ConvNet weights at each epoch for Health Estimation with a simple Linear Regression trained with a 40-fold configuration. We can see in Fig. 6 how the training on a different, but related, task can increase

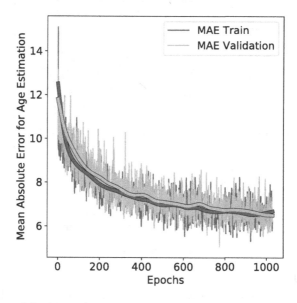

Fig. 3. Decrease of the Mean Absolute Error during the training for the train set and the validation set.

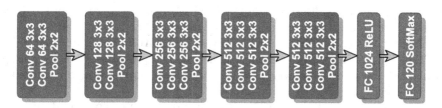

Fig. 4. Our architecture takes a 224×224 image and produces a probability distribution over all possible ages. The blue part has not been modified from the original VGG-16 architecture.

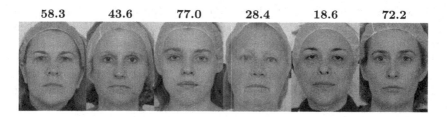

Fig. 5. An excerpt of our database with their corresponding perceived health scores. Our database contains 140 photos of women faces with a neutral expression in a controlled environment.

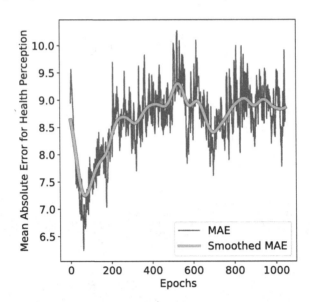

Fig. 6. Variation of the Mean Absolute Error in function of the epoch at which the weights are chosen. Epoch 0 corresponds to VGG-16 just trained on ImageNet. The red curve has been Gaussian smoothed with $\sigma = 25$.

performance on our health estimation problem. At epoch 0, learning for biological age hasn't started yet and we get a relatively high MAE (9.0). In a second stage, learning for biological age greatly decreases Mean Absolute Error from 9.0 to 6.2. Finally, as learning progresses and the model specializes in biological age estimation, the error increases. An optimal period is found around epoch 60 to take the weights for health estimation.

Now that we found the ConvNet weights to compute representations from faces, we test several estimators to asses health scores from representations. For each estimator, we evaluate a broad range of parameters and report those producing the best performance in Table 1. In the table, the Multi Layer Perceptron is composed of two layers containing n neurons for the first layer and 120 for the output layer.

As we can see on Table 1, simple estimators as a Linear Regression or a Linear Regression regularized with a low ℓ_2 penalty (Ridge Regression) can achieve the best performance given our dataset and the feature extraction method we chose earlier. We can explain the fact that simpler estimators perform better than more complex estimators as Random Forests or Multi Layer Perceptron by the scarce number of samples $n = 140$ in regard of the dimensionality of our features $d = 512 * 7 * 7 = 25088$. The final architecture of our system is described in Fig. 7.

Table 1. List of tested estimators. The estimator with the lowest Mean Absolute Error is bolded.

Estimator	MAE
Linear Regression	6.240
Ridge $\alpha = 10^{-3}$	**6.232**
Lasso $\alpha = 10^{-2}$	6.437
Linear SVR $C = 10^3$	6.355
RBF SVR $C = 10^4, \gamma = 10^{-4}$	6.269
PLS Regression $n = 100$	14.64
Multi Layer Perceptron $n = 2048$	8.543
Extremely Randomized Trees $n = 200$	8.446
K-NN $K = 15$	8.778

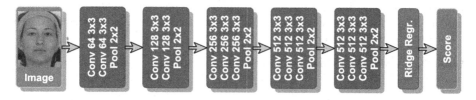

Fig. 7. The whole computation chain. The blue part and the green part are trained separately on different datasets.

3   Experiment: System Versus Human Performance

We have 140 images of faces and each of them had been rated by 74 judges. For every picture, we asked them to evaluate health and to give a score from 0 to 100; 0 being perceived in very bad health and 100 being perceived in very good health. Finally, for each image, we took the average of the 74 ratings to determine a reliable perceived health score. In this database, the health scores obtained are 60% correlated with biological ages.

Exploiting the previously described system, we trained the Ridge Regression in a 140-fold manner to assess its performance.

As we can see on Fig. 8, we can achieve good performance on our dataset with a scarce amount of data. Using mean absolute error MAE, coefficient of determination R^2 and Pearson correlation PC, Table 2 shows that our system estimates health more accurately than an average human working on the same dataset.

In addition, among the 74 judges, one judge with the lowest MAE (i.e. smallest difference in average between his ratings and the average ratings) is selected and placed in the table below under the name Best Human.

As an additional note, we can observe that health scores are 60% correlated with biological ages, and health estimates outputted by our system are 90%

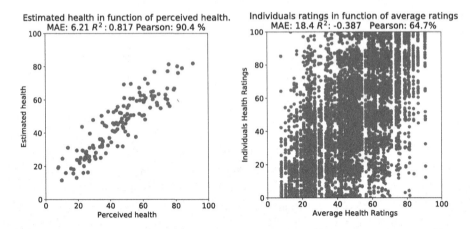

Fig. 8. Left: The predictions of our system compared to the perceived health scores, which is the average health ratings from humans. Right: all individual ratings from humans in function of average ratings. This 2nd graph shows the relatively high variance of human ratings for each image.

Table 2. Performance of our health estimation system compared to human performance.

	MAE	PC	R^2
System	**6.21**	**90.4%**	**0.817**
Average Human	18.4	64.7%	−0.387
Best Human	9.37	81.3%	0.637

correlated with health scores. Hence, we confirm that our system estimates health from faces, and not just biological age.

4   Conclusion

This paper describes how we manage to develop an automatic system able to imitate human judgments of health. We trained a Convolutional Neural Network to estimate biological age and we used representations produced by the network of our scarce database to train a simpler estimator. We observed a very good performance of the system when we compared it to human judgments of health.

Nevertheless, we identified several areas of improvement.

First, the use of a Linear Regression to rank the different ConvNet weights (Fig. 6) tends to favor this type of estimators in the next step where we compare the performance of different estimators (Table 1). We could have ranked the different weights using a multitude of estimators.

Moreover, by using more images annotated with health ratings, we could improve the performance of our system and make it more robust to variations in pose and illumination.

Additional work will be necessary to test its performance on other demographic groups such as other ethnicities and men.

To conclude, we developed the first automatic health estimation system able to reproduce human judgments. Such a system could be used in institutions such as hospitals or retirement homes to automatically predict a potential future sickness from earlier visual signs present in a face. Similarly, it could be used for the remote monitoring of patients, to detect a sudden drop in health perception and prevent behaviors that negatively impact health.

References

1. Efran, M.G.: The effect of physical appearance on the judgment of guilt, interpersonal attraction, and severity of recommended punishment in a simulated jury task. J. Res. Pers. **8**(1), 45–54 (1974)
2. Marlowe, C.M., Schneider, S.L., Nelson, C.E.: Gender and attractiveness biases in hiring decisions: Are more experienced managers less biased? J. Appl. Psychol. **81**(1), 11–21 (1996)
3. Ritts, V., Patterson, M.L., Tubbs, M.E.: Expectations, impressions, and judgments of physically attractive students: a review. Rev. Educ. Res. **62**(4), 413–426 (1992)
4. Spisak, B.R., Blaker, N.M., Lefevre, C.E., Moore, F.R., Krebbers, K.F.B.: A face for all seasons: Searching for context-specific leadership traits and discovering a general preference for perceived health. Front. Hum. Neurosci. **8**, 792 (2014)
5. Feingold, A.: Good-looking people are not what we think. Psychol. Bull. **111**(2), 304 (1992)
6. Henderson, A.J., Holzleitner, I.J., Talamas, S.N., Perrett, D.I.: Perception of health from facial cues. Philos. Trans. R. Soc. B: Biol. Sci. **371**(1693), 20150380 (2016)
7. Whitehead, R.D., Re, D., Xiao, D., Ozakinci, G., Perrett, D.I.: You are what you eat: within-subject increases in fruit and vegetable consumption confer beneficial skin-color changes. PLOS ONE **7**(3), e32988 (2012)
8. Zebrowitz, L.A., et al.: Older and younger adults' accuracy in discerning health and competence in older and younger faces. Psychol. Aging **29**(3), 454 (2014)
9. Stephen, I.D., Coetzee, V., Smith, L.M., Perrett, D.I.: Skin blood perfusion and oxygenation colour affect perceived human health. PLoS ONE **4**(4), e5083 (2009)
10. Re, D.E., Whitehead, R.D., Xiao, D., Perrett, D.I.: Oxygenated-blood colour change thresholds for perceived facial redness, health, and attractiveness. PLoS ONE **6**(3), e17859 (2011)
11. Axelsson, J., Sundelin, T., Ingre, M., Someren, E.J.W.V., Olsson, A., Lekander, M.: Beauty sleep: experimental study on the perceived health and attractiveness of sleep deprived people. BMJ **341**, c6614 (2010)
12. Axelsson, J., Sundelin, T., Axelsson, C., Lasselin, J., Lekander, M.: Identification of acutely sick people and facial cues of sickness. Brain Behav. Immun. **66**, e38 (2017)
13. Fink, B., Matts, P., D'Emiliano, D., Bunse, L., Weege, B., Röder, S.: Colour homogeneity and visual perception of age, health and attractiveness of male facial skin: perception of male skin colour. J. Eur. Acad. Dermatol. Venereol. **26**(12), 1486–1492 (2011)
14. Lanitis, A., Taylor, C.J., Cootes, T.F.: Toward automatic simulation of aging effects on face images. IEEE Trans. Pattern Anal. Mach. Intell. **24**(4), 442–455 (2002)

15. Lanitis, A., Draganova, C., Christodoulou, C.: Comparing different classifiers for automatic age estimation. IEEE Trans. Syst., Man, Cybern. Part B Cybern. **34**, 621–628 (2004)
16. Guo, G., Mu, G., Fu, Y., Huang, T.S.: Human age estimation using bio-inspired features. In: IEEE Conference on Computer Vision and Pattern Recognition, CVPR 2009, pp. 112–119. IEEE (2009)
17. Rothe, R., Timofte, R., Van Gool, L.: DEX: deep expectation of apparent age from a single image. In: Proceedings of the IEEE International Conference on Computer Vision Workshops, pp. 10–15 (2015)
18. Qin, R., Gao, W., Xu, H., Hu, Z.: Modern physiognomy: an investigation on predicting personality traits and intelligence from the human face. arXiv:1604.07499 [cs], April 2016
19. Fan, Y.Y., Liu, S., Li, B., Guo, Z., Samal, A., Wan, J., Li, S.Z.: Label distribution-based facial attractiveness computation by deep residual learning. IEEE Trans. Multimed. **PP**(99), 1 (2017)
20. Chen, F., Zhang, D.: Combining a causal effect criterion for evaluation of facial attractiveness models. Neurocomputing **177**, 98–109 (2016)
21. Liu, S., Fan, Y.Y., Samal, A., Guo, Z.: Advances in computational facial attractiveness methods. Multimed. Tools Appl. **75**(23), 16633–16663 (2016)
22. Chen, F., Xiao, X., Zhang, D.: Data-driven facial beauty analysis: prediction, retrieval and manipulation. IEEE Trans. Affect. Comput. **PP**(99), 1 (2017)
23. Zhang, Z., Luo, P., Loy, C.C., Tang, X.: Learning social relation traits from face images. arXiv:1509.03936 [cs], September 2015
24. Simonyan, K., Zisserman, A.: Very deep convolutional networks for large-scale image recognition. arXiv preprint arXiv:1409.1556 (2014)

Xmonet: A Fully Convolutional Network for Cross-Modality MR Image Inference

Sophia Bano[1(✉)], Muhammad Asad[2], Ahmed E. Fetit[3], and Islem Rekik[4]

[1] Wellcome/EPSRC Centre for Interventional and Surgical Sciences and Department of Computer Science, University College London, London, UK
sophia.bano@ucl.ac.uk
[2] Imagination Technologies, Kings Langley, UK
[3] Biomedical Image Analysis Group, Imperial College London, London, UK
[4] BASIRA Lab, CVIP, School of Science and Engineering (Computing), University of Dundee, Dundee, UK

Abstract. Magnetic resonance imaging (MRI) can generate multi-modal scans with complementary contrast information, capturing various anatomical or functional properties of organs of interest. But whilst the acquisition of multiple modalities is favourable in clinical and research settings, it is hindered by a range of practical factors that include cost and imaging artefacts. We propose XmoNet, a deep-learning architecture based on fully convolutional networks (FCNs) that enables cross-modality MR image inference. This multiple branch architecture operates on various levels of image spatial resolutions, encoding rich feature hierarchies suited for this image generation task. We illustrate the utility of XmoNet in learning the mapping between heterogeneous T1- and T2-weighted MRI scans for accurate and realistic image synthesis in a preliminary analysis. Our findings support scaling the work to include larger samples and additional modalities.

Keywords: Fully convolutional networks · MRI · Multimodal
Image generation

1 Introduction

Magnetic resonance imaging (MRI) is the key imaging technology used to aid the diagnosis and management of a wide range of diseases. Visual characteristics of tissues of interest can be acquired via a variety of MR modalities (e.g. T1-weighted, T2-weighted, FLAIR, diffusion-weighted and diffusion-tensor imaging), each offering complementary contrast mechanisms. For instance in neuro-oncology, T1-weighted scans are favourable for observing brain structures whereas T2-weighted scans can provide rich information for tumour localisation. However, a number of factors impede acquisition of multimodal scans in clinical settings; particularly cost, limited availability of scanning time and patient discomfort [7]. In research settings and imaging clinical trials, it is common to face

© Springer Nature Switzerland AG 2018
I. Rekik et al. (Eds.): PRIME 2018, LNCS 11121, pp. 129–137, 2018.
https://doi.org/10.1007/978-3-030-00320-3_16

heterogeneous or incomplete datasets due to similar reasons, as well as acquisition artefacts and data corruption. This has motivated various efforts in the MR literature that can broadly be divided into two categories: (i) improving image acquisition and reconstruction strategies, and (ii) synthesising a target modality given a separate source modality; also known as cross-modality generation.

Cross-modality generation has attracted the attention of the medical image computing community in recent years. Work by D. H. Ye *et al.* [14] investigated a modality propagation approach, where for each point in the target image a patch-based search is carried out across a database of images, utilising nearest neighbours' information for estimating target modality values. The work was motivated by the observation that local and contextual similarities observed in one modality can often extend to other modalities. Evaluation of the approach illustrated effectiveness in synthesising T2-weighted and DTI signals given a source T1-weighted input, including successful application on brain tumour scans. Y. Lu *et al.* [10] proposed a novel distance measure that used patch based intensity histogram and Weber Local Descriptor features to search the most similar patch from the database for modality synthesis.

Recently, Y. Huang *et al.* [7] proposed a weakly supervised technique that requires only a few registered multi-modal image pairs for effective cross-modality generation. The technique works through mapping different image features of the underlying tissues, preserving global statistical image properties across modalities, and subsequently refining the features to ensure local geometrical structures are preserved within each modality. Additionally, manifold matching is used to select target-modality features from the most similar source-modality subjects; thus complementing unpaired data with the original training pairs. Effectiveness of the technique was illustrated in cross modality generation between T1- and T2-weighted scans, as well as T2- and PD-weighted scans.

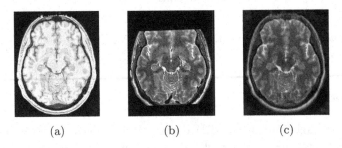

(a)   (b)   (c)

Fig. 1. The proposed XmoNet enables cross-modality MR image inference, as demonstrated here with an example. The architecture takes as input a T1-weighted slice in (a) and predicts the corresponding T2-weighted slice in (c). Ground-truth T2-weighted slice is shown in (b) for reference. Visual inspection of (b) and (c) illustrates practical utility of XmoNet in achieving cross-modality mapping, along with generation of areas which have missing ground-truth data; a high-value application in clinical and research settings.

Deep learning algorithms, particularly Convolutional Neural Networks (CNNs), have rapidly gained widespread adoption within the medical image computing community. Work by Bahrami *et al.* [2] studied the utility of CNNs for mapping cross-domain scans, albeit for a resolution mapping problem (3T to 7T MRI) as opposed to generation of missing modalities. In their earlier work, Bahrami *et al.* [3] made use of high- and low-frequency visual features, thus capturing variations among 3 T scans with various levels of quality. Evaluation was carried out on various paired MR datasets of healthy subjects, as well as patients with epilepsy and MCI. A. Ben-Cohen *et al.* [4] combined a fully convolutional network (FCN) with a conditional generative adversarial network (GAN) to generate PET data from CT for improving automated lesion detection. Y. Hiasa *et al.* [5] proposed CycleGAN-based MR to CT orthopedic image synthesis method in which the accuracy at the bone boundaries was improved by adding the gradient consistency loss.

We contribute XmoNet, a deep learning architecture for rapid and accurate cross(X)-MOdality learning; and carry out a preliminary analysis to examine its effectiveness on heterogeneous MR data. The architecture is based on fully convolutional networks (FCN) and utilises parallel pathways to encode low- and high-frequency visual features, allowing mapping of rich feature hierarchies. Preliminary analysis demonstrated accurate and realistic synthesis of target T2-weighted images from source T1-weighted data (see Fig. 1); our findings support scaling the work to include larger samples and additional modalities.

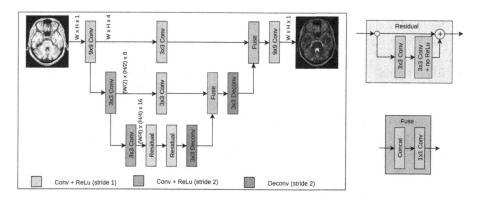

Fig. 2. Flowchart of the proposed XmoNet. The input T1-weighted slice is convolved using multiple pathways at different resolutions. The output from each pathway is upsampled with a deconvolution operation and then fed into a fusion layer. The multiple higher resolution pathways allows high-frequency patterns to be preserved. Multiple residual layers are added to the lowest resolution path, which ensures mapping of low-frequency visual patterns from the source data.

2   Proposed Method

Inspired by recent successes of fully convolutional networks (FCNs) [1,9,11] the XmoNet utilises a FCN architecture that learns the cross-modality mapping from T1- onto T2-weighted MR data. Figure 2 shows a flowchart of the proposed architecture. Given an input slice, the network utilises several strided-convolutional layers to reduce spatial dimensionality whilst increasing the number of activation channels at every branch, following intuition from the well-established VGG architecture [12]. Through the use of multiple pathways, we map different frequency levels of visual features from the input scan. The use of multiple pathways is inspired by FCN methods proposed for semantic segmentation [1,9], and ensures capturing of high-frequency visual patterns. Merging with deconvolution layers is carried out in order to spatially upsample the activations whilst reducing the number of channels. These are followed by fuse layers for pathway concatenation. Residual layers are also used for cross-modality mapping of low-frequency visual patterns. The network uses 4, 8 and 16 filters in the first, second and third convolutional pathways respectively. The two residual blocks use 16 filters each and the filters in the upsampling layers are reduced to 8 and 4 in the first and second branch, respectively. L2 loss is used for the network training.

3   Experimental Analysis

3.1   Dataset

In this preliminary analysis we used the public MNI-HISUB25 dataset by Kulaga-Yoskovitz *et al.* [8] which includes submillimetric, high-resolution T1- and T2-weighted brain scans of 25 healthy subjects. The dataset is available in NIfTI format and is labelled for hippocampal subfields. Resolutions are $0.6 \times 0.6 \times 0.6 \, \mathrm{mm}^2$ and $0.45 \times 0.45 \times 2.0 \, \mathrm{mm}^2$ for T1- and T2-weighted scans, respectively. Kulaga-Yoskovitz *et al.* [8] pre-processed the captured scans for spatial normalisation to MNI152-space as well as registration of the two modalities. The final, pre-processed T1- and T2-weighted scans have a $0.4 \times 0.4 \times 0.4 \, \mathrm{mm}^3$ resolution in MNI152-space which are used in our experiments.

3.2   Experimental Setup

We used the open-source med2image[1] tool for MRI axial slice extraction. This was then followed by extracting only those slices that contained hippocampi since region around hippocampi is of high relevance to the diagnosis of brain disorders such as Alzheimers' disease. In total, 2431 slices (452×542 pixels) contained hippocampi regions; these formed the data for our experiments. We performed two experiments: (i) input to XmoNet was the whole T1-weighted image (452×542 pixels), and (ii) input to XmoNet was a cropped region selected around right hippocampus of the T1-weighted image (128×128 pixels).

---

[1] https://github.com/FNNDSC/med2image. last access: 20072018.

T2-weighted images in the dataset failed to capture complete brain structures; most of them had zero-pixel regions in place of lower or/and upper parts of the images (Fig. 1). Incorporating corrupted regions into the learning process would obscure network training; we alleviated this through generating exclusion masks obtained by detecting regions in the T2-weighted images where no signal was present. A blob size threshold was used to ensure zero-pixel brain structures were not included within the masks. Such masks were subsequently used during model training, ensuring the loss is computed only for pixels within which an anatomical signal was present. Similarly, the masks were used during the validation stage when computing evaluation metrics.

3.3 Validation Protocol

(a) 80% of the data was selected (first 20 subjects; 1961 slices in total) for model training. The remaining data (5 subjects; 470 slices) were completely unseen during the training process but held out for evaluation. (b) Furthermore, we performed k-fold cross-validation (k=5) to provide additional reassurance; each fold contained an average of 485 slices representing the scans of 5 subjects. The cross-validation loop consisted of model training over 4 folds and subsequent testing on the remaining fold. An i7-CPU workstation with NVIDIA 1080 GTX card installed was used for the analysis. The training process took place over 20 hours (approx. 5 hours per fold) for 5-fold validation. Observed testing rate was 48 slices per second.

3.4 Evaluation Metrics

Peak signal-to-noise ratio (PSNR) and structural similarity (SIMM) [13] metrics are used in existing method [2,3,6] for the quantitative evaluation of reconstructed images/patches, hence we used the same evaluation metrics. Given a ground-truth X and a generated image Y both of height H and width W; mean square error (MSE) is first obtained:

$$MSE = \frac{1}{HW} \sum_{i=0}^{H-1} \sum_{i=0}^{W-1} [X(i,j) - Y(i,j)]^2 \qquad (1)$$

PSNR (in dB) is then computed as follows (MAX$_X$ is the maximum possible pixel intensity; 255 here):

$$PSNR = 10 \log_{10} \left(\frac{MAX_X^2}{MSE} \right) \qquad (2)$$

SIMM measures the perceived change in Y relative to X and is computed as:

$$SIMM(x,y) = \frac{(2\mu_x\mu_y + c_1)(2\sigma_{xy} + c_2)}{\left(\mu_x^2 + \mu_y^2 + c_1\right)\left(\sigma_x^2 + \sigma_y^2 + c_2\right)} \qquad (3)$$

where μ_x and μ_y are the mean, σ_x and σ_y are the variance and σ_{xy} are the covariances of X and Y. c_1 and c_2 depend on the dynamic range of pixel intensities; needed to stabilise division on weak denominators [13]. Increase in PSNR suggests an improvement in signal to noise ratio i.e. lower noise and/or better image generation. SIMM, on the other hand, captures the structural similarity between a synthesised and a ground-truth image. PSNR and SIMM were computed for only those pixels that lie outside the defined exclusion masks. Visual inspection was further carried out to assess realism of synthesised images, particularly regions where no T2 ground-truth is available.

Table 1. Mean and standard deviation (Std) for PSNR and SIMM obtained via 5-fold cross validation for synthesis of T2-weighted (i) complete images and (ii) right hippocampus subregions.

fold#		1		2		3		4		5	
		Mean	Std	Mean	Std	Mean	Std	Mean	Std	Mean	Std
Complete slice	PSNR	30.48	0.58	30.74	0.56	30.98	0.67	30.96	0.53	31.11	1.21
	SIMM	0.77	0.09	0.79	0.10	0.80	0.10	0.80	0.10	0.78	0.11
Hippocampi region	PSNR	28.45	0.78	27.75	0.14	27.83	0.34	27.76	0.22	29.24	0.72
	SIMM	0.60	0.12	0.61	0.13	0.61	0.12	0.60	0.13	0.63	0.14

4   Results and Discussion

Table 1 shows the result for the 5-fold validation for the complete and right-hippocampus T2-weighted sub-region generation. Both PSNR and SIMM measures are higher for the complete T2-weighted image synthesis compared to the T2-weighted sub-region synthesis as complete image synthesis managed to better capture high resolution details resulting in relatively accurate and sharp image generation. This is because the variance of each pixel in complete T2-weighted image is low during training compared to the sub-region image.

Figure 3 shows a set of original images (T1-weighted network input and noisy T2-weighted ground-truth) as well as synthesised T2-weighted images for 8 different subjects. The proposed XmoNet is capable of achieving cross-modality mapping from T1 onto T2. Visual inspection of these figures suggests that synthesised images better capture overall brain structures (with respect to source T1-weighted images) than the original T2 scans; successful synthesis of regions with heavily missing T2 signal is achieved (Fig. 3(d)–(f)).

A number of limitations exist in this study. Firstly, the generated brain regions for which no T2 baseline exists require thorough validation and assessment by medical experts. Additionally, network input-output is currently a T1-T2 generation route; exploring the opposite scenario of T2-T1 generation was not carried out. Furthermore, testing data used in the study was obtained from the same source as the training/fine-tuning data; studying network's generalisability to different acquisition settings was not carried out.

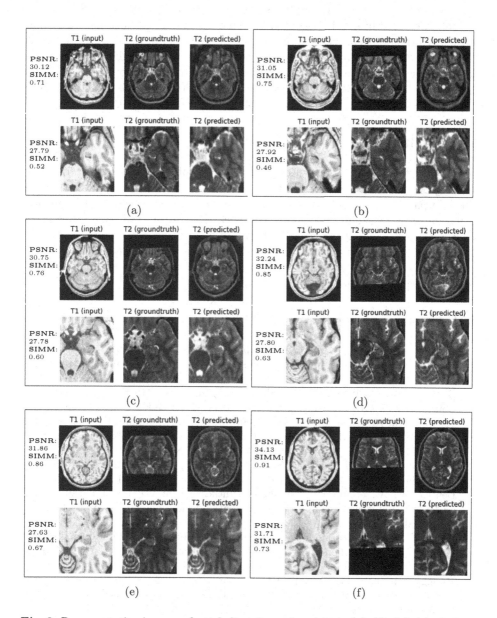

Fig. 3. Representative images of axial slices from six subjects (a)–(f); (a)–(c) sections at the level of Pons showing missing frontal lobe parts in the T2 (ground-truth) scans, (d)–(f) showing missing frontal and parietal lobe parts in the T2 (ground-truth) scans. XmoNet automatically generated the missing parts as shown in T2 (predicted). For each subject, upper row shows complete image synthesis while lower row shows results on the hippocampus sub-region images.

In addition to the above, validating XmoNet on larger datasets will drive our future efforts. Additionally, rigorous comparison against performance of state-of-the-art methods is crucial. An interesting application of the work is synthesis of images of non-healthy regions e.g. brain tumours. Although the model was designed for MR image generation, it can be adopted to incorporate non-MR based modalities (e.g. CT). Moreover, cross modality inference in 3D images is also of interest [6], hence adopting our model to 3D images can also be considered.

5   Conclusions

We proposed XmoNet, a CNN designed for the problem of cross-modality MR image generation. The network utilises a fully convolutional architecture, where multiple pathways are used to capture a hierarchy of low- and high-frequency visual patterns. A preliminary analysis was carried out on brain MR scans of 25 healthy subjects. Quantitative evaluation and qualitative visual inspection illustrated the utility of XmoNet for accurate and realistic synthesis of T2-weighted images from source T1-weighted data. Our findings support extending the analysis to incorporate larger datasets and additional modalities.

References

1. Badrinarayanan, V., Kendall, A., Cipolla, R.: SegNet: a deep convolutional encoder-decoder architecture for image segmentation. IEEE Trans. Pattern Anal. Mach. Intell. **39**(12), 2481–2495 (2017)
2. Bahrami, K., Rekik, I., Shi, F., Shen, D.: Joint Reconstruction and segmentation of 7T-like MR images from 3T MRI based on cascaded convolutional neural networks. In: Descoteaux, M., Maier-Hein, L., Franz, A., Jannin, P., Collins, D.L., Duchesne, S. (eds.) MICCAI 2017. LNCS, vol. 10433, pp. 764–772. Springer, Cham (2017). https://doi.org/10.1007/978-3-319-66182-7_87
3. Bahrami, K., Shi, F., Zong, X., Shin, H.W., An, H., Shen, D.: Reconstruction of 7T-like images from 3T MRI. IEEE Trans. Med. Imaging **35**(9), 2085 (2016)
4. Ben-Cohen, A., et al.: Cross-modality synthesis from CT to PET using FCN and GAN networks for improved automated lesion detection. arXiv preprint arXiv:1802.07846 (2018)
5. Hiasa, Y., et al.: Cross-modality image synthesis from unpaired data using Cycle-GAN: Effects of gradient consistency loss and training data size. arXiv preprint arXiv:1803.06629 (2018)
6. Huang, Y., Shao, L., Frangi, A.F.: Simultaneous super-resolution and cross-modality synthesis of 3D medical images using weakly-supervised joint convolutional sparse coding. arXiv preprint arXiv:1705.02596 (2017)
7. Huang, Y., Shao, L., Frangi, A.F.: Cross-modality image synthesis via weakly coupled and geometry co-regularized joint dictionary learning. IEEE Trans. Med. Imaging **37**(3), 815–827 (2018)
8. Kulaga-Yoskovitz, J., et al.: Multi-contrast submillimetric 3 tesla hippocampal subfield segmentation protocol and dataset. Sci. Data **2**, 150059 (2015)
9. Long, J., Shelhamer, E., Darrell, T.: Fully convolutional networks for semantic segmentation. In: Proceedings of the IEEE Conference on Computer Vision and Pattern Recognition, pp. 3431–3440 (2015)

10. Lu, Y., Sun, Y., Liao, R., Ong, S.H.: A modality synthesis framework: using patch based intensity histogram and weber local descriptor features. In: International Symposium on Biomedical Imaging (ISBI), pp. 1126–1129. IEEE (2015)
11. Ronneberger, O., Fischer, P., Brox, T.: U-Net: convolutional networks for biomedical image segmentation. In: Navab, N., Hornegger, J., Wells, W.M., Frangi, A.F. (eds.) MICCAI 2015. LNCS, vol. 9351, pp. 234–241. Springer, Cham (2015). https://doi.org/10.1007/978-3-319-24574-4_28
12. Simonyan, K., Zisserman, A.: Very deep convolutional networks for large-scale image recognition. arXiv preprint arXiv:1409.1556 (2014)
13. Wang, Z., Simoncelli, E.P., Bovik, A.C.: Multiscale structural similarity for image quality assessment. In: Conference Record of the Thirty-Seventh Asilomar Conference on Signals, Systems and Computers, vol. 2, pp. 1398–1402. IEEE (2003)
14. Ye, D.H., Zikic, D., Glocker, B., Criminisi, A., Konukoglu, E.: Modality propagation: coherent synthesis of subject-specific scans with data-driven regularization. In: Mori, K., Sakuma, I., Sato, Y., Barillot, C., Navab, N. (eds.) MICCAI 2013. LNCS, vol. 8149, pp. 606–613. Springer, Heidelberg (2013). https://doi.org/10.1007/978-3-642-40811-3_76

3D Convolutional Neural Network and Stacked Bidirectional Recurrent Neural Network for Alzheimer's Disease Diagnosis

Chiyu Feng[1], Ahmed Elazab[1], Peng Yang[1], Tianfu Wang[1],
Baiying Lei[1(✉)], and Xiaohua Xiao[2(✉)]

[1] National-Regional Key Technology Engineering Laboratory for Medical
Ultrasound, Guangdong Key Laboratory for Biomedical Measurements
and Ultrasound Imaging, School of Biomedical Engineering,
Health Science Center, Shenzhen University, Shenzhen, China
leiby@szu.edu.cn
[2] The Affiliated Hospital of Shenzhen University, Shenzhen, China
tu_xi8888@163.com

Abstract. Alzheimer's disease (AD) is the leading cause of dementia in the elderly and the number of sufferers increases year by year. Early detection of AD is highly beneficial to provide timely treatment and possible medication, which is still an open challenge. To meet challenges of the early diagnosis of AD and its early stage (e.g., progressive MCI (pMCI) and stable MCI (sMCI)) in clinical practice, we present a novel deep learning framework in this paper. The proposed framework exploits the merits of 3D convolutional neural network (CNN) and stacked bidirectional recurrent neural network (SBi-RNN). Specifically, we devise simple 3D-CNN architecture to obtain the deep feature representation from magnetic resonance imaging (MRI) and positron emission tomography (PET) images, respectively. We further apply SBi-RNN on the local deep cascaded and flattened descriptors for performance boosting. Extensive experiments are performed on the ADNI dataset to investigate the effectiveness of the proposed method. Our method achieves an average accuracy of 94.29% for AD vs. normal classification (NC), 84.66% of pMCI vs. NC and 64.47% sMCI vs. NC, which outperforms the related algorithms. Also, our method is simpler and more compact compared with the existing methods with complex preprocessing and feature engineering processes.

Keywords: Alzheimer's disease · 3D-CNN · SBi-RNN · Multi-modality

1 Introduction

Alzheimer's disease (AD) is a progressive neurodegenerative disorder, which leads to dementia in the elderly. Mild cognitive impairment (MCI) is a transitional state between normal control (NC) and dementia, which is divided into progressive MCI (pMCI) and stable MCI (sMCI) [1]. According to a report released by the international Alzheimer's Association, there are about 47 million AD patients worldwide, and this number reaches 131 million in 2050 [2]. However, there is no cure for AD. If AD can be diagnosed at an early stage, we can effectively prevent deterioration of patients.

© Springer Nature Switzerland AG 2018
I. Rekik et al. (Eds.): PRIME 2018, LNCS 11121, pp. 138–146, 2018.
https://doi.org/10.1007/978-3-030-00320-3_17

Therefore, early diagnosis of AD/MCI is quite meaningful for patient care and future treatment. Medical imaging techniques such as magnetic resonance images (MRI) and positron emission tomography (PET) are effective to boost the diagnosis performance by providing powerful imaging information. However, the early diagnosis of AD is not trivial even for health care professionals. Furthermore, early diagnosis of AD via human visual inspection is often subjective.

To tackle these issues, numerous automatic algorithms are proposed to discover the anatomical and functional neural changes related to AD [3]. For example, Liu *et al.* [4] extracted a set of latent features from regions of interest (ROI) of MRI and PET scans, which trained several multi-layer auto-encoders to combine multimodal features for classification. Gray *et al.* presented a multi-modal classification framework, which used coordinates from this joint embedding via pairwise similarity measures derived from random forest classifiers [5]. And Zhang *et al.* propose a Multi-Layer Multi-View Classification approach, which regards the multi-view input as the first layer, and constructs a latent representation to explore the complex correlation between the features and class labels [6]. However, these traditional methods of extracting features are limited since they require the complex preprocessing. The information is loss due to feature reduction, which causes undesirable performance.

To solve this problem and further improve the performance, convolutional neural network (CNN) is an effective way. CNN has witnessed great success especially in natural image classification (e.g., ImageNet) and recently attracted much attention for AD diagnosis. For example, Li *et al.* reduced a 3 layers 3D CNN to perform AD diagnosis [7]. Liu *et al.* proposed a multi-modality classification algorithm based on cascaded CNNs model that combined the multi-level and multi-modal features for AD diagnosis [8]. Generally, CNN structure relies on stacked fully connected (FC) layers and SoftMax classifier after getting the feature maps. However, the FC layers always ignore the 2D information in the feature map.

To solve these problems, we take the feature map from CNN. The conventional method focused on extracting higher-level semantic information through a 2D CNN [8]. However, this feature map is very thin and long, because there are 400 features after 7 convolutional layers and the size of each one is only 8. To handle it, we use the sliding window of CNN to scan directly from one side to the other side. When using 2DCNN to process this feature map, the convolutional layer core will trace the feature along the long side, which loses a lot of information from short side. As a powerful neural sequence learning model, recurrent neural network (RNN) is designed for sequence analysis. It processes input sequence one element at a time. It maintains a "*state*" vector in their hidden units, which implicitly contains information of all past elements of the sequence [9]. Compared with RNN, bidirectional recurrent neural network (Bi-RNN) can access context in both directions [10] to explore the contextual information hidden in features. Using Bi-RNN not only can get more information, but also can avoid the influence of the choice of the scanning direction. Further, we also raise the depth of Bi-RNN by stacking the RNN cell in Bi-RNN which can help us to get deeper semantic information. For this reason, we use the stacked bidirectional recurrent neural network (SBi-RNN) instead of the traditional RNN. Similar to the scanner's line-by-line method in RNN, it can effectively discover more information by progressively learning.

In summary, we propose a new method for the diagnosis of AD based on 3D CNN and Bi-RNN. 3D CNN extracts the primary features of MRI and PET. The SBi-RNN is used to learn the advanced semantic features from 3D CNN. The experimental results show that the proposed method can achieve higher diagnosis accuracy than the existing methods.

2 Methodology

Figure 1 shows our novel, compact, and efficient framework based on 3D- CNN and SBi-RNN. We first obtain the preprocessed MRI and PET using two independent 3D CNNs. Next, we cascade the features of MRI and PET into a 2D feature map and normalize them. Last, we use SBi-RNN to get further advanced semantic information. The final diagnosis results are obtained by the SoftMax classifier.

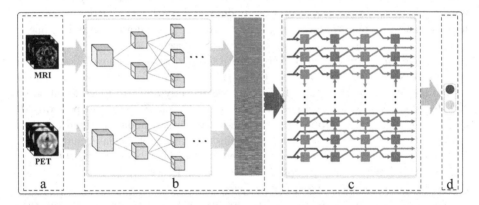

Fig. 1. The proposed framework for AD diagnosis. (a) MRI and PET input; (b) Dual CNN architecture to get deep and normalized feature map; (c) SBi-RNN for feature enhancement; (d) Classification by SoftMax classifier.

2.1 Data Preprocessing

Firstly, we preprocess the MRI images by applying the typical procedures of Anterior Commissure (AC)–Posterior Commissure (PC) correction, skull-stripping, and cere-bellum removal. Then, we segment the anatomical MRI images into three tissue types of gray matter (GM), white matter (WM), and cerebrospinal fluid (CSF) by using FAST in FSL package7. Finally, we use a brain atlas already aligned with the MNI coordinate space for normalizing the three tissues of MRI data into a standard space. It has been confirmed that GM is highly related to AD/MCI compared with WM and CSF [11]. In this regard, we choose GM for feature representation. For PET images, they are rigidly registered to the respective MRI. Same as [12], we downsample both GM density maps and PET images into $64 \times 64 \times 64$ voxels, which reduces computational time and memory cost without sacrificing the classification accuracy.

2.2   Feature Learning with 3D CNN

CNN is a special multi-layer neural networks, which are trained with the backpropagation algorithm. However, most of CNN architectures are designed for 2D image, which is inefficient to encode the spatial information of 3D image. Therefore, we use the 3D convolution kernel. The 3D convolution kernel is built by alternatively stacking convolutional sub-sampling layers that can hierarchically learn the multi-level features. Finally, we use FC and SoftMax classifier for classification.

Convolutional layer convolves the input image with the learned kernel filters. Then, we add a bias term in the convolutional and a non-linear activation function. In this work, we use the ReLU as activation function. Finally, we can get a series of feature maps by each filter. The 3D convolutional operation is defined as:

$$u_{kj}^l(x,y,z) = \sum_{\delta_x}\sum_{\delta_y}\sum_{\delta_z} F_k^{l-1}\left(x+\delta_x, y+\delta_y, z+\delta_z\right) \times W_{kj}^l\left(\delta_x, \delta_y, \delta_z\right), \quad (1)$$

where x, y and z denote the voxel positions for a given 3D data. $W_{kj}^l(\delta_x, \delta_y, \delta_z)$ is the j-th 3D kernel weight, which connects the k-th feature map of the l-1 layer and the j-th feature map of the l layer. F_k^{l-1} is the k-th feature map of the l-1 layer, the $\delta_x, \delta_y, \delta_z$ are the kernel size corresponding to the x, y and z, respectively. The $u_{kj}^l(x,y,z)$ is the convolutional response of the kernel filter. After convolution, ReLU is used to the activation function of each convolution layer:

$$F_j^l(x,y,z) = \max\left(0, b_j^l + \sum_k u_{jk}^l(x,y,z)\right), \quad (2)$$

where b_j^l is the bias term from the j-th feature map of the l-th layer. The $F_j^l(x,y,z)$ is obtained by summation of the response maps of different convolution kernels of the j-th 3D feature map.

After each convolutional layer, we add a pooling layer such as average or maximum pooling. In this paper, we use max pooling to obtain more compact and efficient features. Max pooling replaces each cube with their maximum to reduce the feature map along the spatial dimensions. It can keep the most important feature for discrimination. In addition, the features become more compact from low-level to high-level, which can achieve the robustness against some variations.

Apart from alternatively stacking 6 convolutional layers and 6 pooling layers, the features of MRI and PET will be cascaded and flattened followed by 2 FC layers. Here, we extract features from the last convolutional layer. All the features from the FC layer are flattened into 1D vector. Finally, the features are imported in SoftMax classifier and get the final result.

2.3   SBi-RNN Based Classification

Normally, the high-level reasoning in the CNN depends on FC layers. However, the FC layer just simply connects all neurons, which are unable to fuse all the information effectively. Therefore, we use the SBi-RNN instead of traditional FC layer.

In a CNN model, layers are connected between layers. However, nodes between hidden layers in RNN are linked, and the input of the hidden layer includes not only the output of the input layer, but also the output of the hidden layer of the previous node. Mathematically, each node is defined as s_t, which can be expressed as:

$$s_t = f(Ux_t + Ws_{t-1}), \tag{3}$$

where x_t is the input of the t-th unit, U is the weight from the input layer to the hidden layer, and W is the connection weight from previous unit to current unit. The $f(\cdot)$ is activation function. We choose the *tanh* as the activation function in this paper. After getting all the s_t, SoftMax is used to get the final result (o_t):

$$o_t = SoftMax(Vs_t). \tag{4}$$

The V is the weights from the hidden layer to the output layer. Then, the calculation process for the entire RNN is illustrated in the following sections.

2.3.1 Forward Calculation

For an input x of length T, the network has I input unit, hidden units, and K output units. Defining x_i^t as the i-th input at time t. Let a_j^t and b_j^t represent the input of network element j at time t and the output of the nonlinear identifiable activation function of element j at time t, respectively. For the complete sequence of implicit units, we can start with $t = 1$ and get it by recursively calling the following formula:

$$a_h^t = \sum_{i=1}^{I} w_{ih}x_i^t + \sum_{h'=1}^{H} w_{h'h}b_{h'}^{t-1}, \tag{5}$$

$$b_h^t = \theta(a_h^t). \tag{6}$$

Meanwhile, the output unit for the network can also be calculated as:

$$a_k^t = \sum_{h=1}^{H} w_{hk}b_n^t. \tag{7}$$

2.3.2 Backward Calculation

For RNNs, the objective function depends on the activation function of the hidden layer (not only by its effect on the output layer, but also on its impact on the next time step hidden layer), that is:

$$\frac{\partial o}{\partial a_j^t} = \theta'(a_h^t)\left(\sum_{k=1}^{K} \delta_k^t w_{hk} + \sum_{h'=1}^{H} \delta_{h'}^{t+1} w_{hh'}\right). \tag{8}$$

Finally, the weights of the inputs and outputs of the hidden layer units are the same in each step. We sum this sequence to obtain the derivative of each network weight:

$$\frac{\partial o}{\partial w_{ij}} = \sum_{t=1}^{T} \frac{\partial o}{\partial a_j^t} \frac{\partial a_j^t}{\partial w_{ij}} = \sum_{t=1}^{T} \delta_j^t b_j^t, \qquad (9)$$

2.3.3   Constitute SBi-RNN

The basic idea of a Bi-RNN assumes that each training sequence is forward and backward via two RNNs, which are connected to one output layer. This structure provides complete previous and future contextual information for each point in the output layer. The SBi-RNN is used to obtain deeper information by superimposing a basic RNN in both forward and backward RNN of Bi-RNN. For the hidden layer of SBi-RNN, forward calculation is the same as RNN except that the input sequence is opposite to the two hidden layers. The output layer does not update until all hidden sequences have processed all the input sequences. SBi-RNN's backward estimation is similar to RNN's inverse propagation through time except that all output layer δ terms are first calculated and then returned to two hidden layers in different directions.

3   Experimental Setting and Results

3.1   Dataset and Implementation

In this paper, we use the Alzheimer's Disease Neuroimaging Initiative (ADNI) publicly available dataset (http://adni.loni.usc.edu/). We only consider the baseline MRI data and 18-Fluoro-DeoxyGlucose PET data acquired from 93 AD, 76pMCI, 128sMCI and 100 NC. To alleviate the overfitting problem, ten percent neurons are randomly cut off

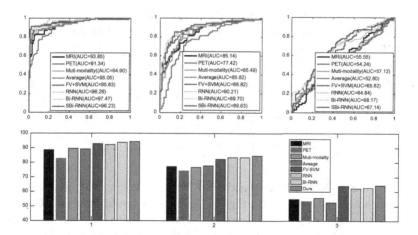

Fig. 2. Results of different methods and modalities. The upper half is the ROC curve for different classification tasks, the under is the Acc bar chart results of the different classification.

during training. In order to speed up training, we use root mean square prop to train SBi-RNN. For evaluating the classification performance, we use different performance metrics. These metrics include the accuracy (Acc), the area under receive operation curve (AUC), the sensitivity (Sen) and the specificity (Spec) to compare the experiments. Here, 10-fold evaluation is performed 10 times to avoid any bias. All the experiments are conducted on a computer with GPU NVIDIA TITAN Xt and implemented using Keras library in Python.

3.2 Results

Firstly, we test the results of the proposed method based on the different modalities. For the single modality, we use a 14 layers CNN architecture to get the deep features. Then, the flatten feature is utilized as the input of the SBi-RNN, while the output is the final prediction result. For the multi-modality, we add the fusion and flattening between CNN and SBi-RNN to maximize the use of data.

The results are listed in Table 1 and the receivers of curves (ROC) are illustrated in Fig. 2. From these results, it is clear that the multi-modality performs better than single modality. The results also show that our MRI has better result than PET. Because the MRI can capture structural information of brain regions and the information of structural and subject's mental state at the time of testing may not be unified.

Then, we compare the proposed multimodal classification algorithm by SBi-RNN to other multimodal methods. One combination method is the direct concatenation, which is the baseline method. The combination method via the average between two modal features can enhance the multi-modal representation. We use the fisher vector (FV) to encode the feature and use support victor machine (SVM) as classifier, which can get advanced semantic information from two modalities [13].

Table 1. Comparison of classification performance on different methods (%).

Method	AD vs. NC			pMCI vs. NC			sMCI vs. NC		
	Acc	Sen	Spec	Acc	Sen	Spec	Acc	Sen	Spec
MRI	88.60	92.77	85.45	77.27	80.00	75.86	54.82	58.17	48.00
PET	82.78	83.33	82.52	74.43	70.13	77.78	53.51	55.61	40.63
Muti-modality	89.64	90.11	89.22	76.70	78.69	75.65	55.70	58.60	49.30
Average	89.13	90.00	88.35	77.84	80.33	76.52	52.63	56.76	45.00
FV-SVM	92.75	94.38	91.35	82.39	**83.58**	81.65	64.04	65.54	**61.25**
RNN	92.23	**97.56**	88.29	83.52	79.01	**87.37**	62.28	68.10	56.25
Bi-RNN	93.76	95.51	92.31	83.52	81.33	85.15	62.72	68.38	56.76
Ours	**94.29**	96.59	**92.38**	**84.66**	83.56	85.44	**64.47**	**70.43**	48.41

Also, we use the RNN, Bi-RNN and SBi-RNN for encoding and classification. The results are shown in Table 1 and Fig. 2. From these results, the Full Connection performs better than each individual modality. The results also show that in our model, the MRI can have better results compared with the PET. Experiments show that our proposed method can get better result than other methods.

Finally, we compare the performance of the proposed method with other multi-modal methods, and the result is shown in Table 2. We find that our method can get better results than the existing methods especially [8], which uses 2D CNN to extract advanced semantic information from joint feature maps. The reason is that the SBi-RNN with progressive scans is more effective than direct convolution using 2D convolution kernels to identify the informative features.

Table 2. Algorithm comparison of the classification performance (%).

	Method	Data	Acc	Sen	Spec	AUC
AD vs. NC	Gray *et al.* 2013 [5]	51AD + 52NC	89.00	87.90	90.00	–
	Li *et al.* 2014 [7]	198AD + 229NC	92.87	–	–	89.82
	Liu *et al.* 2015 [4]	85AD + 77NC	91.40	92.32	90.42	87.09
	Liu *et al.* 2018 [8]	91AD + 100NC	93.26	92.55	**93.94**	95.68
	Ours	91AD + 100NC	**94.29**	**96.59**	92.38	**96.23**
pMCI vs. NC	Liu *et al.* 2018 [8]	76pMCI + 100NC	82.95	81.08	84.31	88.43
	Ours	76pMCI + 100NC	**84.66**	**83.56**	**85.44**	**89.63**
sMCI vs. NC	Liu *et al.* 2018 [8]	128sMCI + 100NC	64.04	63.07	**67.31**	67.05
	Ours	128sMCI + 100NC	**64.47**	**70.43**	48.41	**67.14**

4 Conclusion

In this paper, we propose a new hybrid framework for AD diagnosis based on 3D CNN and SBi-RNN. We get deep features via 3D-CNN from MRI and PET images and exploit Bi-RNN to obtain discriminative features. The focus of this paper is to explore obtaining the joint information after CNN feature extractions, which can be retrained to be more useful. The simple FC layer completely ignores 2D feature information. Our proposed method outperforms the related algorithm and achieves good results on the public ADNI dataset. In future, we will focus on improving the diagnostic performance for early MCI with more advanced deep learning techniques such as convolutional RNN.

References

1. Minati, L., Edginton, T., Bruzzone, M.G., Giaccone, G.: Current concepts in Alzheimer's disease: a multidisciplinary review. Am. J. Alzheimers Dis. Other Demen **24**, 95–121 (2009)
2. Herrera, A.C., Prince, M., Knapp, M., Karagiannidou, M., Guerchet, M.: World Alzheimer report 2016: improving healthcare for people with dementia. Coverage, quality and costs now and in the future (2016)
3. Lei, B., Yang, P., Wang, T., Chen, S., Ni, D.: Relational-regularized discriminative sparse learning for Alzheimer's disease diagnosis. IEEE Trans. Cybern. **47**, 1102–1113 (2017)
4. Liu, S., et al.: ADNI: multimodal neuroimaging feature learning for multiclass diagnosis of Alzheimer's disease. IEEE Trans. Biomed. Eng. **62**, 1132–1140 (2015)

5. Gray, K.R., Aljabar, P., Heckemann, R.A., Hammers, A., Rueckert, D.: Random forest-based similarity measures for multi-modal classification of Alzheimer's disease. Neuroimage **65**, 167–175 (2013)
6. Zhanga, C., Adelic, E., Zhoua, T., Chena, X., Shena, D.: Multi-layer multi-view classification for Alzheimer's disease diagnosis (2018)
7. Li, R., et al.: Deep learning based imaging data completion for improved brain disease diagnosis. In: International Conference on Medical Image Computing and Computer-Assisted Intervention, pp. 305–312 (2014)
8. Liu, M., Cheng, D., Wang, K., Wang, Y.: Multi-modality cascaded convolutional neural networks for Alzheimer's disease diagnosis. Neuroinformatics, 1–14 (2018)
9. Lecun, Y., Bengio, Y., Hinton, G.: Deep learning. Nature **521**, 436 (2015)
10. Fan, B., Xie, L., Yang, S., Wang, L., Soong, F.K.: A deep bidirectional LSTM approach for video-realistic talking head. Multimedia Tools Appl. **75**, 5287–5309 (2016)
11. Liu, M., Zhang, D., Shen, D.: Ensemble sparse classification of Alzheimer's disease. Neuroimage **60**, 1106–1116 (2012)
12. Liu, M., Zhang, D., Shen, D.: Hierarchical fusion of features and classifier decisions for Alzheimer's disease diagnosis. Hum. Brain Mapp. **35**, 1305–1319 (2014)
13. Lei, B., Chen, S., Ni, D., Wang, T.: Discriminative learning for Alzheimer's disease diagnosis via canonical correlation analysis and multimodal fusion. Front. Aging Neurosci. **8**, 77 (2016)

Generative Adversarial Training for MRA Image Synthesis Using Multi-contrast MRI

Sahin Olut[✉], Yusuf H. Sahin, Ugur Demir, and Gozde Unal

ITU Vision Laboratory, Istanbul Technical University, Istanbul, Turkey
oluts@itu.edu.tr

Abstract. Magnetic Resonance Angiography (MRA) has become an essential MR contrast for imaging and evaluation of vascular anatomy and related diseases. MRA acquisitions are typically ordered for vascular interventions, whereas in typical scenarios, MRA sequences can be absent in the patient scans. This motivates the need for a technique that generates inexistent MRA from existing MR multi-contrast, which could be a valuable tool in retrospective subject evaluations and imaging studies. We present a generative adversarial network (GAN) based technique to generate MRA from T1- and T2-weighted MRI images, for the first time to our knowledge. To better model the representation of vessels which the MRA inherently highlights, we design a loss term dedicated to a faithful reproduction of vascularities. To that end, we incorporate steerable filter responses of the generated and reference images as a loss term. Extending the well-established generator-discriminator architecture based on the recent PatchGAN model with the addition of steerable filter loss, the proposed steerable GAN (sGAN) method is evaluated on the large public database IXI. Experimental results show that the sGAN outperforms the baseline GAN method in terms of an overlap score with similar PSNR values, while it leads to improved visual perceptual quality.

Keywords: MR angiography · GANs · Steerable filters
Image synthesis

1 Introduction

Due to recent improvements in hardware and software technologies of Magnetic Resonance Imaging (MRI) the use of MRI has become ubiquitous in examination and evaluation of patients in hospitals. Non-Contrast Enhanced (NCE) time-of-flight (TOF) MR Angiography (MRA) has become an established modality for evaluating vascular diseases throughout intracranial, peripheral, abdominal, renal and thoracic imaging procedures [3,8]. In a majority of the MRI examinations, T1- and T2-weighted MRI contrast sequences are the main structural imaging sequences. Unless specifically required by endovascular concerns, MRA images are often absent due to lower cost and shorter scan time considerations.

© Springer Nature Switzerland AG 2018
I. Rekik et al. (Eds.): PRIME 2018, LNCS 11121, pp. 147–154, 2018.
https://doi.org/10.1007/978-3-030-00320-3_18

When a need for a retrospective inspection of vascular structures arises, generation of the missing MRA contrast based on the available contrast could be a valuable tool in the clinical examinations.

Recent advances in convolutional neural networks (CNNs), particularly deep generative networks have started to be successfully applied to reconstruction [16], image generation and synthesis problems [1] in medical imaging. The main purpose of this work is to employ those image generative networks to synthesize a new MRI contrast from the other existing multi-modal MRI contrast. Our method relies on well-established idea of generative adversarial networks (GANs) [2]. The two main contributions of this paper can be summarized as follows:

- We provide a GAN framework for generation of MRA images from T1 and T2 images, for the first time to our knowledge.
- We present a dedicated new loss term, which measures fidelity of directional features of vascular structures, for an increased performance in MRA generation.

2   Related Works

We refer to relatively recent techniques based on convolutional deep neural networks.

Image synthesis, which is also termed as image-to-image translation, relied on auto-encoders or its variations like denoising auto-encoders [14], variational auto-encoders [7]. Those techniques often lead to blurry or not adequately realistic outputs because of their classical loss measure, which is based on the standard Euclidean (L2) distance or L1 distance between the target and produced output images [12]. Generative adversarial networks (GANs) [2] address this issue by adding a discriminator to the network in order to perform adversarial training. The goal is to improve the performance of the generator in learning a realistic data distribution while trying to counterfeit the discriminator.

Recently, inspired from the Markov random fields [11], PatchGAN technique, which slides a window over the input image, evaluates and aggregates realness of patches, is proposed [4]. Isola *et al*'s PatchGAN method, also known as `pix2pix`, is applied to various problems in image-to-image translation.

Medical image synthesis is currently an emerging area of interest for application of the latest image generation techniques mentioned above. Wolterink *et al.* [15] synthesized Computed Tomography (CT) images from T1-weighted MR images using the cyclic loss proposed in the CycleGAN technique [17]. Nie and Trullo *et al.* [13] proposed a context-aware technique for medical image synthesis, where they added a gradient difference as a loss term to the generator to emphasize edges. Similarly, [1] utilized CycleGAN and `pix2pix` technique in generating T1-weighted MR contrast from T2-weighted MR contrast or vice versa.

In this paper, we create a pipeline for generating MR Angiography (MRA) contrast based on multiple MRI contrast, particularly the joint T1-weighted and T2-weighted MRI using `pix2pix` framework. As MRA imaging mainly targets visualization of vasculature, we modify the `pix2pix` in order to adapt it to the MRA generation by elucidating vessel structures through a new loss term in its objective function. We are inspired from the **steerable filters** which arose from the idea of orientation selective excitations in the human visual cortex. Steerable filters involve a set of detectors at different orientations [9]. In our work, the addition of the steerable filter responses to the GAN objective tailors the generator features to both reveal and stay faithful to vessel-like structures, as will be demonstrated.

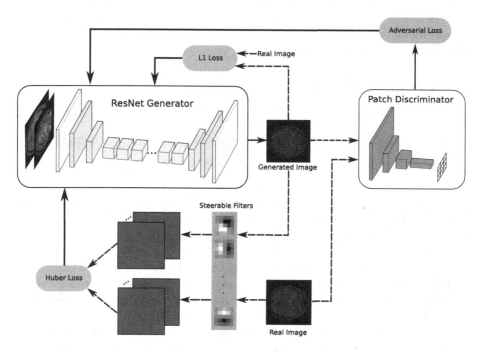

Fig. 1. The sGAN architecture. ResNet generator takes concatenation of T1- and T2-weighted MR images and transforms them into an MRA image slice.

3   Method

The proposed method for generating a mapping from T1- and T2- weighted MRI to MRA images, which is named as steerable filter GAN (sGAN), is illustrated in Fig. 1. The generator and the discriminator networks are conditioned on T1- and T2-weighted MRI, which are fed to the network as two channels of the input. The details of the proposed architecture are described next.

3.1   Network Architecture

As illustrated in Fig. 1, our architecture consists of a generator and a discriminator network. A generator network which is similar to architecture in [6] is adopted for our setting. In generator network, we used 3 down-sampling layers with strided convolutions of stride 2, which is followed by 9 residual blocks. In residual blocks, the channel size of input and output are the same. At the up-sampling part, 3 convolutions with fractional strides are utilized.

In a GAN setting, the adversarial loss obtained from the discriminator network D forces the generator network G to produce more realistic images, while it updates itself to distinguish real images from synthetic images. As shown in [4], the Markovian discriminator (PatchGAN) architecture leads to more refined outputs with detailed texture as both the input is divided to patches and the network evaluates patches instead of the whole image at once. Our discriminator architecture consists of 3 down-sampling layers with strides of 2 which are followed by 2 convolutional layers.

3.2   Objective Functions

In sGAN, we employ three different objective functions to optimize parameters of our network.

Adversarial loss, which is based on the GAN framework, is defined as:

$$\mathcal{L}_{GAN}(G, D) = \mathbb{E}_{x,y}[\log D(x, y)] + \mathbb{E}_x[\log(1 - D(x, G(x)))] \qquad (1)$$

where G is generator network and D is discriminator network, x is the two channel input consisting of T1-weighted and T2-weighted MR images, $G(x)$ is the generated MRA image, and y is the reference (target) MRA image, respectively. We utilize the PatchGAN approach, where similarly, the adversarial loss evaluates whether its input patch is real or synthetically generated [4]. The generator is trained $\mathcal{L}_{adv}$ which consists of the second term in Eq. 1.

Reconstruction loss helps the network to capture global appearance characteristics as well as relatively coarse features of the target image in the reconstructed image. For that purpose, we utilize the $L1$ distance, which is we term as $\mathcal{L}_{rec} = ||y - \hat{y}||_1$, where y is the target, $\hat{y} = G(x)$ is the produced output.

Steerable filter response loss is another metric in our work for better MR Angiography (MRA) generation. Since MRA specifically targets imaging of the vascular anatomy, faithful reproduction of vessel structures is of utmost importance. We design additional loss term for emphasizing vesselness properties by incorporating with steerable filters by comparing filters responses of target image and the synthesized output through a Huber loss function 3:

$$\mathcal{L}_{steer} = \frac{1}{K} \sum_{k=1}^{K} \rho(f_k * y, f_k * \hat{y}) \qquad (2)$$

where $*$ denotes the convolution operator, K is the number of filters, f_k is the kth steerable filter kernel. The Huber function with its parameter set to unity is defined as:

$$\rho(x, y) = \begin{cases} (x - y)^2 * 0.5 & if \ |x - y| \leq 1 \\ |x - y| - 0.5 & otherwise \end{cases} \qquad (3)$$

Fig. 2. Top two rows: generated steerable filter kernel weights (5 × 5); Bottom row: two examples of steerable filter responses (k = 7, 18) to the input MRA image on the left.

Figure 2 depicts the K = 20 steerable filters of size 5 × 5. We also show sample filter responses to an MRA image to illustrate different characteristics highlighted by the steerable filters.

In the sGAN setting, the overall objective is defined as follows:

$$\mathcal{L} = \lambda_1 \mathcal{L}_{adv} + \lambda_2 \mathcal{L}_{rec} + \lambda_3 \mathcal{L}_{steer} \tag{4}$$

where $\mathcal{L}_{adv}, \mathcal{L}_{rec}, \mathcal{L}_{steer}$ refer to Eqs. 1, 3.2 and 2, respectively, with corresponding weights $\lambda_1, \lambda_2, \lambda_3$.

4 Experiments and Results

4.1 Dataset and Experiment Settings

We used 440 subjects from IXI dataset (http://brain-development.org/ixi-dataset). 400 images used for training, randomly selected 40 images are used for testing. The parameters used in the model are: learning rate 0.0002, loss term constants $\lambda_1 = 0.8$, $\lambda_2 = 0.005$ and $\lambda_3 = 0.145$ in Eq. 4.

4.2 Evaluation Metrics

We utilize two different measures for performance evaluation. First one is the peak signal-to-noise ratio (PSNR) which is defined by $10 \log_{10} \frac{(\max y)^2}{\frac{1}{n} \sum_i^n (y_i - \hat{y}_i)^2}$, where n is the number of pixels in an image. The PSNR is calculated between the original MRA and the generated MRA images.

In the MRA modality generation, it is important to synthesize vessel structures correctly. We utilize Dice score as the second measure in order to highlight the fidelity of the captured vascular anatomy in the synthesized MRA images. The Dice score is defined by $\frac{2|y \cap \hat{y}|}{|y|+|\hat{y}|}$. In order to calculate the Dice score, the segmentation maps are produced by an automatic vessel segmentation algorithm presented in [5] over both the original MRA images and the generated MRA images using the same set of parameters in the segmentation method.

4.3   Quantitative and Qualitative Results

To our knowledge, no previous works attempted synthetic MRA generation. To evaluate our results, we compare the generated MRA images corresponding to the baseline, which is the PatchGAN with ResNet architecture against the sGAN, which is the baseline with added steerable loss term. The PSNR and Dice scores are tabulated in Table 1.

Table 1. Performance measures (mean PSNR and mean Dice scores) on the test set: first row corresponds to the baseline PatchGAN; second row shows the sGAN results.

Method	PSNR (dB)	Dice score (%)
Baseline: $\mathcal{L}_{adv} + \mathcal{L}_{rec}$	29.40	74.8
sGAN: $\mathcal{L}_{adv} + \mathcal{L}_{rec} + \mathcal{L}_{steer}$	**29.51**	**76.8**

We show sample visual results of representative slices in Fig. 3. Sample 3D visual results are given as surface renderings of segmentation maps in Fig. 3.

5   Discussion and Conclusion

The presented sGAN method is a data-driven approach to generation of MRA contrast, from the multi-contrast T1- and T2-weighted MRI, which are based on spin-lattice and spin-spin relaxation effects. The sGAN relies on the recent popular pix2pix framework as the baseline. In the adaptation of the baseline method to MRA generation, the steerable-filter response based loss term included in the sGAN method highlights the directional features of vessel structures. This leads to an enhanced smoothing along vessels while improving their continuity. This is demonstrated qualitatively through visual inspection. In quantitative evaluations, the sGAN performs similarly with a slight increase (statistically insignificant) in PSNR values compared to those of the baseline. However, it is well-known that PSNR measure does not necessarily correspond to perceptual quality in image evaluations [10,12]. In terms of the vascular segmentation maps extracted from the generated MRAs and the original MRA, the sGAN improves the overlap scores by 2% against the baseline. This is a desirable output, as the MRA targets imaging of vascular anatomy. The proposed sGAN has the potential to be useful in retrospective studies of existing MR image databases that lack MRA contrast. Furthermore, after extensive validation, it could lead to cost and time effectiveness where it is needed, by construction of the MRA based on relatively more common sequences such as T1- and T2-weighted MR contrast.

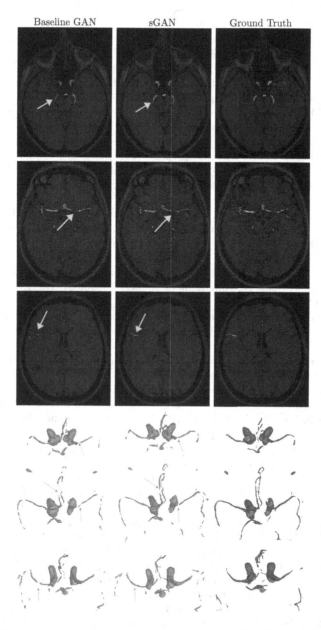

Fig. 3. Top three rows: visual comparison of generated 2D MRA axial slices to the original MRA slices by both the baseline and the sGAN methods.

Bottom three rows: visual comparison of segmentation maps over generated MRA to those over the original MRA in surface rendering format using both the baseline and the sGAN methods. Arrows indicate the increased fidelity in vessel structure with new loss term.

References

1. Dar, S.U.H., Yurt, M., Karacan, L., Erdem, A., Erdem, E., Çukur, T.: Image synthesis in multi-contrast MRI with conditional generative adversarial networks. arXiv preprint arXiv:1802.01221 (2018)
2. Goodfellow, I., et al.: Generative adversarial nets. In: Advances in Neural Information Processing Systems, pp. 2672–2680 (2014)
3. Hartung, M.P., Grist, T.M., François, C.J.: Magnetic resonance angiography: current status and future directions. J. Cardiovasc. Magn. Reson. **13**(1), 19 (2011)
4. Isola, P., Zhu, J.Y., Zhou, T., Efros, A.A.: Image-to-image translation with conditional adversarial networks. arXiv preprint (2017)
5. Jerman, T., Pernuš, F., Likar, B., Špiclin, Ž.: Enhancement of vascular structures in 3D and 2D angiographic images. IEEE Trans. Med. Imaging **35**(9), 2107–2118 (2016)
6. Johnson, J., Alahi, A., Fei-Fei, L.: Perceptual losses for real-time style transfer and super-resolution. In: European Conference on Computer Vision (2016)
7. Kingma, D.P., Welling, M.: Auto-encoding variational Bayes. arXiv preprint arXiv:1312.6114 (2013)
8. Kiruluta, A.J., González, R.G.: Magnetic resonance angiography: physical principles and applications. In: Handbook of Clinical Neurology, vol. 135, pp. 137–149. Elsevier (2016)
9. Knutsson, H., Wilson, R., Granlund, G.: Anisotropic nonstationary image estimation and its applications: part i-restoration of noisy images. IEEE Trans. Commun. **31**(3), 388–397 (1983)
10. Ledig, C., et al.: Photo-realistic single image super-resolution using a generative adversarial network. arXiv preprint (2016)
11. Li, C., Wand, M.: Precomputed real-time texture synthesis with Markovian generative adversarial networks. In: Leibe, B., Matas, J., Sebe, N., Welling, M. (eds.) ECCV 2016. LNCS, vol. 9907, pp. 702–716. Springer, Cham (2016). https://doi.org/10.1007/978-3-319-46487-9_43
12. Mathieu, M., Couprie, C., LeCun, Y.: Deep multi-scale video prediction beyond mean square error. arXiv preprint arXiv:1511.05440 (2015)
13. Nie, D., et al.: Medical image synthesis with context-aware generative adversarial networks. In: Descoteaux, M., Maier-Hein, L., Franz, A., Jannin, P., Collins, D.L., Duchesne, S. (eds.) MICCAI 2017. LNCS, vol. 10435, pp. 417–425. Springer, Cham (2017). https://doi.org/10.1007/978-3-319-66179-7_48
14. Vincent, P., Larochelle, H., Bengio, Y., Manzagol, P.A.: Extracting and composing robust features with denoising autoencoders. In: Proceedings of the 25th International Conference on Machine Learning, pp. 1096–1103. ACM (2008)
15. Wolterink, J.M., Dinkla, A.M., Savenije, M.H.F., Seevinck, P.R., van den Berg, C.A.T., Išgum, I.: Deep MR to CT synthesis using unpaired data. In: Tsaftaris, S.A., Gooya, A., Frangi, A.F., Prince, J.L. (eds.) SASHIMI 2017. LNCS, vol. 10557, pp. 14–23. Springer, Cham (2017). https://doi.org/10.1007/978-3-319-68127-6_2
16. Yang, G., et al.: Dagan: deep de-aliasing generative adversarial networks for fast compressed sensing MRI reconstruction. IEEE Trans. Med. Imaging **37**(6), 1310–1321 (2017)
17. Zhu, J.Y., Park, T., Isola, P., Efros, A.A.: Unpaired image-to-image translation using cycle-consistent adversarial networks. arXiv preprint arXiv:1703.10593 (2017)

Diffusion MRI Spatial Super-Resolution Using Generative Adversarial Networks

Enes Albay[(⊠)], Ugur Demir, and Gozde Unal

Istanbul Technical University, Istanbul 34469, Turkey
{albay,ugurdemir,gozde.unal}@itu.edu.tr

Abstract. Spatial resolution is one of the main constraints in diffusion Magnetic Resonance Imaging (dMRI). Increasing resolution leads to a decrease in SNR of the diffusion images. Acquiring high resolution images without reducing SNRs requires larger magnetic fields and long scan times which are typically not applicable in the clinical settings. Currently feasible voxel size is around 1 mm^3 for a diffusion image. In this paper, we present a deep neural network based post-processing method to increase the spatial resolution in diffusion MRI. We utilize Generative Adversarial Networks (GANs) to obtain a higher resolution diffusion MR image in the spatial dimension from lower resolution diffusion images. The obtained real data results demonstrate a first time proof of concept that GANs can be useful in super-resolution problem of diffusion MRI for upscaling in the spatial dimension.

Keywords: Magnetic resonance imaging (MRI)
Diffusion MRI (dMRI) · Super resolution
Generative adversarial networks (GANs)

1 Introduction

Water molecules undergo random movement and diffuse in an environment due to second law of thermodynamics. Diffusion phenomenon enables us to map fibrous substances using principles of magnetic resonance imaging (MRI). Diffusion magnetic resonance imaging (dMRI) takes advantage of signal attenuation that takes place due to diffusion of water molecules in a tissue that is being imaged. Although the signal attenuates isotropically in a free water environment, the signal shows varying attenuations in a restricted environment. This gives an opportunity of in vivo imaging of the internal structure of the human brain white matter, which contains fibrous material that restricts water molecules movements in some directions while water molecules move freely in other directions [10].

Even though dMRI allows microscopic imaging of the white matter at very high magnetic fields, spatial resolution of dMRI is restricted clinically because with the current technology, very high magnetic fields cannot be used ante-mortem. Furthermore, long scan times are not clinically feasible for microscopic

---

E. Albay and U. Demir—Equal contribution.

I. Rekik et al. (Eds.): PRIME 2018, LNCS 11121, pp. 155–163, 2018.
https://doi.org/10.1007/978-3-030-00320-3_19

resolution. At lower magnetic fields, signal to noise ratio (SNR) becomes problematic for small voxel sizes. Currently, for diffusion image volumes, clinically applicable voxel size is about 1 mm^3 [11], which is relatively coarse with respect to underlying microstructure of brain tissue. Diameter of neuronal axons in brain white matter is at most 30 µm [7], therefore, a typical voxel contains thousands of fiber populations, possibly lying along different directions with crossings, splaying, or kissing architectures. Hence, increasing both spatial resolution and angular resolution of dMRI using post-processing techniques is desirable and would aid in post-analysis of dMRI data.

In this paper, we present a post-processing method to generate higher spatial resolution dMRI volumes based on an end-to-end generative adversarial network (GAN) framework [5]. GANs learn a mapping from low resolution diffusion MRI data to synthesize a high resolution counterpart. Its main difference from conventional methods is that GANs learn a non-linear model from pairs of low resolution-high resolution data rather than performing a blind interpolation.

2　Related Works

Only a few spatial super resolution methods for diffusion MRI were presented in the literature. Conventional methods for super resolution are typically based on up-sampling with interpolation of low resolution data. An early super resolution approach to diffusion data is based on combination of two shifted images to create an up-sampled image [14], which led to blurry results. Alternatively, a track density approach was presented to obtain super resolution in white matter fiber tracts based on tractography information, however, this method does not up-sample the underlying spatial structure of the diffusion images [1]. A Markov chain Monte Carlo method, the Metropolis-Hastings algorithm is utilized by [19] to create a generative model of local information and sharpens images according to local structure while increasing spatial resolution. This is different from our approach as it does not actually directly learn the data distribution. A recently suggested method proposes using RGB image enhancement method with diffusion images, however, not leading to clear results [18]. It is observed that diffusion weighted images are blurry and ODFs are corrupted with respect to the ground truth data. Recent studies on texture synthesis have shown that convolutional neural networks and adversarial training can be successfully applied to super-resolve images at high upscale factors [3,12]. This was the motivation of our method, which is presented next.

3　Method

We introduce a deep GAN based single slice super-resolution model that takes a down-sampled low resolution dMRI axial slice I_{LR} and synthesizes its high resolution counterpart $\hat{I}_{HR}$. Each down-sampled axial slice from a brain volume is upscaled to the desired resolution with a certain scale factor through bi-cubic interpolation, which is called I_{LR}^{bc}. In this paper, we exemplify the spatial super resolution model with an up-sampling factor of two. The generative model takes I_{LR}^{bc}, and tries to expose the high frequency details by exploring the context of low-resolution image. The trained network resolves the blurriness and generates sharp images filled with estimated missing details. Overall flow of our method is depicted in Fig. 1.

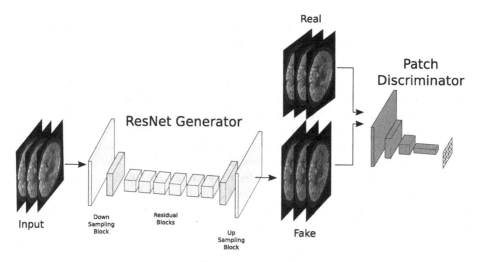

Fig. 1. General structure of architecture. Input slices are x2 upscaled by bi-cubic interpolation. Generator network takes input I_{LR}^{bc} images and synthesizes "fake" high-resolution slices I_{HR}. Discriminator network evaluates artificially generated slices and produces an adversarial loss.

During training of the generative model, an adversarial training [5] approach is used in order to produce more realistic looking outputs. Training procedure intends to minimize the combination of an adversarial loss produced by the discriminator network, and a pixel-wise reconstruction loss (an L2 Loss) to conditionally generate samples from the high resolution image distribution. Details of this procedure are described next.

3.1 Generative Adversarial Networks

GANs have been used to figure out distribution of the input data by learning a mapping from a noise variable to the data space [5]. Recent studies show that once the distribution is learned, the model can be used to generate realistic looking samples [6,12]. Apart from sample generation, GANs are also used to learn a mapping between contextually paired two images [6]. In our super-resolution problem, low resolution image I_{LR}^{bc} is given as a condition to the generator and it is expected that our model learns a mapping G that translates I_{LR}^{bc} to I_{HR}.

There are two different neural networks in the adversarial training phase. The generative network G corresponds to mapping function between the input and the output. The purpose of the discriminator network D is distinguishing the real images from the artificially synthesized ones. While the network G aims to fool D, at the same time, D is trained to improve its accuracy. This optimization problem corresponds to a minimax game, which can be formulated as:

$$\min_{\theta_G} \max_{\theta_D} E[\log D(I_{HR})] + E[\log(1 - D(G(I_{LR}^{bc})))]. \tag{1}$$

As long as D successfully classifies its input, G benefits from the gradient provided by the D network via its adversarial loss.

Generator Network. The architecture of the generative network is ResNet, which is composed by following the guidelines described in [8]. It consists of down-sampling layers, residual blocks and up-sampling layers. There are two down-sampling layers and each one consists of a convolution layer with stride set to 2, batch normalization layer and Leaky ReLU (LReLU) activation. There are six residual blocks in the architecture. The up-sampling blocks recover spatial resolution of the activation maps in order to reach desired height and width for a slice. An up-sampling layer contains resized convolution [13], batch normalization and LReLU activation. Additionally, a 7×7 convolution layer with a Tanh activation is added to end of the network.

Discriminator Network. We utilize a patch based discriminator network PatchGAN [6] design which evaluates local patches of the generated image and gives an average score as a measure instead of considering the whole input. This gives more robust results than the vanilla GAN. Our patch based discriminator has 6 convolution layers followed by batch normalization except the first and the last layers. First 5 layers have LReLU activation and the last convolution layer pass its outputs to Sigmoid activation.

3.2 Training Objective

The main objective function is formed by combining the reconstruction and adversarial losses. The total loss function is optimized with back-propagation by using Adam optimizer [9]. L2 pixel-wise distances between the synthesized image and the ground truth are used as reconstruction loss. Even though it forces the network to produce a blurry output, it guides the network to roughly predict texture colors and low frequency details. Discriminator network computes a score according to quality of the generator outputs and, and is used as an adversarial loss as described in Eq. 1.

Total loss function defines the objective used in the training phase. Each component of the total loss function is governed by a coefficient λ:

$$\mathcal{L} = \lambda_1 \mathcal{L}_{rec} + \lambda_2 \mathcal{L}_{adv}. \tag{2}$$

where $\mathcal{L}_{rec}$ is reconstruction loss and $\mathcal{L}_{adv}$ is adversarial loss.

4   Experiments

4.1   Dataset

A diffusion dataset obtained from the Human Connectome Project (HCP) is used [17], where 29 diffusion subjects are randomly selected, and 25 are used to train the network and four of them are used in testing. HCP diffusion images are multi-shell, from which a single shell is extracted for each subject, which resulted in 108 diffusion volumes per subject. It was shown that the best b-value with an SNR of 30 for a non-diffusion weighted volume is between 3000 and 4000 s/mm^2 [16]. As the SNR of the HCP data is greater than 30 for the non-diffusion weighted volume, a single shell that has b-value 2000 s/mm^2 is selected. DIPY [4] library is used in all the analysis. All 108 diffusion-weighted volumes including non-diffusion weighted volumes are used in training the network, and the super resolution model is applied for up-sampling of all diffusion volumes in the test stage. In Fig. 2, sample visual results for diffusion-weighted images with I_{LR}^{bc}, $\hat{I}_{HR}$ and I_{HR} from a selected subject are shown. It can be seen that I_{LR}^{bc} is blurry and our network produces $\hat{I}_{HR}$ image with a success.

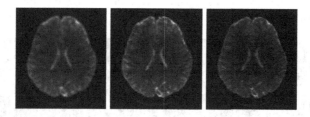

Fig. 2. Diffusion-weighted images for I_{LR}^{bc}, $\hat{I}_{HR}$ and I_{HR} of selected one subject, respectively.

4.2   SNR Comparison and FA (Fractional Anisotropy) Maps

SNR values of I_{LR}^{bc}, $\hat{I}_{HR}$ and I_{HR} are compared to measure how image generation introduced noise to diffusion data. The same ROI is used to compare each of the images. SNR values are computed according to most signal attenuation direction approach [2].

Corpus Callosum (CC) is segmented automatically using fractional anisotropy (FA) values. SNR values in the CC region in x, y ad z-directions are compared for four different subjects in Table 1. It can be observed that $\hat{I}_{HR}$ shows closer SNR values to I_{HR} than those of the I_{LR}^{bc}.

As a second quantitative evaluation, FA histograms are calculated for each subject. Figure 3 depicts the histograms for two of the subjects. The histograms show that I_{HR} and $\hat{I}_{HR}$ exhibit very similar distributions for FA values that are greater than 0.4. Other two subjects displayed similar distributions.

The generated FA maps and color FA maps are shown in Fig. 4 for one of the subjects. It can be observed that I_{HR} and $\hat{I}_{HR}$ have similar FA and color FA

Table 1. SNR values comparison in the various directions. Generated output has similar SNR values with the ground truth.

	Subject 1			Subject 2			Subject 3			Subject 4		
Direction	I_{LR}^{bc}	$\hat{I}_{HR}$	I_{HR}	I_{LR}^{bc}	$\hat{I}_{HR}$	I_{HR}	I_{LR}^{bc}	$\hat{I}_{HR}$	I_{HR}	I_{LR}^{bc}	$\hat{I}_{HR}$	I_{HR}
b0	76.05	**62.64**	50.19	72.52	**63.04**	51.02	40.8	**37.26**	29.1	113.47	**92.87**	83.51
x-dir	12.15	**10.92**	9.2	12.39	**11.59**	10.3	5.99	**4.62**	5.24	16.08	**12.82**	14.29
y-dir	39.27	**32.14**	27.44	36.05	**34.21**	28.7	18.91	**16.35**	15.25	52.0	**43.43**	45.52
z-dir	33.75	**25.79**	25.99	31.44	**26.42**	27.95	18.78	**14.12**	15.89	56.57	**43.44**	49.33

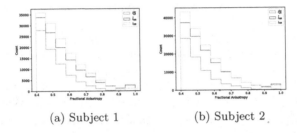

(a) Subject 1   (b) Subject 2

Fig. 3. FA distributions for two subjects. Green shows I_{HR} distribution, blue shows $\hat{I}_{HR}$ and red shows I_{LR}^{bc} (Color figure online)

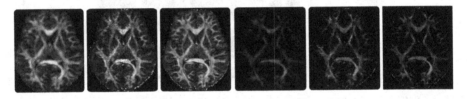

Fig. 4. Color FA maps are shown for I_{LR}^{bc}, $\hat{I}_{HR}$ and I_{HR} images respectively. Red indicates right-left axis, green for anterior-posterior axis and blue for inferior-superior axis diffusion. (Color figure online)

maps while the baseline bi-cubic interpolation introduces attenuation and blur in the FA maps.

4.3 Tensor and ODF Analysis

For further evaluation of the quality of the reconstructed high resolution diffusion volumes, the diffusion tensor models are constructed for $\hat{I}_{HR}$, I_{LR}^{bc} and I_{HR}. Figure 5 shows the results for one of the subjects. Similar tensor orientations and strengths at the crossing points of CC and corticospinal tracts (CST) are observed for the $\hat{I}_{HR}$ and I_{HR} of test subjects.

The orientation distribution functions (ODFs) are generated using constrained spherical deconvolution (CSD) [15] over the high resolution diffusion volumes. In Fig. 6, reconstructed ODFs are shown for one subject. It was observed that I_{LR}^{bc} has bigger artifactual side lobes.

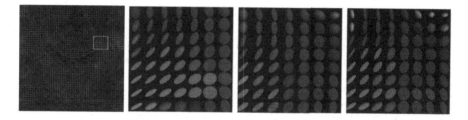

Fig. 5. Reconstructed tensors of diffusion image for one selected subject. Leftmost image is a general coronal view. Other views show I_{LR}^{bc}, $\hat{I}_{HR}$ and I_{HR} images at the area of crossing between CC and CST, respectively. Red indicates right-left axis, green for anterior-posterior axis and blue for inferior-superior axis diffusion. (Color figure online)

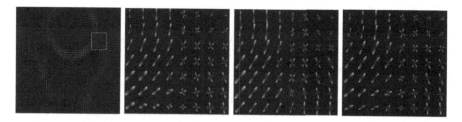

Fig. 6. Reconstructed ODFs over high resolution diffusion images. Leftmost image is a general coronal view. Crossing between CC and CST is shown in the yellow rectangle. Other views show ODFs of I_{LR}^{bc}, $\hat{I}_{HR}$ and I_{HR} images at the area of crossing between CC and CST, respectively. (Color figure online)

5 Conclusions

In this paper, for the first time, an end-to-end super-resolution method based on GANs is presented for dMRI data. This approach does not assume any model, does not simply interpolate existing data but learns a data-driven generative mapping. The experimental quantitative results such as distribution of FA values and SNR as well as qualitative results such as FA maps, color FA maps, reconstructed tensors and ODFs demonstrate that GANs produce promising results to create higher resolution data using low resolution dMRI input. Although our work shows a preliminary proof of concept with GANs to increase the spatial resolution of dMRI twofold, our future work investigates further tuning of networks with larger training sets, increasing the resolution to triple, quadruple, or higher scale factors, and extending our work to angular up-sampling.

References

1. Calamante, F., Tournier, J.D., Heidemann, R.M., Anwander, A., Jackson, G.D., Connelly, A.: Track density imaging (TDI): validation of super resolution property. Neuroimage **56**(3), 1259–1266 (2011)
2. Descoteaux, M., Deriche, R., Le Bihan, D., Mangin, J.F., Poupon, C.: Multiple q-shell diffusion propagator imaging. Med. Image Anal. Front. Neuroinformatics **15**(4), 603–621 (2011)
3. Dong, C., Loy, C.C., He, K., Tang, X.: Learning a deep convolutional network for image super-resolution. In: Fleet, D., Pajdla, T., Schiele, B., Tuytelaars, T. (eds.) ECCV 2014. LNCS, vol. 8692, pp. 184–199. Springer, Cham (2014). https://doi.org/10.1007/978-3-319-10593-2_13
4. Garyfallidis, E.: Dipy, a library for the analysis of diffusion MRI data. Front. Neuroinformatics **8**, 8 (2014)
5. Goodfellow, I., et al.: Generative adversarial nets. In: Ghahramani, Z., Welling, M., Cortes, C., Lawrence, N.D., Weinberger, K.Q. (eds.) Advances in Neural Information Processing Systems, vol. 27, pp. 2672–2680. Curran Associates, Inc. (2014)
6. Isola, P., Zhu, J.Y., Zhou, T., Efros, A.A.: Image-to-image translation with conditional adversarial networks. arxiv (2016)
7. Johansen-Berg, H., Behrens, T.E.: Diffusion MRI: From Quantitative Measurement to In Vivo Neuroanatomy. Academic Press (2013)
8. Johnson, J., Alahi, A., Fei-Fei, L.: Perceptual losses for real-time style transfer and super-resolution. In: Leibe, B., Matas, J., Sebe, N., Welling, M. (eds.) ECCV 2016. LNCS, vol. 9906, pp. 694–711. Springer, Cham (2016). https://doi.org/10.1007/978-3-319-46475-6_43
9. Kingma, D.P., Ba, J.: Adam: a method for stochastic optimization. CoRR abs/1412.6980 (2014). http://arxiv.org/abs/1412.6980
10. Le Bihan, D., Basser, P.J.: Molecular diffusion and nuclear magnetic resonance. In: Diffusion and Perfusion Magnetic Resonance Imaging, pp. 5–17 (1995)
11. Le Bihan, D., Iima, M.: Diffusion magnetic resonance imaging: what water tells us about biological tissues. PLoS Biol. **13**(7), e1002203 (2015)
12. Ledig, C., et al.: Photo-realistic single image super-resolution using a generative adversarial network. CoRR abs/1609.04802 (2016)
13. Odena, A., Dumoulin, V., Olah, C.: Deconvolution and checkerboard artifacts. Distill (2016). https://doi.org/10.23915/distill.00003, http://distill.pub/2016/deconv-checkerboard
14. Peled, S., Yeshurun, Y.: Superresolution in MRI: application to human white matter fiber tract visualization by diffusion tensor imaging. Magn. Reson. Med. **45**(1), 29–35 (2001)
15. Tournier, J.D., Calamante, F., Connelly, A.: Robust determination of the fibre orientation distribution in diffusion mri: non-negativity constrained super-resolved spherical deconvolution. Neuroimage **35**(4), 1459–1472 (2007)
16. Tournier, J.D., Calamante, F., Gadian, D.G., Connelly, A.: Direct estimation of the fiber orientation density function from diffusion-weighted MRI data using spherical deconvolution. NeuroImage **23**(3), 1176–1185 (2004)
17. Van Essen, D.C., et al.: The human connectome project: a data acquisition perspective. Neuroimage **62**(4), 2222–2231 (2012)

18. Yang, Z., He, P., Zhou, J., Wu, X.: Non-local diffusion-weighted image super-resolution using collaborative joint information. Exp. Ther. Med. **15**(1), 217–225 (2018)

19. Yap, P.-T., An, H., Chen, Y., Shen, D.: A generative model for resolution enhancement of diffusion MRI data. In: Mori, K., Sakuma, I., Sato, Y., Barillot, C., Navab, N. (eds.) MICCAI 2013. LNCS, vol. 8151, pp. 527–534. Springer, Heidelberg (2013). https://doi.org/10.1007/978-3-642-40760-4_66

Prediction to Atrial Fibrillation Using Deep Convolutional Neural Networks

Jungrae Cho[1], Yoonnyun Kim[2], and Minho Lee[1(✉)]

[1] School of Electronics Engineering, Kyungpook National University,
Daegu, Republic of Korea
zzemb6@gmail.com, mholee@gmail.com
[2] Department of Internal Medicine (Cardiology),
Keimyung University Dongsan Medical Center, Daegu, Republic of Korea
ynkim@dsmc.or.kr

Abstract. Recently, many researchers have attempted to apply deep neural networks to detect Atrial Fibrillation (AF). In this paper, we propose an approach for prediction of AF instead of detection using Deep Convolutional Neural Networks (DCNN). This is done by classifying electrocardiogram (ECG) before AF into normal and abnormal states, which is hard for the cardiologists to distinguish from the normal sinus rhythm. ECG is transformed into spectrogram and trained using VGG16 networks to predict normal and abnormal signals. By changing the time length of abnormal signals and making up their own datasets for preprocessing, we investigate the changes in F1-score for each dataset to explore the right time to alert the occurrence of AF.

Keywords: Atrial fibrillation · Arrhythmia · Deep neural networks
Convolutional neural networks

1 Introduction

Atrial Fibrillation (AF) is one of the common cardiac arrythmia in patients, which is usually accompanied by other serious symptoms such as stroke [1]. This irregular heart rhythm also increases the chance of occurrence of heart failures and mortality in arrythmia patients [2]. Then, it is crucial to detect and predict AF as early as possible. Many machine learning approaches have been used to classify normal sinus rhythm and cardiac arrythmias from electrocardiogram (ECG) [3–5]. Recently, deep learning has reported its successful contributions to various areas such as image classification [6–9]. Many researchers have applied deep neural networks to monitor the occurrence of AF. Among which, convolutional neural networks (CNN) and recurrent neural networks (RNN) have been popular in feature extraction to detect AF and other arrythmias [10–13]. However, they have been focused on detection and not prediction of AF. A few researches have challenged to predict AF before it happens using machine learning and neural networks [14, 15]. In this paper, we propose a new AF prediction algorithm to explore the prelude of AF that is difficult for the cardiologists to identify using Deep Convolutional Neural Networks (DCNN). The ECG signals before AF are divided into normal and abnormal signals, and the time length of each of these

I. Rekik et al. (Eds.): PRIME 2018, LNCS 11121, pp. 164–171, 2018.
https://doi.org/10.1007/978-3-030-00320-3_20

two classes are different. Then, we train VGG16 networks [16] and measure F1-scores for each different label case to check the dynamics of ECG before AF.

2 Scenario of Prediction to AF

Figure 1 shows the scenario of predicting normal and abnormal states from ECG. To predict prelude of AF, we divide the ECG signals (before the occurrence of AF) into normal signal and abnormal signal. Normal signal is the same as regular sinus rhythm, however, abnormal signal is difficult to be distinguished from normal signal with human eye. The goal of the scenario is to alert arrythmia patients 4–5 min ahead the possibility of occurrence of AF by monitoring their ECG continuously.

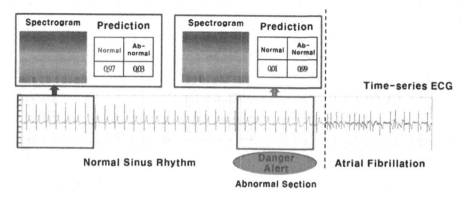

Fig. 1. Scenario for prediction of AF. ECG signal is divided into normal and abnormal signals before occurrence of AF. DCNN learns and predicts if the signal is in normal state or in abnormal state.

3 Data Preprocessing

3.1 Dataset

We use single-lead ECG dataset provided by Keimyung University Dongsan Medical Center (KUDMC), which is private and anonymized. We use ECG signals that are about 10 min long to predict normal and abnormal signals before AF to predict normal and abnormal signals as mentioned in Fig. 1. We choose to train each patient's data separately because hemodynamic response i.e. the average rhythm and characteristic of the heart beat is unique to each patient [2]. So, the dataset for patient-dependent model requires long sequences of each patient which contains both normal sinus rhythm and AF. From the restricted condition, we choose ECG signals of three patients because ECG records have very few cases of the continuation of normal and AF signals. To provide more experiments, we additionally use two records of paroxysmal AF (PAF) from PhysioNet dataset [15, 17]. Table 1 illustrates the number of obtained spectrograms from ECG signals, duration of ECG, and data source.

Table 1. Dataset information

Patients	# of spectrograms	Duration of ECG [minutes]	Source of data
Patient 1	1879	23	KUDMC
Patient 2	272	9	KUDMC
Patient 3	363	10	KUDMC
Patient 4	299	30	PhysioNet
Patient 5	299	30	PhysioNet

3.2 Preprocessing

Figure 2 shows the preprocessing of ECG signals. Since ECG is a time-series data, we transform ECG into spectrograms to be used as the input for CNN. Spectrograms are generated using short-time Fourier transform of every 30 s ECG signals with an overlap of 1 s [14].

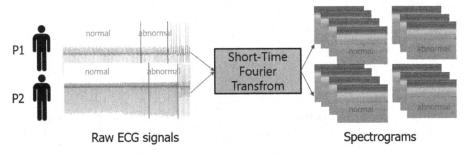

Fig. 2. Preprocessing of the ECG signals convert to spectrograms. P1, P2 are patients. From their ECG records, we divide normal and abnormal periods. The divided ECG signals are transformed in to spectrograms to use them as input to CNN. Each patient's dataset is used to train its own subject specific model.

3.3 VGG16

To classify very similar but different signals, i.e. normal and abnormal states, we utilizes DCNN because it is considered as the powerful algorithm in image processing field for its successful performance to image classification in ImageNet Large Scale Visual Recognition Challenge (ILSVRC) in 2012 [7]. VGG16 network is one of the DCNN which consists of 13 convolution and pooling layers and 3 fully-connected layers [16]. In this paper, VGG16 is considered to predict normal and abnormal states since it has a deep architecture with good performance for image classification. We use VGG16 networks implemented with Keras [18]. To overcome the paucity of data samples, pretrained weights from ImageNet [7] are considered and fine-tuned for normal and abnormal classes. The architecture of VGG16 is as shown in Fig. 3.

Layer (type)	Output Shape	Param #
input_1 (InputLayer)	(None, 128, 128, 3)	0
block1_conv1 (Conv2D)	(None, 128, 128, 64)	1792
block1_conv2 (Conv2D)	(None, 128, 128, 64)	36928
block1_pool (MaxPooling2D)	(None, 64, 64, 64)	0
block2_conv1 (Conv2D)	(None, 64, 64, 128)	73856
block2_conv2 (Conv2D)	(None, 64, 64, 128)	147584
block2_pool (MaxPooling2D)	(None, 32, 32, 128)	0
block3_conv1 (Conv2D)	(None, 32, 32, 256)	295168
block3_conv2 (Conv2D)	(None, 32, 32, 256)	590080
block3_conv3 (Conv2D)	(None, 32, 32, 256)	590080
block3_pool (MaxPooling2D)	(None, 16, 16, 256)	0
block4_conv1 (Conv2D)	(None, 16, 16, 512)	1180160
block4_conv2 (Conv2D)	(None, 16, 16, 512)	2359808
block4_conv3 (Conv2D)	(None, 16, 16, 512)	2359808
block4_pool (MaxPooling2D)	(None, 8, 8, 512)	0
block5_conv1 (Conv2D)	(None, 8, 8, 512)	2359808
block5_conv2 (Conv2D)	(None, 8, 8, 512)	2359808
block5_conv3 (Conv2D)	(None, 8, 8, 512)	2359808
block5_pool (MaxPooling2D)	(None, 4, 4, 512)	0
global_average_pooling2d_1 (	(None, 512)	0
dropout_1 (Dropout)	(None, 512)	0
dense_1 (Dense)	(None, 128)	65664
dropout_2 (Dropout)	(None, 128)	0
batch_normalization_1 (Batch	(None, 128)	512
dense_2 (Dense)	(None, 2)	258

Total params: 14,781,122
Trainable params: 14,780,866
Non-trainable params: 256

Fig. 3. Architecture of VGG16 network. To solve AF prediction problem, we modified fully connected layers and the dimension of the output layer.

3.4   Training Configuration

The input of VGG16 is spectrograms obtained from ECG of size 256×256. The output is two classes with normal ([1 0]) and abnormal ([0 1]) signals. Optimizer is ADAM [19]. We applied dropout [20] and batch normalization [21] to fully-connected layers to stabilize training and validation loss.

4   Experiments

Not only to predict normal and abnormal ECG signals but also to find proper time to alert the occurrence of AF, we make up abnormal states as 4, 5, and 6 min before AF. By varying abnormal periods, we obtain 3 cases of datasets for each patient as shown in Fig. 4.

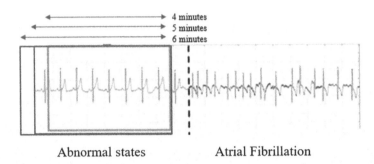

Fig. 4. Varying the length of abnormal states to explore proper alert time for AF.

We train VGG16 network for each dataset and every patient. We measure the F1-scores after the training process and test the accuracies to investigate the discrimination of each case of abnormal states. Each F1-score is the average of F1-scores calculated from three times experiments with the same training and test set. We additionally prepare several baseline models to compare them to VGG16. Since Multi-Layer Perceptron (MLP) and Support Vector Machine (SVM) are not suitable for high dimensional data i.e. spectrograms, we consider standard CNN and Long-Short Term Memory (LSTM) networks [22] as baseline models. The simple CNN consists of two convolution layers, one max pooling layer, and fully connected layers. The LSTM model has 1 LSTM cell and fully connected layers.

4.1   Model Performance

For each case of abnormal state, we measure F1-scores of each model as shown in Table 2. VGG16 reports higher F1-scores compared to standard CNN and LSTM. LSTM fails to learn the data for patient 3, 4 and 5 with low F1-scores as mentioned in Table 2, whereas standard CNN and VGG16 converge their train losses. The better F1-scores of VGG16 shows that the deeper CNN architecture is good for learning our datasets.

As shown in the table, every patient shows different F1-scores. The diversity in dynamics of F1-score is considered since patients can have their own hemodynamic consequences in their ECG records [2]. The lower F1-score indicates that normal and abnormal states are hard to believe the prediction results by the DCNN. Whereas, the higher F1-score indicates that normal and abnormal states are easy to distinguish with high reliability. In Fig. 4, Patient 1 and 5 show a monotonic decrease of F1-scores.

It indicates that the 4-min case has higher discrimination compared to 5 and 6-min cases. Patients 4 is the opposite case of Patient 1 and 5, which means that the prediction accuracy is more believable through time. For Patients 2 and 3, the prediction of AF is more believable in 4 and 6 min. Those results show that the change in F1-scores implies the relative reliability of prediction results for existence of abnormal state before AF happens.

Table 2. F1-scores of VGG16 and baseline models (standard CNN and LSTM) for various case of abnormal states

Model	Case of Abnormal states [minutes]	Patient 1	Patient 2	Patient 3	Patient 4	Patient 5
VGG16	4	**0.6**	**0.76**	0.57	0.65	**0.72**
	5	0.57	0.57	0.41	0.69	0.62
	6	0.54	0.70	**0.61**	**0.72**	0.56
CNN	4	**0.5**	0.56	0.36	0.42	**0.57**
	5	0.4	0.54	**0.46**	**0.55**	0.53
	6	0.44	**0.59**	0.39	0.4	0.42
LSTM	4	0.46	**0.6**	0.33	0.33	0.33
	5	0.36	0.52	**0.38**	0.33	0.33
	6	**0.6**	0.49	0.33	0.33	0.33

4.2   Application to Alert the Occurrence of AF

Figure 5 shows the change of test accuracies and F1-scores for datasets which have different length of abnormal states for each patient. In each figure, the markers indicate the highest accuracy and F1-score to predict test data as normal or abnormal signals.

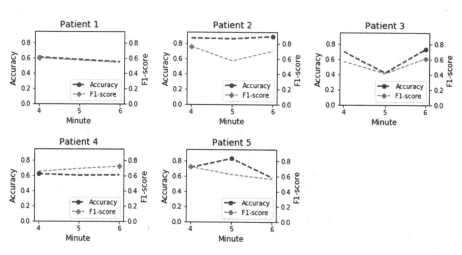

Fig. 5. Change of test accuracies and F1-scores for 4, 5, 6 minute-dataset for patients. The Markers in each figure indicate the highest accuracy and F1-score for its abnormal section.

Since F1-score considers both precision and recall unlike the accuracy, the dynamics between accuracies and F1-scores looks different for each patient as shown in Fig. 5. By considering the abnormal periods from the highest accuracy verified by its F1-score as the confidence for the prelude of AF, it has chance for application to alert the occurrence of AF to both doctors and patients to determine if AF could happen.

5 Conclusion and Future Works

Prediction of AF is a crucial task to save the patient's life because AF could lead to fatal diseases. In this paper, we attempted to predict the prelude of AF using DCNN. We trained VGG16 network to predict normal sinus rhythm and abnormal signals, and measured F1-scores for different length of abnormal states. The F1-score range of patients showed that it had subject specific discriminant patterns. DCNN suggests that there are some abnormal signals before AF that are difficult to distinguish from normal signals.

For future work, it is possible to analyze wider range of abnormal sections to explore F1-score dynamics and additional experiments with more patients can be considered. Also, we are considering a new DCNN learning algorithm to detect very sensitive variation of AF signals in normal and abnormal conditions. Finally, the research to automate the exploration of proper alert time is recommended.

Acknowledgements. This work was partly supported by Institute for Information & communications Technology Promotion (IITP) grant funded by the Korea government (MSIT) (2016-0-00564, Development of Intelligent Interaction Technology Based on Context Awareness and Human Intention Understanding) (30%), Institute for Information & communications Technology Promotion (IITP) grant funded by the Korea government (MSIT) (2018-2-00861, Intelligent SW Technology Development for Medical Data Analysis) (40%) and the Ministry of Trade, Industry & Energy (MOTIE, Korea) under Industrial Technology Innovation Program. No.1063553, 'Self-directed portable safety kits and application based living environment service system' (30%).

References

1. Wolf, P.A., Abbott, R.D., Kannel, W.B.: Atrial fibrillation as an independent risk factor for stroke: the Framingham Study. Stroke **22**(8), 983–988 (1991)
2. Dries, D., Exner, D., Gersh, B., Domanski, M., Waclawiw, M., Stevenson, L.: Atrial fibrillation is associated with an increased risk for mortality and heart failure progression in patients with asymptomatic and symptomatic left ventricular systolic dysfunction: a retrospective analysis of the SOLVD trials. J. Am. Coll. Cardiol. **32**(3), 695–703 (1998)
3. Polat, K., Güneş, S.: Detection of ECG Arrhythmia using a differential expert system approach based on principal component analysis and least square support vector machine. Appl. Math. Comput. **186**(1), 898–906 (2007)
4. Bost, R., Popa, R.A., Tu, S., Goldwasser, S.: Machine learning classification over encrypted data. In: NDSS, p. 4325 (2015)
5. Li, Q., Rajagopalan, C., Clifford, G.D.: Ventricular fibrillation and tachycardia classification using a machine learning approach. IEEE Trans. Biomed. Eng. **61**(6), 1607–1613 (2014)

6. LeCun, Y., Bengio, Y., Hinton, G.: Deep learning. Nature **521**(7553), 436 (2015)
7. Krizhevsky, A., Sutskever, I., Hinton, G.E.: Imagenet classification with deep convolutional neural networks. In: Advances in Neural Information Processing Systems, pp. 1097–1105 (2012)
8. Russakovsky, O., et al.: Imagenet large scale visual recognition challenge. Int. J. Comput. Vision **115**(3), 211–252 (2015)
9. He, K., Zhang, X., Ren, S., Sun, J.: Deep residual learning for image recognition. In: Proceedings of the IEEE Conference on Computer Vision and Pattern Recognition, pp. 770–778 (2016)
10. Rajpurkar, P., Hannun, A.Y., Haghpanahi, M., Bourn, C., Ng, A.Y.: Cardiologist-level arrhythmia detection with convolutional neural networks. arXiv preprint arXiv:170701836 (2017)
11. Poh, M.-Z., et al.: Diagnostic assessment of a deep learning system for detecting atrial fibrillation in pulse waveforms. Heart:heartjnl-2018-313147 (2018)
12. Oh, S.L., Ng, E.Y., San Tan, R., Acharya, U.R.: Automated diagnosis of arrhythmia using combination of CNN and LSTM techniques with variable length heart beats. Comput. Biol. Med. (2018)
13. Xia, Y., Wulan, N., Wang, K., Zhang, H.: Detecting atrial fibrillation by deep convolutional neural networks. Comput. Biol. Med. **93**, 84–92 (2018)
14. Kim, J., Sangjun, O., Kim, Y., Lee, M.: Convolutional neural network with biologically inspired retinal structure. Procedia Comput. Sci. **88**, 145–154 (2016)
15. Bianchi, F.M., Livi, L., Ferrante, A., Milosevic, J., Malek, M.: Time series kernel similarities for predicting Paroxysmal Atrial Fibrillation from ECGs. arXiv preprint arXiv:180106845 (2018)
16. Simonyan, K., Zisserman, A.: Very deep convolutional networks for large-scale image recognition. arXiv preprint arXiv:14091556 (2014)
17. PhysioNet: The PAF Prediction Challenge Database (2001). https://physionet.org/physiobank/database/afpdb/
18. Chollet, F.: Keras (2015)
19. Kingma, D.P., Ba, J.: Adam: a method for stochastic optimization. arXiv preprint arXiv: 14126980 (2014)
20. Srivastava, N., Hinton, G., Krizhevsky, A., Sutskever, I., Salakhutdinov, R.: Dropout: a simple way to prevent neural networks from overfitting. J. Mach. Learn. Res. **15**(1), 1929–1958 (2014)
21. Ioffe, S., Szegedy, C.: Batch normalization: accelerating deep network training by reducing internal covariate shift. arXiv preprint arXiv:150203167 (2015)
22. Sak, H., Senior, A., Beaufays, F.: Long short-term memory recurrent neural network architectures for large scale acoustic modeling. In: Fifteenth Annual Conference of the International Speech Communication Association (2014)

Author Index

Printed in the United States
By Bookmasters